Britain Great, William Wheelhouse

The Corrupt Practices Prevention act, 1883 (46 & 47 Vict.c.51)

With an Analysis, Table of Penalties, Notes and an Appendix of Statutes and Rules Affecting the Same

Britain Great, William Wheelhouse

The Corrupt Practices Prevention act, 1883 (46 & 47 Vict.c.51)
With an Analysis, Table of Penalties, Notes and an Appendix of Statutes and Rules Affecting the Same

ISBN/EAN: 9783337159955

Printed in Europe, USA, Canada, Australia, Japan

Cover: Foto ©Suzi / pixelio.de

More available books at **www.hansebooks.com**

THE

CORRUPT PRACTICES PREVENTION ACT

1883 (46 & 47 Vict. c. 51)

WITH AN

Analysis, Table of Penalties, Notes,

AND AN

APPENDIX OF STATUTES AND RULES AFFECTING THE SAME, AND GENERAL INDEX.

BY

SIR WILLIAM WHEELHOUSE,

ONE OF HER MAJESTY'S COUNSEL

(And formerly Member of Parliament for Leeds).

Second Edition.

LONDON:

REEVES & TURNER, 100, CHANCERY LANE,

Law Booksellers and Publishers.

1885

CONTENTS.

APPENDIX.

INTRODUCTION.

The Editor of the following Notes has not put them together so much with a view of producing what is commonly termed a "Law Book," as for the purpose of giving a ready analysis of the New Statute, intending such analysis, moreover, rather as a Guide-Book to those, whether lawyers or laymen, who will have hereafter to act upon its provisions.

The Index has been compiled more especially with this view, and he sincerely trusts that it will be found valuable as an adjunct to the Work, containing as it does nearly a rescript of the statute itself.

The Appendix contains a copy of or a reference to all the Statutes affected by the late Act, as well as the General Rules made in pursuance of the Representation of the People Act, 1867—such sections of either as have been repealed being printed in italics.

He has thought it unnecessary to quote more than very few of the "Leading Cases," especially as these have been most carefully tabulated in Mr. J. C. Carter's excellent edition of "Rogers on Elections."

It is not any part of the Editor's duty to say more in reference to the Statute than to observe that its provisions are in some cases so stringent as to be in considerable danger, he fears, of defeating their proposed object, a consequence which he sincerely hopes may not however arise.

W. St. J. W.

ANALYSIS.

The Act is divided into what may be termed thirteen different parts:—

1 to 6.— The first six sections, inclusive, are devoted to Corrupt Practices.

7 to 12.—The next six, inclusive, to Illegal Practices.

13 to 21.—The following nine, inclusive, to Illegal Payment, Employment and Hiring.

22 to 23.—The next two to *Excuses* (if any can be shown) in reference to Corrupt and Illegal Practices, Payment, Employment and Hiring.

24 to 35.—The following twelve, inclusive, to Election Expenses.

36 to 39.—The next four, inclusive, to Disqualification of Electors.

40 to 44.—The next five to Proceedings on Election Petitions.

45 to 49.—The following five to "Miscellaneous" matters.

50 to 58.—The next nine to Legal Proceedings.

59 to 67.—The following nine to Supplemental Matters, Repeal of former Statutes, &c., &c.

68, 69.—The two next sections make the Act apply to Scotland and Ireland respectively.

70.—One section as to the Continuance of other Acts, and Schedules.

The thirteenth part consists of the Schedules to this Act.

PENALTIES UNDER THE NEW STATUTE, 1883.

Personation: or aiding in or committing it. (Sect. 6, sub-sects. 2 and 3.)	Felony: imprisonment not exceeding 2 years with hard labour.	Incapable of holding a seat in the House for 7 years, incapable of being registered as an elector; or voting at any (Parliamentary or other public) election for the like length of time; and incapable to hold any office, public or judicial: If magistrate, barrister, solicitor, or licensed person, also subject to penalties mentioned in sect. 38.
Corrupt Practice: *i.e.* bribery, treating or undue influence. (Sect. 6, sub-sect. 1.)	Indictable Misdemeanor: imprisonment not exceeding 1 year, with or without hard labour; or fine not exceeding 200*l*.	The like incapacities.
Illegal Practice .... (Sect. 10.)	Fine not exceeding 100*l*.	Incapacity of being registered as a voter, and voting at any election in the constituency where illegal practice committed for 5 years.
Corrupt withdrawal of Parliamentary Petition. (Sect. 41, sub-sect. 4.)	Indictable Misdemeanor: imprisonment not exceeding 1 year; or fine not exceeding 200*l*.	
Failure by Election Agent to make return of expenses on the order of High Court. (Sect. 34, sub-sect. 2.)	Fine not exceeding 500*l*.	
Illegal Payment, Hiring, or Employment. (Sect. 21, sub-sect. 1.)	Fine not exceeding 100*l*.	
Member sitting or voting after the time has expired for return of expenses, &c., if such returns have not been made. (Sect. 33, sub-sect. 5.)	Fine of 100*l*. a-day to any person suing.	
False Declaration (perjury) .. (Sect. 33, sub-sect. 7.)	Indictable Misdemeanor: penal servitude not exceeding 7 years, together with all the concomitants of a "corrupt practice."	

CORRUPT AND ILLEGAL PRACTICES PREVENTION ACT, 1883.

(46 & 47 VICT. c. 51.)

ARRANGEMENT OF SECTIONS.

---

46 & 47 VICT. c. 51.

An Act for the better prevention of Corrupt and Illegal Practices at Parliamentary Elections.
[25th August, 1883.]

BE it enacted by the Queen's most excellent Majesty, by and with the advice and consent of the lords spiritual and temporal, and commons, in this present Parliament assembled, and by the authority of the same, as follows:

Corrupt Practices.

What is treating.

1. Whereas under section four of the Corrupt Practices Prevention Act, 1854, persons other than candidates at parliamentary elections are not liable to any punishment for treating, and it is expedient to make such persons liable; be it therefore enacted in substitution for the said section four as follows:—

(1) Any person who corruptly by himself or by any other person, either before, during, or after an election, directly or indirectly gives

or provides, or pays, wholly or in part the expense of giving or providing, any meat drink entertainment or provision to or for any person, for the purpose of corruptly influencing that person or any other person to give or refrain from giving his vote at the election, or on account of such person or any other person having voted or refrained from voting, or being about to vote or refrain from voting at such election, shall be guilty of treating.

(2) And every elector who corruptly accepts or takes any such meat drink entertainment or provision shall also be guilty of treating.

Mr. Justice Willes, in *The Lichfield case* (1 O'M. & H. 365 *et seq.*), said he had doubt as to whether treating, without any corrupt motive, at an election had ever been held to be an offence at common law; and even when looked upon as an offence, was only so considered in its abuse, but if clearly done with a view of influencing the election, it was dealt with as a form of bribery. (*The Bodmin case*, 1 O'M. & H. 124.) The first treating Act is the 7 & 8 Will. 3, c. 4, which enacts that "on the occurrence of any vacancy, if any person, being a candidate, either by himself, or in any other way or means on his behalf, or at his charge, *before the election*, gives a voter any meat, drink, &c., he shall be guilty of treating," and vacated the seat *ipso facto*. This matter has been somewhat differently modified by the 5 & 6 Vict. c. 132, s. 22. It would also seem, however, that the operation of the Act of William III. was confined to the period between the *teste* of the writ and the election itself (*Ribbons* v. *Crickett*, H. & P. 161), though even this was unsettled by the ruling in *The Dungarvan case*, R. & D. 327. See also *Hughes* v. *Marshall*, 2 C. & J. 118; 17 & 18 Vict. c. 102; and 31 & 32 Vict. c. 125.

To avoid all possibility of question it becomes absolutely necessary not to give any refreshment at all to any one connected with the election—that is, give it in the way of "hospitality."

2. Every person who shall directly or indirectly, by himself or by any other person on his behalf, make use of or threaten to make use of any force, violence, or restraint, or inflict or threaten to

What is undue influence.

inflict, by himself or by any other person, any temporal or spiritual injury, damage, harm, or loss upon or against any person in order to induce or compel such person to vote or refrain from voting, or on account of such person having voted or refrained from voting at any election, or who shall by abduction, duress, or any fraudulent device or contrivance impede or prevent the free exercise of the franchise of any elector, or shall thereby compel, induce, or prevail upon any elector either to give or to refrain from giving his vote at any election, shall be guilty of undue influence.

Although there had been various enactments against undue influence previously, yet it was not until the passing of the 17 & 18 Vict. c. 102, s. 5, that it was specifically defined, and thereby made cognizable as a statutory offence. (See *The Helston case*, 68 Jour. H. C. 344; *The Hertford case*, P. & K. 552 (in the notes); *The Bishop of Cashel's case*, 16 Jour. H. C. 548; *The Lichfield case*, 1 O'M. & H. 25; *The Windsor case*, 2 O'M. & H. 93; *The Bewdley case*, 1 P. R. & D. 69; *Clitheroe*, 2 P. R. & D. 34; *New Windsor case*, 2 P. R. & D. 150; *Stafford*, 1 O'M. & H. 228; *North Norfolk*, 1 O'M. & H. 240. See, too, *The Northallerton case* (1 O'M. & H. 168), where a threat only was used; *Staleybridge*, 1 O'M. & H. 72; *Galway*, 2 O'M. & H. 200; *Morpeth*, 1 Doug. 147; *Pontefract*, 1 Doug. 227; *Knaresborough*, 1 Peck, 85; *Norfolk*, 9 Jour. H. C. 631.) See cases as to undue clerical influence, as by denying some of the services or offices of a church or its priesthood, which its votaries think necessary or essential, *The Mayo case*, W. & D. 1; *Longford*, 2 O'M. & H. 16; *Galway*, 1 O'M. & D. 305.

What is corrupt practice.

3. The expression "corrupt practice" as used in this Act means any of the following offences; namely, treating and undue influence, as defined by this Act, and bribery, and personation, as defined by the enactments set forth in Part III. of the Third Schedule to this Act, and aiding, abetting, counselling, and procuring the commission of the offence of personation, and every offence which is a corrupt practice within the meaning of this Act shall be a corrupt practice within the meaning of the Parliamentary Elections Act, 1868. 31 & 32 Vict. c. 125.

As to bribery, see the 17 & 18 Vict. c. 102, s. 2, substituted for former statute, 49 Geo. 3, c. 118. (*Bodmin*, 1 O'M. & H. 124; *Middlesex*, 2 Peck, 31; *2nd Clitheroe*, 2 P. & D. 279.)

As to personation, see 35 & 36 Vict. c. 33, s. 24, whereby any person found guilty of it, by himself or his agents, or counselling, aiding, abetting or procuring it, is disqualified from sitting in that Parliament. But the personation must be *knowingly* committed, as well as *wilfully*, by the person committing the act, to affect the seat; and see also the Parliamentary Elections Act, 1868 (31 & 32 Vict. c. 125). (*Coventry*, 1 O'M. & H. 105; *Gloucester*, 2 O'M. & H. 62, and Part III. of Schedule 3 to this Act.)

Punishment of candidate found, on election petition, guilty personally of corrupt practices. 31 & 32 Vict. c. 125.

4. Where upon the trial of an election petition respecting an election for a county or borough the election court, by the report made to the speaker in pursuance of section eleven of the Parliamentary Elections Act, 1868, reports that any corrupt practice other than treating or undue influence has been proved to have been committed in reference to such election *by or with the knowledge and consent of any candidate* at such election, or that the offence of treating or undue influence has been proved to have been committed in reference to such election *by any candidate* at such election, that candidate shall not be capable of ever being elected to or sitting in the House of Commons for the said county or borough, and if he has been elected, his election shall be void; and he shall further be subject to the same incapacities as if at the date of the said report he had been convicted on an indictment of a corrupt practice.

If any corrupt practice, that is, bribery, personation, and aiding and abetting personation, be proved against a candidate *personally*, he is thereby rendered incapable for ever sitting for the same constituency, thus considerably increasing the former punishment under 31 & 32 Vict. c. 125, s. 43, which limited the incapacity, in the large majority of cases, to seven years next following.

Punishment of candidate found, on election petition, guilty by agents of corrupt practices.

5. Upon the trial of an election petition respecting an election for a county or borough, in which a charge is made of any corrupt practice having been committed in reference to such election, the election court shall report in writing to the speaker whether any of the candidates at such election has been guilty by his agents of any corrupt practice in reference to such election; and if the report is that any candidate at such election has been guilty *by his agents* of any corrupt practice in reference to such election, that candidate shall not be capable of being elected to or sitting in the House of Commons for such county or borough for seven years after the date of the report, and if he has been elected his election shall be void.

If any candidate has been guilty, *by his agent*, of any corrupt practice, he is incapacitated from sitting for that constituency for the next seven years, and his then election, if he has been chosen, is void.

Punishment of person convicted on indictment of corrupt practices.

6. (1.) A person who commits any corrupt practice other than personation, or aiding, abetting, counselling, or procuring the commission of the offence of personation, shall be guilty of a misdemeanor, and on conviction on indictment shall be liable to be imprisoned, with or without hard labour, for a term not exceeding one year, or to be fined any sum not exceeding two hundred pounds.

(2.) A person who commits the offence of personation, or of aiding, abetting, counselling, or procuring the commission of that offence, shall be guilty of felony, and any person convicted thereof on indictment shall be punished by imprisonment for a term not exceeding two years, together with hard labour.

(3.) A person who is convicted on indictment of any corrupt practice shall (in addition to any punishment as above provided) be not capable during a period of seven years from the date of his conviction:

(a) of being registered as an elector or voting at *any* election in the United Kingdom, whether it be a parliamentary election or an election for any public office within the meaning of this Act; or

(b) of holding any public or judicial office within the meaning of this Act, and if he holds any such office the office shall be vacated.

(4.) Any person so convicted of a corrupt practice in reference to any election shall also be incapable of being elected to and of sitting in the House of Commons during the seven years next after the date of his conviction, and if at that date he has been elected to the House of Commons his election shall be vacated from the time of such conviction.

The summary of penalties under this section (6) are—

1. For any offence, save personation, indictable for *misdemeanor*, liable to imprisonment with or without hard labour for a year, and to a fine of 100*l.*, together with the further disqualification of not being capable of being registered or of holding any judicial office for seven years, and should he have been elected his seat shall, *ipso facto*, be vacated.
2. For personation, or counselling, aiding or abetting it,

indictable for *felony*, imprisonment with or without hard labour for *two* years, and with like additional penalties as above.

See the cases of *Coventry* (1 O'M. & H. 105) and *Gloucester* (2 O'M. & H. 62).

Illegal Practices.

Certain expenditure to be illegal practice.

7. (1.) No payment or contract for payment shall, for the purpose of promoting or procuring the election of a candidate at any election be made—

(a) on account of the conveyance of electors to or from the poll, whether for the hiring of horses or carriages, or for railway fares, or otherwise; or

(b) to an elector on account of the use of any house, land, building, or premises for the exhibition of any address, bill, or notice, or on account of the exhibition of any address, bill, or notice; or

(c) on account of any committee room in excess of the number allowed by the First Schedule to this Act.

(2.) Subject to such exception as may be allowed in pursuance of this Act, if any payment or contract for payment is knowingly made in contravention of this section either before, during, or after an election, the person making such payment or contract shall be guilty of an illegal practice, and any person receiving such payment or being a party to any such contract, knowing the same to be in contravention of this Act, shall also be guilty of an illegal practice.

(3.) Provided that where it is the ordinary business of an elector as an advertising agent to exhibit for payment bills and advertisements, a payment to or contract with such elector, if made in the ordinary course of business, shall not be deemed to be an illegal practice within the meaning of this section.

An alteration of deep importance is made by this section. Previously in county elections, and in one or two very wide-spreading boroughs (Aylesbury, Shoreham, Cricklade and Much Wenlock), the cost of conveyance to the poll was considered a legal charge, and might be defrayed by the candidate for such constituency. The conveyance of voters to the poll in boroughs by hired vehicles, though formerly allowable, was abolished, except in the instances above named, some time previously. It will be noted, under this Act (see sects. 13 and 14, *post*, and especially the two provisoes marked as sub-sects. 3 and 4 of sect. 14), this third sub-section still leaves it perfectly legal for any carriage, horse or other animal to be hired, employed or used by *an elector*, or several electors, at their joint cost, for the purpose of being themselves conveyed to or from the poll; in other words, the electors may use, hire and pay for conveyances for themselves. (See and read carefully sects. 13 and 14, *post*.)

8. (1.) Subject to such exception as may be allowed in pursuance of this Act, no sum shall be paid and no expense shall be incurred by a candidate at an election or his election agent, whether before, during, or after an election, on account of or in respect of the conduct or management of such election, in excess of any maximum amount in that behalf specified in the first schedule to this Act.

Expense in excess of maximum to be illegal practice.

(2.) Any candidate or election agent who knowingly acts in contravention of this section shall be guilty of an illegal practice.

This is the first time when any "maximum" has been fixed.

---

9. (1.) If any person votes or induces or procures any person to vote at any election, knowing

Voting by prohibited persons

and publishing of false statements of withdrawal to be illegal.

that he or such person is prohibited, whether by this or any other Act from voting at such election, he shall be guilty of an illegal practice.

(2.) Any person who before or during an election knowingly publishes a false statement of the withdrawal of a candidate at such election for the purpose of promoting or procuring the election of another candidate shall be guilty of an illegal practice.

(3.) Provided that a candidate shall not be liable, nor shall his election be avoided, for any illegal practice under this section committed by his agent other than his election agent.

The strength of this provision is modified by the proviso that the act complained of must be done by the *election* agent.

Punishment on conviction of illegal practice.

10. A person guilty of an illegal practice, whether under the foregoing sections or under the provisions hereinafter contained in this Act, shall on summary conviction be liable to a fine not exceeding one hundred pounds and be incapable during a period of five years from the date of his conviction of being registered as an elector or voting at any election (whether it be a parliamentary election or an election for a public office within the meaning of this Act) held for or within the county or borough in which the illegal practice has been committed.

It will be noted that, while the offences named in sect. 6 (corrupt practices) are respectively made misdemeanors and felonies—here, for the punishment of illegal practices the proceedings are summary—penalty, a fine not exceeding 100*l.*, and the offender is not allowed to be registered as an elector for five years within the particular constituency.

Report of election court respecting illegal practice, and punishment of candidate found guilty by such report.

11. Whereas by sub-section fourteen of section eleven of the Parliamentary Elections Act, 1868, it is provided that where a charge is made in an election petition of any corrupt practice having been committed at the election to which the petition refers, the judge shall report in writing to the Speaker as follows:— 31 & 32 Vict. c. 125.

(a) "Whether any corrupt practice has or has not been proved to have been committed by or with the knowledge and consent of any candidate at such election, and the nature of such corrupt practice;

(b) "The names of all persons, if any, who have been proved at the trial to have been guilty of any corrupt practice;

(c) "Whether corrupt practices have, or whether there is reason to believe corrupt practices have, extensively prevailed at the election to which the petition relates:"

And whereas it is expedient to extend the said sub-section to illegal practices:

Be it therefore enacted as follows:—

Sub-section fourteen of section eleven of the Parliamentary Elections Act, 1868, shall apply as if that sub-section were herein re-enacted with the substitution of illegal practice within the meaning of this Act for corrupt practice; and upon the trial of an election petition respecting an election for a county or borough, the election court shall report in writing to the speaker the particulars required by the said sub-section as herein re-enacted, and shall also report whether any candidate at such election has been guilty by his agents 31 & 32 Vict. c. 125.

of any illegal practice within the meaning of this Act in reference to such election, and the following consequences shall ensue upon the report by the election court to the speaker; (that is to say),

(a) If the report is that any illegal practice has been proved to have been committed in reference to such election by or with the knowledge and consent of any candidate at such election, that candidate shall not be capable of being elected to or sitting in the House of Commons for the said county or borough for seven years next after the date of the report, and if he has been elected his election shall be void; and he shall further be subject to the same incapacities as if at the date of the report he had been convicted of such illegal practice; and

(b) If the report is that a candidate at such election has been guilty by his agents of any illegal practice in reference to such election, that candidate shall not be capable of being elected to or sitting in the House of Commons for the said county or borough during the Parliament for which the election was held, and if he has been elected, his election shall be void.

This enlarges the scope of the 31 & 32 Vict. c. 125; extending "illegal practice" and including it, as well as the "corrupt practice" of that statute, and may be summarised as follows:—

1. If "illegal practice" be proved to have taken place by the knowledge and with the consent of the candidate himself, he is disqualified (so far as that constituency is concerned) from a seat for it in the House of Commons for the next seven years, and, if elected, his election will be void, with the additional penalties named in a former section; and
2. If the "illegal practice" was brought home to his agent, the election shall be void.

Extension of 15 & 16 Vict. c. 57, respecting election commissioners to illegal practices.

12. Whereas by the Election Commissioners Act, 1852, as amended by the Parliamentary Elections Act, 1868, it is enacted that where a joint address of both Houses of Parliament represents to her Majesty that an election court has reported to the Speaker that corrupt practices have, or that there is reason to believe that corrupt practices have, extensively prevailed at an election in any county or borough, and prays her Majesty to cause inquiry under that Act to be made by persons named in such address (being qualified as therein mentioned), it shall be lawful for her Majesty to appoint the said persons to be election commissioners for the purpose of making inquiry into the existence of such corrupt practices: (15 & 16 Vict. c. 57. 31 & 32 Vict. c. 125.)

And whereas it is expedient to extend the said enactments to the case of illegal practices:

Be it therefore enacted as follows:—

When election commissioners have been appointed in pursuance of the Election Commissioners Act, 1852, and the enactments amending the same, they may make inquiries and act and report as if "corrupt practices" in the said Act and the enactments amending the same included illegal practices; and the Election Commissioners Act, 1852, shall be construed with such modifications as are necessary for giving effect to this section, and the expression "corrupt practice" in that Act shall have the same meaning as in this Act. (15 & 16 Vict. c. 57.)

Illegal Payment, Employment, and Hiring.

Providing of money for illegal

13. Where a person knowingly provides money for any payment which is contrary to the pro-

practice or payment to be illegal payment.

visions of this Act, or for any expenses incurred in excess of any maximum amount allowed by this Act, or for replacing any money expended in any such payment or expenses, except where the same may have been previously allowed in pursuance of this Act to be an exception, such person shall be guilty of illegal payment.

Employment of hackney carriages, or of carriages and horses kept for hire.

14. (1.) A person shall not let, lend, or employ for the purpose of the conveyance of electors to or from the poll, any public stage or hackney carriage, or any horse or other animal kept or used for drawing the same, or any carriage, horse, or other animal which he keeps or uses for the purpose of letting out for hire, and if he lets, lends, or employs such carriage, horse, or other animal, knowing that it is intended to be used for the purpose of the conveyance of electors to or from the poll, he shall be guilty of an illegal hiring.

(2.) A person shall not hire, borrow, or use for the purpose of the conveyance of electors to or from the poll any carriage, horse, or other animal which he knows the owner thereof is prohibited by this section to let, lend, or employ for that purpose, and if he does so he shall be guilty of an illegal hiring.

(3.) Nothing in this Act shall prevent a carriage, horse, or other animal being let to or hired, employed, or used by an elector, or several electors at their joint cost, for the purpose of being conveyed to or from the poll.

In other words, the candidate or his agent may *not* hire—the elector may do so however at his own cost, or the joint cost of himself and other electors. (See sect. 7, *ante*.)

(4.) No person shall be liable to pay any duty or to take out a license for any carriage by reason only of such carriage being used without payment or promise of payment for the conveyance of electors to or from the poll at an election.

It must be borne in mind that this section applies only to the hire of any *public stage* or *hackney carriage*, or for the use of any horse or other animal kept or used for hire.

In reference to sects. 13 and 14, see sect. 7 and the notes thereto.

Payment for cab or coach hire, or for fares by inland steamer or railway, would be clearly an "illegal payment" under this section.

Still, however, conveyance by sea is permissible under certain circumstances (see sect. 48.)

15. Any person who corruptly induces or procures any other person to withdraw from being a candidate at an election, in consideration of any payment or promise of payment, shall be guilty of illegal payment, and any person withdrawing, in pursuance of such inducement or procurement, shall also be guilty of illegal payment.

Corrupt withdrawal from a candidature.

16. (1.) No payment or contract for payment shall, for the purpose of promoting or procuring the election of a candidate at any election, be made on account of bands of music, torches, flags, banners, cockades, ribbons, or other marks of distinction.

Certain expenditure to be illegal payment.

Notwithstanding the words "for the purpose of promoting or procuring the election of a candidate at any election," it is absolutely necessary henceforward to consider that bands, banners, flags, cockades, ribbons or torches, along with any "other mark of distinction," are not allowable, though possibly it would be somewhat difficult to define what would be considered by a judge "any other mark of distinction." (See *Richardson* v. *Webster*, 3 C. & P. 128.)

(2.) Subject to such exception as may be allowed in pursuance of this Act, if any payment or contract for payment is made in contravention of this section, either before, during, or after an election, the person making such payment shall be guilty of illegal payment, and any person being a party to any such contract or receiving such payment shall also be guilty of illegal payment if he knew that the same was made contrary to law.

Considerable difficulty must arise from the insertion into this section of the last few words, "*i. e. if he knew that the same was made contrary to law.*"

Certain employment to be illegal.

17. (1.) No person shall, for the purpose of promoting or procuring the election of a candidate at any election, be engaged or employed for payment or promise of payment for any purpose or in any capacity whatever, except for any purposes or capacities mentioned in the first or second parts of the First Schedule to this Act, or except so far as payment is authorized by the first or second parts of the First Schedule to this Act.

This section does away entirely with paid canvassers, runners, "*et id genus omne.*" See, however, for necessary exceptions, sched. 1, pts. 1 and 2.

(2.) Subject to such exception as may be allowed in pursuance of this Act, if any person is engaged or employed in contravention of this section, either before, during, or after an election, the person engaging or employing him shall be guilty of illegal employment, and the person so engaged or employed shall also be guilty of illegal employment if he knew that he was engaged or employed contrary to law.

Here, again, considerable difficulty must arise by the last few words making the employment illegal in the recipient, "if he knew that he was engaged or employed *contrary to law*."

18. Every bill, placard, or poster having reference to an election shall bear upon the face thereof the name and address of the printer and publisher thereof; and any person printing, publishing, or posting, or causing to be printed, published, or posted, any such bill, placard, or poster as aforesaid, which fails to bear upon the face thereof the name and address of the printer and publisher, shall, if he is the candidate, or the election agent of the candidate, be guilty of an illegal practice, and if he is not the candidate, or the election agent of a candidate, shall be liable on summary conviction to a fine not exceeding one hundred pounds.

Name and address of printer on placards.

19. The provisions of this Act prohibiting certain payments and contracts for payments, and the payment of any sum, and the incurring of any expense in excess of a certain maximum, shall not affect the right of any creditor, who, when the contract was made or the expense was incurred, was ignorant of the same being in contravention of this Act.

Saving for creditors.

20. (a.) Any premises on which the sale by wholesale or retail of any intoxicating liquor is

Use of committee room in

house for sale of intoxicating liquor or refreshment, or in elementary school, to be illegal hiring.

authorized by a licence (whether the licence be for consumption on or off the premises), or

(b.) Any premises where any intoxicating liquor is sold, or is supplied to members of a club, society, or association other than a permanent political club, or

(c.) Any premises whereon refreshment of any kind, whether food or drink, is ordinarily sold for consumption on the premises, or

(d.) The premises of any public elementary school in receipt of an annual parliamentary grant, or any part of any such premises, shall not be used as a committee room for the purpose of promoting or procuring the election of a candidate at an election, and if any person hires or uses any such premises or any part thereof for a committee room he shall be guilty of illegal hiring, and the person letting such premises or part, if he knew it was intended to use the same as a committee room, shall also be guilty of illegal hiring:

Provided that nothing in this section shall apply to any part of such premises which is ordinarily let for the purpose of chambers or offices or the holding of public meetings or of arbitrations, if such part has a separate entrance and no direct communication with any part of the premises on which any intoxicating liquor or refreshment is sold or supplied as aforesaid.

This enactment entirely abolishes the previously existing right of holding a committee room at a public house—why an elementary school should have been involved in the same prohibitive enactment is not so clear—and, moreover, this section declares that both the person or party hiring, and the person or party letting, shall be equally guilty of "illegal hiring," attended with all its penal consequences.

The proviso is, perhaps, in the few cases to which it will be found applicable, a slight modification of the stringency of the main part of the clause itself.

21. (1.) A person guilty of an offence of illegal payment, employment or hiring shall, on summary conviction, be liable to a fine not exceeding one hundred pounds.

Punishment of illegal payment, employment, or hiring.

(2.) A candidate or an election agent of a candidate who is personally guilty of an offence of illegal payment, employment, or hiring shall be guilty of an illegal practice.

Excuse and Exception for Corrupt or Illegal Practice or Illegal Payment, Employment, or Hiring.

22. Where, upon the trial of an election petition respecting an election for a county or borough, the election court report that a candidate at such election has been guilty by his agents of the offence of treating and undue influence, and illegal practice, or of any of such offences, in reference to such election, and the election court further report that the candidate has proved to the court—

Report exonerating candidate in certain cases of corrupt and illegal practice by agents.

(a) That no corrupt or illegal practice was committed at such election by the candidate or his election agent, and the offences mentioned in the said report were committed contrary to the orders and without the sanction or connivance of such candidate or his election agent; and

(b) That such candidate and his election agent took all reasonable means for preventing the commission of corrupt and illegal practices at such election; and

(c) That the offences mentioned in the said report were of a trivial, unimportant, and limited character; and

(d) That in all other respects the election was free from any corrupt or illegal practice on the part of such candidate and of his agents;

then the election of such candidate shall not, by reason of the offences mentioned in such report, be void, nor shall the candidate be subject to any incapacity under this Act.

If the candidate, *by his agents*, has been found, on an election inquiry, guilty of treating and undue influence and illegal practice, or any of them, in reference to such election, and the election court reports that the candidate has proved in court—

(a) That no corrupt or illegal practice was done with the knowledge and consent of the candidate or his *election* agent; and

(b) That all reasonable means were taken by them to prevent illegal or corrupt practices being committed; and

(c) That the offences were trivial, unimportant, and of limited character; and

(d) That in other respects the election was free from any corrupt or illegal practice by such candidate and his agents;

then the election shall be deemed good.

Power of High Court and election court to except innocent act from being illegal practice, &c.

23. Where, on application made, it is shown to the High Court or to an election court by such evidence as seems to the Court sufficient—

(a) That any act or omission of a *candidate* at any election, or of *his election agent or of any other agent or person*, would, by reason of being a payment, engagement, employment, or contract in contravention of this Act, or being the payment of a sum or the incurring of expense in excess of any maximum amount allowed by this Act, or of otherwise being in contravention of any of the provisions of this Act, be but for this section an illegal practice, payment, employment, or hiring; and

(b) That such act or omission arose from inadvertence or from accidental miscalculation, or from some other reasonable cause of a like nature, and in any case did not arise from any want of good faith; and

(c) That such notice of the application has been given in the county or borough for which the election was held as to the Court seems fit;

and under the circumstances it seems to the Court to be just that the candidate and the said election and other agent and person, or any of them, should not be subject to any of the consequences under this Act of the said act or omission, the Court may make an order allowing such act or omission to be an exception from the provisions of this Act which would otherwise make the same an illegal practice, payment, employment, or hiring, and thereupon such candidate, agent, or person shall not be subject to any of the consequences under this Act of the said act or omission.

This seems to be only fair and reasonable, though it would have been desirable to use the word "shall" instead of "may," although, perhaps, it is not of much consequence, as the words must necessarily be construed by the Court itself.

Election Expenses.

Nomination of election agent.

24. (1.) On or before the day of nomination at an election, a person shall be named by or on behalf of each candidate as his agent for such election (in this Act referred to as the election agent).

(2.) A candidate may name himself as election agent, and thereupon shall, so far as circumstances admit, be subject to the provisions of this Act both as a candidate and as an election agent, and any reference in this Act to an election agent shall be construed to refer to the candidate acting in his capacity of election agent.

(3.) On or before the day of nomination the name and address of the election agent of each candidate shall be declared in writing by the candidate or some other person on his behalf to the returning officer, and the returning officer shall forthwith give public notice of the name and address of every election agent so declared.

(4.) One election agent only shall be appointed for each candidate, but the appointment, whether the election agent appointed be the candidate himself or not, may be revoked, and in the event of such revocation or his death, whether such event is before, during, or after the election, then forthwith another election agent shall be appointed, and his name and address declared in writing to the returning officer, who shall forthwith give public notice of the same.

One election agent only shall be nominated by each candidate.

This need only be done *immediately before* the nomination itself, and a candidate may, on his own nomination, undertake the onerous duty of being his own election agent, subject, however, to all the liabilities and responsibilities that would attach to any other person, had such other person been designated to fulfil the office.

It is requisite to send in the name and address in writing to the returning officer of the election agent.

And that the returning officer should give public notice of such name and address.

This nomination may be revoked, and another election agent appointed at any time during the election, and if such new agent be elected, public notice to be given in the same form.

25. (1.) In the case of the elections specified in that behalf in the First Schedule to this Act an election agent of a candidate may appoint the number of deputies therein mentioned (which deputies are in this Act referred to as sub-agents), to act within different polling districts.

Nomination of deputy election agent as sub-agent.

(2.) As regards matters in a polling district the election agent may act by the sub-agent for that district, and anything done for the purposes of this Act by or to the sub-agent in his district shall be deemed to be done by or to the election agent, and any act or default of a sub-agent which, if he were the election agent, would be an illegal practice or other offence against this Act, shall be an illegal practice and offence against this Act committed by the sub-agent, and the sub-agent shall be liable to punishment accordingly; and the candidate shall suffer the like incapacity as if the said act or default had been the act or default of the election agent.

The last words of this sub-section may, and in all probability will, in many cases work considerable hardship upon the candidate, or even upon the election agent himself. Suppose a county election: agent duly appointed, determined to exercise the most watchful possible supervision, and to be equally determined that no wrongful practice shall be tolerated for a moment, yet because, either from want of knowledge, or even from an over-zealous feeling, the *sub*-agent performs some slight act of *legal* wrong—wholly indefensible, it may be—the *candidate* is to be held responsible, and the seat vacated, although the candidate may have known nothing whatever of the matter.

(3.) One clear day before the polling the election agent shall declare in writing the name and address of every sub-agent to the returning officer, and the returning officer shall forthwith give public notice of the name and address of every sub-agent so declared.

(4.) The appointment of a sub-agent shall not be vacated by the election agent who appointed him ceasing to be election agent, but may be revoked by the election agent for the time being of the candidate, and in the event of such revocation or of the death of a sub-agent another sub-agent may be appointed, and his name and address shall be forthwith declared in writing to the returning officer, who shall forthwith give public notice of the same.

Office of election agent and sub-agent.

26. (1.) An election agent at an election for a county or borough shall have within the county or borough, or within any county of a city or town adjoining thereto, and a sub-agent shall have within his district, or within any county of a city or town adjoining thereto, an office or place to which all claims, notices, writs, summons, and documents may be sent, and the address of such office or place shall be declared at the same time as the appointment of the said agent to the returning officer, and shall be stated in the public notice of the name of the agent.

(2.) Any claim, notice, writ, summons, or document delivered at such office or place and addressed to the election agent or sub-agent, as the case may be, shall be deemed to have been served on him, and every such agent may in respect of any matter connected with the election in which he is acting be sued in any court having jurisdiction in the county or borough in which the said office or place is situate.

27. (1.) The election agent of a candidate by himself or by his sub-agent shall appoint every polling agent, clerk, and messenger employed for payment on behalf of the candidate at an election, and hire every committee room hired on behalf of the candidate.

Making of contracts through election agent.

(2.) A contract whereby any expenses are incurred on account of or in respect of the conduct or management of an election shall not be enforceable against a candidate at such election unless made by the candidate himself or by his election agent, either by himself or by his sub-agent; provided that the inability under this section to enforce such contract against the candidate shall not relieve the candidate from the consequences of any corrupt or illegal practice having been committed by his agent.

The early part of this section places, and very rightly places, alike the sole power and responsibility in the hands of the election agent; but the proviso may, in unscrupulous hands, work very great hardship on the candidate.

28. (1.) Except as permitted by or in pursuance of this Act, no payment and no advance or deposit shall be made by a candidate at an election or by any agent on behalf of the candidate or by any other person at any time, whether before, during,

Payment of expenses through election agent.

or after such election, in respect of any expenses incurred on account of or in respect of the conduct or management of such election, otherwise than by or through the election agent of the candidate, whether acting in person or by a sub-agent; and all money provided by any person other than the candidate for any expenses incurred on account of or in respect of the conduct or management of the election, whether as gift, loan, advance, or deposit, shall be paid to the candidate or his election agent and not otherwise;

Provided that this section shall not be deemed to apply to a tender of security to or any payment by the returning officer or to any sum disbursed by any person out of his own money for any small expense legally incurred by himself, if such sum is not repaid to him.

(2.) A person who makes any payment, advance, or deposit in contravention of this section, or pays in contravention of this section any money so provided as aforesaid, shall be guilty of an illegal practice.

Period for sending in claims and making payments for election expenses.

29. (1.) Every payment made by an election agent, whether by himself or a sub-agent, in respect of any expenses incurred on account of or in respect of the conduct or management of an election, shall, except where less than forty shillings, be vouched for by a bill stating the particulars and by a receipt.

(2.) Every claim against a candidate at an election or his election agent in respect of any expenses incurred on account of or in respect of the conduct or management of such election which is not sent in to the election agent within the time limited by this Act shall be barred and shall not be paid; and, subject to such exception as may be allowed in pursuance of this Act, an election agent who pays a claim in contravention of this enactment shall be guilty of an illegal practice.

It must be noticed that the language of this section is peremptory and absolute, "shall be barred, and shall not be paid," on penalty of an "illegal practice," so far as is applicable to an election agent. The time limited for "*sending in the bill*" is only fourteen days; and by sub-sects. 4 and 5 the time limited for *payment* is only twenty-eight days from the day of the declaration (see next section).

(3.) Except as by this Act permitted, the time limited by this Act for sending in claims shall be fourteen days after the day on which the candidates returned are declared elected.

(4.) All expenses incurred by or on behalf of a candidate at an election, which are incurred on account of or in respect of the conduct or management of such election, shall be paid within the time limited by this Act and not otherwise; and, subject to such exception as may be allowed in pursuance of this Act, an election agent who makes a payment in contravention of this provision shall be guilty of an illegal practice.

(5.) Except as by this Act permitted, the time limited by this Act for the payment of such expenses as aforesaid shall be twenty-eight days after the day on which the candidates returned are declared elected.

(6.) Where the election court reports that it has been proved to such court by a candidate that any payment made by an election agent in contravention of this section was made without the sanction or connivance of such candidate, the election of such candidate shall not be void, nor shall he be subject to any incapacity under this Act by reason only of such payment having been made in contravention of this section.

(7.) If the election agent in the case of any claim sent in to him within the time limited by this Act disputes it, or refuses or fails to pay it within the said period of twenty-eight days, such claim shall be deemed to be a disputed claim.

See the note on the last preceding section.

The words "*or fails to pay it*" will be very difficult to construe in many cases, and will probably require judicial ruling for its settlement in nearly every case.

(8.) The claimant may, if he thinks fit, bring an action for a disputed claim in any competent court; and any sum paid by the candidate or his agent in pursuance of the judgment or order of such court shall be deemed to be paid within the time limited by this Act, and to be an exception from the provisions of this Act, requiring claims to be paid by the election agent.

(9.) On cause shown to the satisfaction of the High Court, such Court on application by the claimant or by the candidate or his election agent may by order give leave for the payment by a candidate or his election agent of a disputed claim, or of a claim for any such expenses as aforesaid, although sent in after the time in this section mentioned for sending in claims, or although the same was sent in to the candidate and not to the election agent.

(10.) Any sum specified in the order of leave may be paid by the candidate or his election agent, and when paid in pursuance of such leave shall be deemed to be paid within the time limited by this Act.

30. If any action is brought in any competent court to recover a disputed claim against a candidate at an election, or his election agent, in respect of any expenses incurred on account or in respect of the conduct or management of such election, and the defendant admits his liability, but disputes the amount of the claim, the said amount shall, unless the court, on the application of the plaintiff in the action, otherwise directs, be forthwith referred for taxation to the master, official referee, registrar, or other proper officer of the court, and the amount found due on such taxation shall be the amount to be recovered in such action in respect of such claim.

Reference to taxation of claim against candidates.

31. (1.) The candidate at an election may pay any personal expenses incurred by him on account of or in connection with or incidental to such election to an amount not exceeding one hundred pounds, but any further personal expenses so incurred by him shall be paid by his election agent.

Personal expenses of candidate, and petty expenses.

The *personal* expenses ought never to exceed the 100*l*. here mentioned: and, properly managed, it is difficult to imagine that they could ever amount to so much in a borough, but still it may be found an inconveniently small limit in some of the larger northern county constituencies, where travelling continued for a somewhat lengthened time and over a large district may be absolutely requisite.

(2.) The candidate shall send to the election agent within the time limited by this Act for sending in claims a written statement of the amount of personal expenses paid as aforesaid by such candidate.

It will be advisable *in practice* to consider that this clause is confined to the expense incurred for the candidate's own travelling and charges for living, "postage," "stationery" and "telegrams" sent out by himself, though what the words "and other petty expenses" *may* include, it will be somewhat difficult to interpret.

(3.) Any person may, if so authorized in writing by the election agent of the candidate, pay any necessary expenses for stationery, postage, telegrams, and other petty expenses, to a total amount not exceeding that named in the authority, but any excess above the total amount so named shall be paid by the election agent.

Very great care will be necessary in the exercise of the power given by this sub-section.

(4.) A statement of the particulars of payments made by any person so authorized shall be sent to the election agent within the time limited by this Act for the sending in of claims, and shall be vouched for by a bill containing the receipt of that person.

Remuneration of election

32. (1.) So far as circumstances admit, this Act shall apply to a claim for his remuneration by an election agent and to the payment thereof in like manner as if he were any other creditor, and if any difference arises respecting the amount of such claim the claim shall be a disputed claim within the meaning of this Act, and be dealt with accordingly.

agent and returning officer's expenses.

(2.) The account of the charges claimed by the returning officer in the case of a candidate and transmitted in pursuance of section four of the Parliamentary Elections (Returning Officers) Act, 1875, shall be transmitted within the time specified in the said section to the election agent of the candidate, and need not be transmitted to the candidate.

38 & 39 Vict. c. 84.

This makes a slight change in the course laid down by the Act of 1875 (38 & 39 Vict. c. 84).

33. (1.) Within thirty-five days after the day on which the candidates returned at an election are declared elected, the election agent of every candidate at that election shall transmit to the returning officer a true return (in this Act referred to as a return respecting election expenses), in the form set forth in the Second Schedule to this Act or to the like effect, containing, as respects that candidate,—

Return and declaration respecting election expenses.

(a) A statement of all payments made by the election agent, together with all the bills and receipts (which bills and receipts are in this Act included in the expression "return respecting election expenses");

(b) A statement of the amount of personal expenses, if any, paid by the candidate;

(c) A statement of the sums paid to the returning officer for his charges, or, if the amount is in dispute, of the sum claimed and the amount disputed;

(d) A statement of all other disputed claims of which the election agent is aware;

(e) A statement of all the unpaid claims, if any, of which the election agent is aware, in respect of which application has been or is about to be made to the High Court;

(f) A statement of all money, securities, and equivalent of money received by the election agent from the candidate or any other person for the purpose of expenses incurred or to be incurred on account of or in respect of the conduct or management of the election, with a statement of the name of every person from whom the same may have been received.

A statement, together with "all bills and receipts," which latter words imply the originals—not copies—in such case, and it would therefore be desirable, for mere safety's sake, that every bill and every receipt should be made and signed in "duplicate original," *i.e.* that two copies should be made, one to be transmitted as the Act directs, the other to be kept by the candidate or his election agent. At all events, a very strict and accurate copy of every item, and indeed of every penny spent by the candidate, the election agent, and the sub-agents must be kept, either by the candidate or the election agent.

This, it will be seen, must be transmitted to the returning officer within thirty-five days of the declaration of the election by him.

(2.) The return so transmitted to the returning officer shall be accompanied by a declaration made by the election agent before a justice of the peace in the form in the Second Schedule to this Act (which declaration is in this Act referred to as a declaration respecting election expenses).

(3.) Where the candidate has named himself as his election agent, a statement of all money, securities, and equivalent of money paid by the candidate shall be substituted in the return required by this section to be transmitted by the election agent for the like statement of money, securities, and equivalent of money received by the election agent from the candidate; and the declaration by an election agent respecting election expenses need not be made, and the declaration by the candidate respecting election expenses shall be modified as specified in the Second Schedule to this Act.

Note the distinction enacted between the candidate, when acting as his own election agent, and when some other person acts in such capacity.

If advice may be tendered on such a subject, the Editor would express the most serious doubt as to whether it ever can be advisable for the candidate to nominate himself as his own agent.

(4.) At the same time that the agent transmits the said return, or within seven days afterwards, the candidate shall transmit or cause to be transmitted to the returning officer a declaration made by him before a justice of the peace, in the form in the first part of the Second Schedule to this Act (which declaration is in this Act referred to as a declaration respecting election expenses).

This must be done within *seven* days of the transmission mentioned in the previous part of this section.

(5.) If in the case of an election for any county or borough, the said return and declarations are not transmitted before the expiration of the time limited for the purpose, the candidate shall not, after the expiration of such time, sit or vote in the House of Commons as member for that county or borough until either such return and declarations have been transmitted, or until the date of the allowance of such an authorized excuse for the failure to transmit the same, as in this Act mentioned, and if he sits or votes in contravention of this enactment he shall forfeit one hundred pounds for every day on which he so sits or votes to any person who sues for the same.

Until transmitted, the new member must not sit and vote under a penalty of 100*l*.

(6.) If without such authorized excuse as in this Act mentioned, a candidate or an election agent fails to comply with the requirements of this section he shall be guilty of an illegal practice.

(7.) If any candidate or election agent knowingly makes the declaration required by this section falsely, he shall be guilty of an offence, and on conviction thereof on indictment shall be liable to the punishment for wilful and corrupt perjury; such offence shall also be deemed to be a corrupt practice within the meaning of this Act.

(8.) Where the candidate is out of the United Kingdom at the time when the return is so transmitted to the returning officer, the declaration required by this section may be made by him within fourteen days after his return to the United Kingdom, and in that case shall be forthwith transmitted to the returning officer, but the delay hereby authorized in making such declaration shall not exonerate the election agent from complying with the provisions of this Act as to the return and declaration respecting election expenses.

What is meant by "forthwith" may become the subject of litigation, if not done, that is, immediately on return to this country.

(9.) Where, after the date at which the return respecting election expenses is transmitted, leave is given by the High Court for any claims to be paid, the candidate or his election agent shall, within seven days after the payment thereof, transmit to the returning officer a return of the sums paid in pursuance of such leave accompanied by a copy of the order of the court giving the leave, and in default he shall be deemed to have failed to comply with the requirements of this section without such authorized excuse as in this Act mentioned.

Here again the limit is the very short one of seven days.

34. (1.) Where the return and declarations respecting election expenses of a candidate at an election for a county or borough have not been transmitted as required by this Act, or being transmitted contain some error or false statement, then—

Authorized excuse for non-compliance with provisions as to return and declaration respecting election expenses.

(a) if the candidate applies to the High Court or an election court and shows that the failure to transmit such return and declarations, or any of them, or any part thereof, or any error or false statement therein, has arisen by reason of his illness, or of the absence, death, illness, or misconduct of his election agent or sub-agent or of any clerk or officer of such agent, or by reason of inadvertence or of any reasonable cause of a like nature, and not by reason of any want of good faith on the part of the applicant, or

(b) if the election agent of the candidate applies to the High Court or an election court and shows that the failure to transmit the return and declarations which he was required to transmit, or any part thereof, or any error or false statement therein, arose by reason of his illness or of the death or illness of any prior election agent of the candidate, or of the absence, death, illness, or misconduct of any sub-agent, clerk, or officer of an election agent of the candidate, or by reason of inadvertence or of any reasonable cause of a like nature, and not by reason of any want of good faith on the part of the applicant,

the Court may, after such notice of the application in the said county or borough, and on production of such evidence of the grounds stated in the application, and of the good faith of the application, and otherwise, as to the Court seems fit, make such order for allowing an authorized excuse for the failure to transmit such return and declaration, or for an error or false statement in such return and declaration, as to the Court seems just.

(2.) Where it appears to the Court that any person being or having been election agent or sub-agent has refused or failed to make such return or to supply such particulars as will enable the candidate and his election agent respectively to comply with the provisions of this Act as to the return and declaration respecting election expenses, the Court before making an order allowing the excuse as in this section mentioned shall order such person to attend before the Court, and on his attendance shall, unless he shows cause to the contrary, order him to make the return and declaration, or to deliver a statement of the particulars required to be contained in the return, as to the Court seem just, and to make or deliver the same within such time and to such person and in such manner as the Court may direct, or may order him to be examined with respect to such particulars, and may in default of compliance with any such order order him to pay a fine not exceeding five hundred pounds.

Penalty not exceeding 500*l*. on any election agent or sub-agent.

(3.) The order may make the allowance conditional upon the making of the return and declaration in a modified form or within an extended time, and upon the compliance with such other terms as to the Court seem best calculated for carrying into effect the objects of this Act; and an order allowing an authorized excuse shall relieve the applicant for the order from any liability or consequences under this Act in respect of the matter excused by the order; and where it is proved by the candidate to the Court that any act or omission of the election agent in relation to the return and declaration respecting election expenses was without the sanction or connivance of the candidate, and that the candidate took all reasonable means for preventing such act or omission, the Court shall relieve the candidate from the consequences of such act or omission on the part of his election agent.

(4.) The date of the order, or if conditions and terms are to be complied with, the date at which the applicant fully complies with them, is referred to in this Act as the date of the allowance of the excuse.

Publication of summary of return of election expenses.

35. (1.) The returning officer at an election within ten days after he receives from the election agent of a candidate a return respecting election expenses shall publish a summary of the return in not less than two newspapers circulating in the county or borough for which the election was held, accompanied by a notice of the time and place at which the return and declarations (including the accompanying documents) can be inspected, and may charge the candidate in respect of such publication, and the amount of such charge shall be the sum allowed by the Parliamentary Elections (Returning Officers) Act, 1875.

38 & 39 Vict. c. 84.

(2.) The return and declarations (including the accompanying documents) sent to the returning officer by an election agent shall be kept at the office of the returning officer, or some convenient place appointed by him, and shall at all reasonable times during two years next after they are received by the returning officer be open to inspection by any person on payment of a fee of one shilling, and the returning officer shall on demand furnish copies thereof or any part thereof at the price of twopence for every seventy-two words. After the expiration of the said two years the returning officer may cause the said return and declarations, (including the accompanying documents,) to be destroyed, or, if the candidate or his election agent so require, shall return the same to the candidate.

1. The return must be kept for the next two years by the returning officer.
2. It is to be open to inspection on payment of one shilling as a fee.
3. Copies are to be furnished on demand and offer of twopence for every seventy-two words; and

4. At expiration of two years returning officer may destroy the papers, &c., if not demanded back by the candidate or the election agent.
5. But must return them, if duly applied for by candidate or election agent.

Disqualification of Electors.

36. Every person guilty of a corrupt or illegal practice, or of illegal employment, payment, or hiring at an election is prohibited from voting at such election, and if any such person votes his vote shall be void.

Prohibition of persons guilty of corrupt or illegal practices, &c. from voting.

37. Every person who, in consequence of conviction or of the report of any election court or election commissioners under this Act, or under the Corrupt Practices (Municipal Elections) Act, 1872, or under Part IV. of the Municipal Corporations Act, 1882, or under any other Act for the time being in force relating to corrupt practices at an election for any public office, has become incapable of voting at any election, whether a parliamentary election or an election to any public office, is prohibited from voting at any such election, and his vote shall be void.

Prohibition of disqualified persons from voting. 35 & 36 Vict. c. 60. 45 & 46 Vict. c. 50.

38. (1.) Before a person, not being a party to an election petition nor a candidate on behalf of whom the seat is claimed by an election petition, is reported by an election court, and before any person is reported by election commissioners, to have been guilty, at an election, of any corrupt or illegal practice, the court or commissioners, as the case may be, shall cause notice to be given to such person, and if he appears in pursuance of the notice, shall give him an opportunity of being heard by himself and of calling evidence in his defence to show why he should not be so reported.

Hearing of person before he is reported guilty of corrupt or illegal practice, and incapacity of person reported guilty.

This provision is very reasonable, and applies, as will be seen, to the proceedings before both election *commissioners* and an election *court*.

(2.) Every person reported by election commissioners to have been guilty at an election of any corrupt or illegal practice may appeal against such report to the next court of oyer and terminer or gaol delivery held in and for the county or place in which the offence is alleged to have been committed, and such court may hear and determine the appeal; and subject to rules of court such appeal may be brought, heard, and determined in like manner as if the court were a court of quarter sessions and the said commissioners were a court of summary jurisdiction, and the person so reported had been convicted by a court of summary jurisdiction for an offence under this Act, and notice of every such appeal shall be given to the Director of Public Prosecutions in the manner and within the time directed by rules of court, and subject to such rules then within three days after the appeal is brought.

This gives the right of appeal to anyone found guilty by election commissioners of any corrupt or illegal practice, such appeal being to the next general assizes or gaol delivery for the county or place where such offence is alleged to have been committed.

It will be noted, however, that this section does not give any appeal from the decision of an election *court*.

(3.) Where it appears to the Lord Chancellor that appeals under this section are interfering or are likely to interfere with the ordinary business transacted before any courts of oyer and terminer or gaol delivery, he may direct that the said appeals, or any of them, shall be heard by the judges for the time being on the rota for election petitions, and in such case one of such judges shall proceed to the county or place in which the offences are alleged to have been committed, and shall there hear and determine the appeals in like manner as if such judge were a court of oyer and terminer.

(4.) The provisions of the Parliamentary Elections Act, 1868, with respect to the reception and powers of and attendance on an election court, and to the expenses of an election court, and of receiving and accommodating an election court, shall apply as if such judge were an election court.

Provides the *modus operandi* by which such appeal shall be heard and investigated.

(5.) Every person who after the commencement of this Act is reported by any election court or election commissioners to have been guilty of any corrupt or illegal practice at an election, shall, whether he obtained a certificate of indemnity or not, be subject to the same incapacity as he would be subject to if he had at the date of such election been convicted of the offence of which he is reported to have been guilty: Provided that a report of any election commissioners inquiring into an election for a county or borough shall not avoid the election of any candidate who has been declared by an election court on the trial of a petition respecting such election to have been duly elected at such election or render him incapable of sitting in the House of Commons for the said county or borough during the Parliament for which he was elected.

Note the words "To the *same* incapacity."

(6.) Where a person who is a justice of the peace is reported by any election court or election commissioners to have been guilty of any corrupt practice in reference to an election, whether he has obtained a certificate of indemnity or not, it shall be the duty of the Director of Public Prosecutions to report the case to the Lord High Chancellor of Great Britain with such evidence as may have been given of such corrupt practice, and where any such person acts as a justice of the peace by virtue of his being, or having been, mayor of a borough, the Lord High Chancellor shall have the same power to remove such person from being a justice of the peace as if he was named in a commission of the peace.

Special power as to dealing with the case of justices of the peace found guilty of corrupt practices.

(7.) Where a person who is a barrister or a solicitor, or who belongs to any profession the admission to which is regulated by law, is reported by any election court or election commissioners to have been guilty of any corrupt practice in reference to an election, whether such person has obtained a certificate of indemnity or not, it shall be the duty of the Director of Public Prosecutions to bring the matter before the inn of court, High Court, or tribunal having power to take cognizance of any misconduct of such person in his profession, and such inn of court, High Court, or tribunal may deal with such person in like manner as if such corrupt practice were misconduct by such person in his profession.

The like special power as to dealing with the cases of barristers, solicitors, &c.

(8.) With respect to a person holding a license or certificate under the Licensing Acts (in this section referred to as a licensed person) the following provisions shall have effect:

(a) If it appears to the court by which any licensed person is convicted of the offence of bribery or treating that such offence was committed on his licensed premises, the court shall direct such conviction to be entered in the proper register of licenses.

(b) If it appears to an election court or election commissioners that a licensed person has knowingly suffered any bribery or treating in reference to any election to take place upon his licensed premises, such court or commissioners (subject to the provisions of this Act as to a person having an opportunity of being heard by himself and producing evidence before being reported) shall report the same; and whether such person obtained a certificate of indemnity or not it shall be the duty of the director of public prosecutions to bring such report before the licensing justices from whom or on whose certificate the licensed person obtained his license, and such licensing justices shall cause such report to be entered in the proper register of licenses.

(c) Where an entry is made in the register of licenses of any such conviction of or report respecting any licensed person as above in this section mentioned, it shall be taken into consideration by the licensing justices in determining whether they will or will not grant to such person the renewal of his license or certificate, and may be a ground, if the justices think fit, for refusing such renewal.

The like special powers as to licensed persons generally—

(a) If licensed person be convicted of bribery or treating on his own premises, the court is to direct such conviction to be entered on proper register.

(b) If he have knowingly permitted any bribery or treating to have been done by any other person than himself, the court or commissioners shall report him to the Director of Public Prosecutions, who shall bring the report to the cognizance of the licensing bench, who, in its turn, shall cause it to be registered.

And, on being taken into consideration, *may* form a ground for refusing renewal.

(9.) Where the evidence showing any corrupt practice to have been committed by a justice of the peace, barrister, solicitor, or other professional person, or any licensed person, was given before election commissioners, those commissioners shall report the case to the Director of Public Prosecutions, with such information as is necessary or proper for enabling him to act under this section.

(10.) This section shall apply to an election court under this Act, or under Part IV. of the Municipal Corporations Act, 1882, and the expression election shall be construed accordingly.

List in register of voters of persons incapacitated for voting by corrupt or illegal practices.

39. (1.) The registration officer in every county and borough shall annually make out a list containing the names and description of all persons who, though otherwise qualified to vote at a parliamentary election for such county or borough respectively, are not capable of voting by reason of having, after the commencement of this Act, been found guilty of a corrupt or illegal practice on conviction, or by the report of any election court or election commissioners, whether under this Act, or under Part IV. of the Municipal Corporations Act, 1882, or under any other Act for the time being in force relating to a parliamentary election or an election to any public office; and such officer shall state in the list (in this Act referred to as the corrupt and illegal practices list), the offence of which each person has been found guilty.

45 & 46 Vict. c. 50.

(2.) For the purpose of making out such list he shall examine the report of any election court or election commissioners who have respectively tried an election petition or inquired into an election where the election (whether a parliamentary election or an election to any public office) was held in any of the following places; that is to say,

(a) If he is the registration officer of a county, in that county, or in any borough in that county; and

(b) If he is the registration officer of a borough, in the county in which such borough is situate, or in any borough in that county.

New, so far as the provisions under sub-section 2 (a) and (b) are concerned.

(3.) The registration officer shall send the list to the overseers of every parish within his county or borough, together with his precept, and the overseers shall publish the list together with the list of voters, and shall also, in the case of every person in the corrupt and illegal practices list, omit his name from the list of persons entitled to vote, or, as circumstances require, add "objected" before his name in the list of claimants or copy of the register published by them, in like manner as is required by law in any other cases of disqualification.

(4.) Any person named in the corrupt and illegal practices list may claim to have his name omitted therefrom, and any person entitled to object to any list of voters for the county or borough may object to the omission of the name of any person from such list. Such claims and objections shall be sent in within the same time and be dealt with in like manner, and any such objection shall be served on the person referred to therein in like manner, as nearly as circumstances admit, as other claims and objections under the enactments relating to the registration of parliamentary electors.

(5.) The revising barrister shall determine such claims and objections and shall revise such list in like manner as nearly as circumstances admit as in the case of other claims and objections, and of any list of voters.

(6.) Where it appears to the revising barrister that a person not named in the corrupt and illegal practices list is subject to have his name inserted in such list, he shall (whether an objection to the omission of such name from the list has or has not been made, but) after giving such person an opportunity of making a statement to show cause to the contrary, insert his name in such list and expunge his name from any list of voters.

(7.) A revising barrister in acting under this section shall determine only whether a person is incapacitated by conviction or by the report of any election court or election commissioners, and shall not determine whether a person has or not been guilty of any corrupt or illegal practice.

Mark the restriction contained in this sub-section.

(8.) The corrupt and illegal practices list shall be appended to the register of electors, and shall be printed and published therewith wherever the same is printed or published.

Sub-sect. 8, new.

Proceedings on Election Petition.

Time for presentation of election petitions alleging illegal practice. 31 & 32 Vict. c. 125.

40. (1.) Where an election petition questions the return or the election upon an allegation of an illegal practice, then notwithstanding anything in the Parliamentary Elections Act, 1868, such petition, so far as respects such illegal practice, may be presented within the time following; (that is to say),

(a) At any time before the expiration of fourteen days after the day on which the returning officer receives the return and declarations respecting election expenses by the member to whose election the petition relates and his election agent.

(b) If the election petition specifically alleges a payment of money, or some other act to have been made or done since the said day by the member or an agent of the member, or with the privity of the member or his election agent in pursuance or in furtherance of the illegal practice alleged in the petition, the petition may be presented at any time within twenty-eight days after the date of such payment or other act.

(2.) Any election petition presented within the time limited by the Parliamentary Elections Act, 1868, may for the purpose of questioning the return or the election upon an allegation of an illegal practice be amended with the leave of the High Court within the time within which a petition questioning the return upon the allegation of that illegal practice can under this section be presented.

31 & 32 Vict. c. 125.

(3.) This section shall apply in the case of an offence relating to the return and declarations respecting election expenses in like manner as if it were an illegal practice, and also shall apply notwithstanding that the act constituting the alleged illegal practice amounted to a corrupt practice.

(4.) For the purposes of this section—

(a) Where the return and declarations are received on different days, the day on which the last of them is received, and

(b) Where there is an authorised excuse for failing to make and transmit the return and declarations respecting election expenses, the date of the allowance of the excuse, or if there was a failure as regards two or more of them, and the excuse was allowed at different times, the date of the allowance of the last excuse,

shall be substituted for the day on which the return and declarations are received by the returning officer.

(5.) For the purposes of this section, time shall be reckoned in like manner as it is reckoned for the purposes of the Parliamentary Elections Act, 1868.

41. (1.) Before leave for the withdrawal of an election petition is granted, there shall be produced affidavits by all the parties to the petition and their solicitors, and by the election agents of all of the said parties who were candidates at the election, but the High Court may on cause shown dispense with the affidavit of any particular person if it seems to the court on special grounds to be just so to do.

Withdrawal of election petition.

(2.) Each affidavit shall state that, to the best of the deponent's knowledge and belief, no agreement or terms of any kind whatsoever has or have been made, and no undertaking has been entered into, in relation to the withdrawal of the petition; but if any lawful agreement has been made with respect to the withdrawal of the petition, the affidavit shall set forth that agreement, and shall make the foregoing statement subject to what appears from the affidavit.

(3.) The affidavits of the applicant and his solicitor shall further state the ground on which the petition is sought to be withdrawn.

(4.) If any person makes any agreement or

terms, or enters into any undertaking, in relation to the withdrawal of an election petition, and such agreement, terms, or undertaking is or are for the withdrawal of the election petition in consideration of any payment, or in consideration that the seat shall at any time be vacated, or in consideration of the withdrawal of any other election petition, or is or are (whether lawful or unlawful) not mentioned in the aforesaid affidavits, he shall be guilty of a misdemeanor, and shall be liable on conviction on indictment to imprisonment for a term not exceeding twelve months, and to a fine not exceeding two hundred pounds.

Persons thus acting to be indictable, and on conviction liable to imprisonment for a term not exceeding twelve months and 200*l*. fine.

(5.) Copies of the said affidavits shall be delivered to the Director of Public Prosecutions a reasonable time before the application for the withdrawal is heard, and the Court may hear the Director of Public Prosecutions or his assistant or other representative (appointed with the approval of the Attorney-General), in opposition to the allowance of the withdrawal of the petition, and shall have power to receive the evidence on oath of any person or persons whose evidence the Director of Public Prosecutions or his assistant, or other representative, may consider material.

New; the Director of Public Prosecutions to be served with notice, and given him power to intervene.

(6.) Where in the opinion of the Court the proposed withdrawal of a petition was the result of any agreement, terms, or undertaking prohibited by this section, the Court shall have the same power with respect to the security as under section thirty-five of the Parliamentary Elections Act, 1868, where the withdrawal is induced by a corrupt consideration. 31 & 32 Vict. c. 125.

(7.) In every case of the withdrawal of an election petition the Court shall report to the Speaker whether, in the opinion of such Court, the withdrawal of such petition was the result of any agreement, terms, or undertaking, or was in consideration of any payment, or in consideration that the seat should at any time be vacated, or in consideration of the withdrawal of any other election petition, or for any other consideration, and if so, shall state the circumstances attending the withdrawal.

(8.) Where more than one solicitor is concerned for the petitioner or respondent, whether as agent for another solicitor or otherwise, the affidavit shall be made by all such solicitors.

(9.) Where a person not a solicitor is lawfully acting as agent in the case of an election petition, that agent shall be deemed to be a solicitor for the purpose of making an affidavit in pursuance of this section.

42. The trial of every election petition so far as is practicable, consistently with the interests of justice in respect of such trial, shall be continued de die in diem on every lawful day until its conclusion, and in case the rota of judges for the year shall expire before the conclusion of the trial, or

Continuation of trial of election petition.

of all the proceedings in relation or incidental to the petition, the authority of the said judges shall continue for the purpose of the said trial and proceedings.

Attendance of Director of Public Prosecutions on trial of election petition, and prosecution by him of offenders.

43. (1.) On every trial of an election petition the Director of Public Prosecutions shall by himself or by his assistant, or by such representative as hereinafter mentioned, attend at the trial, and it shall be the duty of such Director to obey any directions given to him by the election court with respect to the summoning and examination of any witness to give evidence on such trial, and with respect to the prosecution by him of offenders, and with respect to any person to whom notice is given to attend with a view to report him as guilty of any corrupt or illegal practice.

Wholly new; indeed, the Director of Public Prosecutions is now, for the first time, imported officially into election business, and, as will be seen, his duties and requirements are exceedingly specific.

He *must* act sometimes on the directions of other "authorities," sometimes he himself *may* take the initiative, sometimes he will have to exercise his powers compulsorily and by "order," sometimes by "direction of others," and sometimes again, voluntarily. It is needless to add, that these distinctions must be carefully noted and considered.

It may be stated that the whole of sect. 43, including, of course, its several sub-sections, is of the utmost importance, and cannot be too carefully studied.

(2.) It shall also be the duty of such director, without any direction from the election court, if it appears to him that any person is able to give material evidence as to the subject of the trial, to cause such person to attend the trial, and with the leave of the Court to examine such person as a witness.

(3.) It shall also be the duty of the said director, without any direction from the election court, if it appears to him that any person who has not received a certificate of indemnity has been guilty of a corrupt or illegal practice, to prosecute such person for the offence before the said Court, or if he thinks it expedient in the interests of justice before any other competent court.

It will be noticed that it is for the Director himself to choose the "competent court" where the trial is to be held.

(4.) Where a person is prosecuted before an election court for any corrupt or illegal practice, and such person appears before the Court, the Court shall proceed to try him summarily for the said offence, and such person, if convicted thereof upon such trial, shall be subject to the same incapacities as he is rendered subject to under this Act upon conviction, whether on indictment or in any other proceeding for the said offence; and further, may be adjudged by the Court, if the offence is a corrupt practice, to be imprisoned with or without hard labour, for a term not exceeding six months, or to pay a fine not exceeding two hundred pounds, and if the offence is an illegal practice, to pay such fine as is fixed by this Act for the offence;

Provided that, in the case of a corrupt practice, the Court, before proceeding to try summarily any person, shall give such person the option of being tried by a jury.

Note the proviso for giving accused the option of having a jury.

(5.) Where a person is so prosecuted for any such offence, and either he elects to be tried by a jury or he does not appear before the Court, or the Court thinks it in the interests of justice expedient that he should be tried before some other Court, the Court, if of opinion that the evidence is sufficient to put the said person upon his trial for the offence, shall order such person to be prosecuted on indictment or before a Court of summary jurisdiction, as the case may require, for the said offence; and in either case may order him to be prosecuted before such Court as may be named in the order; and for all purposes preliminary and of and incidental to such prosecution the offence shall be deemed to have been committed within the jurisdiction of the Court so named.

An additional provision for transferring the inquiry, if deemed advisable, to some other Court or tribunal.

(6.) Upon such order being made,

(a) if the accused person is present before the Court, and the offence is an indictable offence, the Court shall commit him to take his trial, or cause him to give bail to appear and take his trial for the said offence; and

(b) if the accused person is present before the Court, and the offence is not an indictable offence, the Court shall order him to be brought before the Court of summary jurisdiction before whom he is to be prosecuted, or cause him to give bail to appear before that Court; and

(c) if the accused person is not present before the Court, the Court shall as circumstances require issue a summons for his attendance, or a warrant to apprehend him and bring him, before a Court of summary jurisdiction, and that Court, if the offence is an indictable offence, shall, on proof only of the summons or warrant and the identity of the accused, commit him to take his trial, or cause him to give bail to appear and take his trial for the said offence, or if the offence is punishable on summary conviction, shall proceed to hear the case, or if such Court be not the Court before whom he is directed to be prosecuted, shall order him to be brought before that Court.

Surely, it would have been better in an offence of this gravity and magnitude to have provided that here, too, if the accused himself desired it, he might have the option of a jury, instead of allowing any Court of summary jurisdiction, especially surrounded, as it may be, with local feelings, and saturated in local politics, to have exclusive control over the matter, as is done by the latter part of this section.

(7.) The Director of Public Prosecutions may nominate, with the approval of the Attorney-General, a barrister or solicitor of not less than ten years standing to be his representative for the purpose of this section, and that representative shall receive such remuneration as the Commissioners of Her Majesty's Treasury may approve. There shall be allowed to the director and his assistant or representative, for the purposes of this section, such allowance for expenses as the Commissioners of Her Majesty's Treasury may approve.

(8.) The costs incurred in defraying the expenses of the Director of Public Prosecutions under this section (including the remuneration of his representative) shall, in the first instance, be paid by the Commissioners of Her Majesty's Treasury, and so far as they are not in the case of any prosecution paid by the defendant shall be deemed to be expenses of the election court; but if for any reasonable cause it seems just to the Court so to do, the Court shall order all or part of the said costs to be repaid to the Commissioners of Her Majesty's Treasury by the parties to the petition, or such of them as the Court may direct.

Power to election court to order payment by county or borough or individual of costs of election petition.

44. (1.) Where upon the trial of an election petition respecting an election for a county or borough it appears to the election court that a corrupt practice has not been proved to have been committed in reference to such election by or with the knowledge and consent of the respondent to the petition, and that such respondent took all reasonable means to prevent corrupt practices being committed on his behalf, the Court may make one or more orders with respect to the payment either of the whole or such part of the costs of the petition as as the Court may think right as follows:

(a) if it appears to the Court that corrupt practices extensively prevailed in reference to the said election, the Court may order the whole or part of the costs to be paid by the county or borough; and

(b) if it appears to the Court that any person or persons is or are proved, whether by providing money or otherwise, to have been extensively engaged in corrupt practices, or to have encouraged or promoted extensive corrupt practices in reference to such election, the Court may, after giving such person or persons an opportunity of being heard by counsel or solicitor and examining and cross-examining witnesses to show cause why the order should not be made, order the whole or part of the costs to be paid by that person, or those persons or any of them, and may order that if the costs cannot be recovered from one or more of such persons they shall be paid by some other of such persons or by either of the parties to the petition.

(2.) Where any person appears to the Court to have been guilty of the offence of a corrupt or illegal practice, the Court may, after giving such person an opportunity of making a statement to show why the order should not be made, order the whole or any part of the costs of or incidental to any proceeding before the Court in relation to the said offence or to the said person to be paid by the said person.

(3.) The rules and regulations of the Supreme Court of Judicature with respect to costs to be allowed in actions, causes, and matters in the High Court shall in principle and so far as practicable apply to the costs of petition and other proceedings under the Parliamentary Elections Act, 1868, and under this Act, and the taxing officer shall not allow any costs, charges, or expenses on a higher scale than would be allowed in any action, cause, or matter in the High Court on the higher scale, as between solicitor and client.

Miscellaneous.

Inquiry by Director of Public Prosecutions into alleged corrupt or illegal practices.

45. Where information is given to the Director of Public Prosecutions that any corrupt or illegal practices have prevailed in reference to any election, it shall be his duty, subject to the regulations under the Prosecution of Offences Act, 1879, to make such inquiries and institute such prosecutions as the circumstances of the case appear to him to require.

His duty to *inquire*, but any further proceedings are optional with the director.

Removal of incapacity on proof that it was procured by perjury.

46. Where a person has, either before or after the commencement of this Act, become subject to any incapacity under the Corrupt Practices Prevention Acts or this Act by reason of a conviction or of a report of any election court or election commissioners, and any witness who gave evidence against such incapacitated person upon the proceeding for such conviction or report is convicted of perjury in respect of that evidence, the incapacitated person may apply to the High Court, and the Court, if satisfied that the conviction or report so far as respects such person was based upon perjury, may order that such incapacity shall thenceforth cease, and the same shall cease accordingly.

Amendment of law as to

47. (1.) Every county shall be divided into polling districts, and a polling place shall be assigned to each district in such manner that, so far as is reasonably practicable, every elector resident in the county shall have his polling place within a distance not exceeding three miles from his residence, so nevertheless that a polling district need not in any case be constituted containing less than one hundred electors.

Polling districts and polling places.

This may operate to disfranchise many voters in the more sparsely populated districts of Scotland and Ireland, or in cases of permanent lameness or disability to travel, since payment for conveyances has been abolished by this Act.

(2.) In every county the local authority who have power to divide that county into polling districts shall from time to time divide the county into polling districts, and assign polling places to those districts, and alter those districts and polling places in such manner as may be necessary for the purpose of carrying into effect this section.

(3.) The power of dividing a borough into polling districts vested in a local authority by the Representation of the People Act, 1867, and the enactments amending the same, may be exercised by such local authority from time to time, and as often as the authority think fit, and the said power shall be deemed to include the power of altering any polling district, and the said local authority shall from time to time, where necessary for the purpose of carrying this section into effect, divide the borough into polling districts in such manner that—

(a) Every elector resident in the borough, if other than one hereinafter mentioned, shall be enabled to poll within a distance not exceeding one mile from his residence, so nevertheless that a polling district need not be constituted containing less than three hundred electors; and

(b) Every elector resident in the boroughs of East Retford, Shoreham, Cricklade, Much Wenlock, and Aylesbury, shall be enabled to poll within a distance not exceeding three miles from his residence, so nevertheless that a polling district need not be constituted containing less than one hundred electors.

(4.) So much of section five of the Ballot Act, 1872, and the enactments amending the same as in force and is not repealed by this Act, shall apply as if the same were incorporated in this section.

(5.) The expenses incurred by the local authority of a county or borough under this or any other Act in dividing their county or borough into polling districts, and, in the case of a county, assigning polling places to such districts, and in altering any such districts or polling places, shall be defrayed in like manner as if they were expenses incurred by the registration officer in the execution of the enactments respecting the registration of electors in such county or borough, and those enactments, so far as is consistent with the tenor thereof, shall apply accordingly.

Conveyance of voters by sea in certain cases.

48. Where the nature of a county is such that any electors residing therein are unable at an election for such county to reach their polling place without crossing the sea or a branch or arm thereof, this Act shall not prevent the provision of means for conveying such electors by sea to their polling place, and the amount of payment for such means of conveyance may be in addition to the maximum amount of expenses allowed by this Act.

Election commissioners not to inquire into elections before the passing of this Act.

49. Notwithstanding the provisions of the Act 15 and 16 Vict. cap. 57, or any amendment thereof, in any case where, after the passing of this Act, any commissioners have been appointed, on a joint address of both Houses of Parliament, for the purpose of making inquiry into the existence of corrupt practices in any election, the said commissioners shall not make inquiries concerning any election that shall have taken place prior to the passing of this Act, and no witness called before such commissioners, or at any election petition after the passing of this Act, shall be liable to be asked or bound to answer any question for the purpose of proving the commission of any corrupt practice at or in relation to any election prior to the passing of this Act: Provided that nothing herein contained shall affect any proceedings that shall be pending at the time of such passing.

This section is evidently inserted, perhaps quite rightly, to settle all doubts as to the rectitude of inquiring into the conduct of antecedent elections; some election tribunals having considered that they had the right to examine into such matters, with a view of showing or proving the prevalence of general corrupt practices in the constituency.

Legal Proceedings.

Trial in Central Criminal Court of indictment

50. Where an indictment as defined by this Act for any offence under the Corrupt Practices Prevention Acts or this Act is instituted in the High

for corrupt practice at instance of Attorney-General.

Court or is removed into the High Court by a writ of certiorari issued at the instance of the Attorney-General, and the Attorney-General suggests on the part of the Crown that it is expedient for the purposes of justice that the indictment should be tried in the Central Criminal Court, or if a special jury is ordered, that it should be tried before a judge and jury at the Royal Courts of Justice, the High Court may, if it think fit, order that such indictment shall be so tried upon such terms as the Court may think just, and the High Court may make such orders as appear to the Court necessary or proper for carrying into effect the order for such trial.

Limitation of time for prosecution of offence.

51. (1.) A proceeding against a person in respect of the offence of a corrupt or illegal practice or any other offence under the Corrupt Practices Prevention Acts or this Act shall be commenced within one year after the offence was committed, or if it was committed in reference to an election with respect to which an inquiry is held by election commissioners shall be commenced within one year after the offence was committed, or within three months after the report of such commissioners is made, whichever period last expires, so that it be commenced within two years after the offence was committed, and the time so limited by this section shall, in the case of any proceeding under the Summary Jurisdiction Acts for any such offence, whether before an election court or otherwise, be substituted for any limitation of time contained in the last-mentioned Acts.

(2.) For the purposes of this section the issue of a summons, warrant, writ, or other process shall be deemed to be a commencement of a proceeding, where the service or execution of the same on or against the alleged offender is prevented by the absconding or concealment or act of the alleged offender, but save as aforesaid the service or execution of the same on or against the alleged offender, and not the issue thereof, shall be deemed to be the commencement of the proceeding.

Persons charged with corrupt practice may be found guilty of illegal practice.

52. Any person charged with a corrupt practice may, if the circumstances warrant such finding, be found guilty of an illegal practice, (which offence shall for that purpose be an indictable offence,) and any person charged with an illegal practice may be found guilty of that offence, notwithstanding that the act constituting the offence amounted to a corrupt practice, and a person charged with illegal payment, employment, or hiring, may be found guilty of that offence, notwithstanding that the act constituting the offence amounted to a corrupt or illegal practice.

Application of enactments of 17 & 18 Vict. c. 102, and 26 & 27 Vict. c. 29, relating to prosecutions for bribery.

17 & 18 Vict. c. 102.

26 & 27 Vict. c. 29.

53. (1.) Sections ten, twelve, and thirteen of the Corrupt Practices Prevention Act, 1854, and section six of the Corrupt Practices Prevention Act, 1863 (which relate to prosecutions for bribery and other offences under those Acts), shall extend to any prosecution on indictment for the offence of any corrupt practice within the meaning of this Act, and to any action for any pecuniary forfeiture for an offence under this Act, in like manner as if such offence were bribery within the meaning of those Acts, and such indictment or action were the indictment or action in those sections mentioned, and an order under the said section ten may be made on the defendant; but the Director of Public Prosecutions or any person instituting any prosecution in his behalf or by direction of an election court shall not be deemed to be a private prosecutor, nor required under the said sections to give any security.

(2.) On any prosecution under this Act, whether on indictment or summarily, and whether before an election court or otherwise, and in any action for a pecuniary forfeiture under this Act, the person prosecuted or sued, and the husband or wife of such person, may, if he or she think fit, be examined as an ordinary witness in the case.

(3.) On any such prosecution or action as aforesaid it shall be sufficient to allege that the person charged was guilty of an illegal practice, payment, employment, or hiring within the meaning of this Act, as the case may be, and the certificate of the returning officer at an election that the election mentioned in the certificate was duly held, and that the person named in the certificate was a candidate at such election, shall be sufficient evidence of the facts therein stated.

Prosecution on summary conviction, and appeal to quarter sessions.

54. (1.) All offences under this Act punishable on summary conviction may be prosecuted in manner provided by the Summary Jurisdiction Acts.

(2.) A person aggrieved by a conviction by a

court of summary jurisdiction for an offence under this Act may appeal to general or quarter sessions against such conviction.

Application of Summary Jurisdiction and Indictable Offences Acts to proceedings before election courts.

55. (1.) Except that nothing in this Act shall authorize any appeal against a summary conviction by an election court, the Summary Jurisdiction Acts shall, so far as is consistent with the tenor thereof, apply to the prosecution of an offence summarily before an election court, in like manner as if it were an offence punishable only on summary conviction, and accordingly the attendance of any person may be enforced, the case heard and determined, and any summary conviction by such court be carried into effect and enforced, and the costs thereof paid, and the record thereof dealt with under those Acts in like manner as if the court were a petty sessional court for the county or place in which such conviction took place.

(2.) The enactments relating to charges before justices against persons for indictable offences shall, so far as is consistent with the tenor thereof, apply to every case where an election court orders a person to be prosecuted on indictment in like manner as if the court were a justice of the peace.

Exercise of jurisdiction of High Court, and making of rules of court.

56. (1.) Subject to any Rules of Court, any jurisdiction vested by this Act in the High Court may, so far as it relates to indictments or other criminal proceedings, be exercised by any judge of the Queen's Bench Division, and in other respects may either be exercised by one of the judges for the time being on the rota for the trial of election petitions, sitting either in court or at chambers, or may be exercised by a master of the Supreme Court of Judicature in manner directed by and subject to an appeal to the said judges:

Provided that a master shall not exercise jurisdiction in the case either of an order declaring any act or omission to be an exception from the provisions of this Act with respect to illegal practices, payments, employments, or hirings, or of an order allowing an excuse in relation to a return or declaration respecting election expenses.

(2.) Rules of Court may from time to time be made, revoked, and altered for the purposes of this Act, and of the Parliamentary Elections Act, 1868, and the Acts amending the same, by the same authority by whom Rules of Court for procedure and practice in the Supreme Court of Judicature can for the time being be made.

Director of Public Prosecutions, and expenses of prosecutions.

42 & 43 Vict. c. 22.

57. (1) The Director of Public Prosecutions in performing any duty under this Act shall act in accordance with the regulations under the Prosecution of Offences Act, 1879, and subject thereto in accordance with the directions (if any) given to him by the Attorney-General; and any assistant or representative of the Director of Public Prosecutions in performing any duty under this Act shall act in accordance with the said regulations and directions, if any, and with the directions given to him by the Director of Public Prosecutions.

(2.) Subject to the provisions of this Act, the

costs of any prosecution on indictment for an offence punishable under this Act, whether by the Director of Public Prosecutions or his representative or by any other person, shall, so far as they are not paid by the defendant, be paid in like manner as costs in the case of a prosecution for felony are paid.

This, of course, is new, arising from the Director of Public Prosecutions being imported into the operation of this Act.

58. (1.) Where any costs or other sums (not being costs of a prosecution on indictment) are, under an order of an election court, or otherwise under this Act, to be paid by a county or borough, the Commissioners of Her Majesty's Treasury shall pay those costs or sums, and obtain repayment of the amount so paid, in like manner as if such costs and sums were expenses of election commissioners paid by them, and the Election Commissioners Expenses Acts, 1869 and 1871, shall apply accordingly as if they were herein re-enacted, and in terms made applicable to the above-mentioned costs and sums.

Recovery of costs payable by county or borough or by person.

32 & 33 Vict. c. 21.
34 & 35 Vict. c. 61.

(2.) Where any costs or other sums are, under the order of an election court or otherwise under this Act, to be paid by any person, those costs shall be a simple contract debt due from such person to the person or persons to whom they are to be paid, and if payable to the Commissioners of Her Majesty's Treasury shall be a debt to Her Majesty, and in either case may be recovered accordingly.

Supplemental Provisions, Definitions, Savings, and Repeal.

Obligation of witness to answer, and certificate of indemnity.

59. (1.) A person who is called as a witness respecting an election before any election court shall not be excused from answering any question relating to any offence at or connected with such election, on the ground that the answer thereto may criminate or tend to criminate himself or on the ground of privilege;

Provided that—

(a) a witness who answers truly all questions which he is required by the election court to answer shall be entitled to receive a certificate of indemnity under the hand of a member of the court stating that such witness has so answered: and

(b) an answer by a person to a question put by or before any election court shall not, except in the case of any criminal proceeding for perjury in respect of such evidence, be in any proceeding, civil or criminal, admissible in evidence against him:

The witness *must* answer, but he may avoid self-incrimination so far as any penalty is concerned, except that of obloquy and disgrace, provided he "makes a clean breast of it" by answering the questions put to him without equivocation, as in such case undoubtedly he would become "entitled" to his certificate under (a), and to his indemnification, such as it may be, under (b).

(2.) Where a person has received such a certificate of indemnity in relation to an election, and any legal proceeding is at any time instituted against him for any offence under the Corrupt

Practices Prevention Acts or this Act committed by him previously to the date of the certificate at or in relation to the said election, the court having cognisance of the case shall on proof of the certificate stay the proceeding, and may in their discretion award to the said person such costs as he may have been put to in the proceeding.

(3.) Nothing in this section shall be taken to relieve a person receiving a certificate of indemnity from any incapacity under this Act or from any proceeding to enforce such incapacity (other than a criminal prosecution).

Sub-sect. 3 carefully confines the operation of this enactment to providing against *criminal* prosecutions only.

(4.) This section shall apply in the case of a witness before any election commissioners, in like manner as if the expression "election court" in this section included election commissioners.

Sub-sect. 4 thus puts election commissioners into the same position as an election court in their power of dealing with a witness.

(5.) Where a solicitor or person lawfully acting as agent for any party to an election petition respecting any election for a county or borough has not taken any part or been concerned in such election, the election commissioners inquiring into such election shall not be entitled to examine such solicitor or agent respecting matters which came to his knowledge by reason only of his being concerned as solicitor or agent for a party to such petition.

This is an endeavour—possibly a successful one—to carry out the old legal arrangement that no solicitor is at liberty to disclose affairs committed to his keeping by his client.

Submission of report of election court or commissioners to Attorney-General.

60. An election court or election commissioners, when reporting that certain persons have been guilty of any corrupt or illegal practice, shall report whether those persons have or not been furnished with certificates of indemnity; and such report shall be laid before the Attorney-General (accompanied in the case of the commissioners with the evidence on which such report was based) with a view to his instituting or directing a prosecution against such persons as have not received certificates of indemnity, if the evidence should, in his opinion, be sufficient to support a prosecution.

Breach of duty by officer.

35 & 36 Vict. c. 33.

61. (1.) Section eleven of the Ballot Act, 1872, shall apply to a returning officer or presiding officer or clerk who is guilty of any wilful misfeasance or wilful act or omission in contravention of this Act in like manner as if the same were in contravention of the Ballot Act, 1872.

6 Vict. c. 18.

(2.) Section ninety-seven of the Parliamentary Registration Act, 1843, shall apply to every registration officer who is guilty of any wilful misfeasance or wilful act of commission or omission contrary to this Act in like manner as if the same were contrary to the Parliamentary Registration Act, 1843.

Publication and service of notices.

35 & 36 Vict. c. 33.

62. (1.) Any public notice required to be given by the returning officer under this Act shall be given in the manner in which he is directed by the Ballot Act, 1872, to give a public notice.

(2.) Where any summons, notice, or document is required to be served on any person with reference to any proceeding respecting an election for a county or borough, whether for the purpose of causing him to appear before the High Court or any election court, or election commissioners, or otherwise, or for the purpose of giving him an opportunity of making a statement, or showing cause, or being heard by himself, before any court or commissioners, for any purpose of this Act, such summons, notice, or document may be served either by delivering the same to such person, or by leaving the same at, or sending the same by post by a registered letter to, his last known place of abode in the said county or borough, or if the proceeding is before any court or commissioners, in such other manner as the court or commissioners may direct, and in proving such service by post it shall be sufficient to prove that the letter was prepaid, properly addressed, and registered with the post office.

(3.) In the form of notice of a parliamentary election set forth in the second schedule to the Ballot Act, 1872, the words "or any illegal practice" shall be inserted after the words "or other corrupt practices," and the words the "Corrupt and Illegal Practices Prevention Act, 1883," shall be inserted after the words "Corrupt Practices Prevention Act, 1854."

Definition of candidate, and saving for persons nominated without consent.

63. (1.) In the Corrupt Practices Prevention Acts, as amended by this Act, the expression "candidate at an election" and the expression "candidate" respectively mean, unless the context otherwise requires, any person elected to serve in Parliament at such election, and any person who is nominated as a candidate at such election, or is declared by himself or by others to be a candidate, on or after the day of the issue of the writ for such election, or after the dissolution or vacancy in consequence of which such writ has been issued;

(2.) Provided that where a person has been nominated as a candidate or declared to be a candidate by others, then—

(a) If he was so nominated or declared without his consent, nothing in this Act shall be construed to impose any liability on such person, unless he has afterwards given his assent to such nomination or declaration or has been elected; and

(b) If he was so nominated or declared, either without his consent or in his absence and he takes no part in the election, he may, if he thinks fit, make the declaration respecting election expenses contained in the second part of the Second Schedule to this Act, and the election agent shall, so far as circumstances admit, comply with the provisions of this Act with respect to expenses incurred on account of or in respect of the conduct or management of the election in like manner as if the candidate had been nominated or declared with his consent.

General interpretation of terms.

64. In this Act, unless the context otherwise requires—

The expression "election" means the election

of a member or members to serve in Parliament:

The expression "election petition" means a petition presented in pursuance of the Parliamentary Elections Act, 1868, as amended by this Act: 31 & 32 Vict. c. 125.

The expression "election court" means the judges presiding at the trial of an election petition, or, if the matter comes before the High Court, that Court:

The expression "election commissioners" means commissioners appointed in pursuance of the Election Commissioners Act, 1852, and the enactments amending the same: 15 & 16 Vict. c. 57.

The expression "High Court" means her Majesty's High Court of Justice in England:

The expressions "court of summary jurisdiction," "petty sessional court," and "Summary Jurisdiction Acts" have the same meaning as in the Summary Jurisdiction Act, 1879: 42 & 43 Vict. c. 49.

The expression the "attorney general" includes the solicitor general in cases where the office of the attorney general is vacant or the attorney general is interested or otherwise unable to act:

The expression "registration officer" means the clerk of the peace in a county, and the town clerk in a borough, as respectively defined by the enactments relating to the registration of parliamentary electors:

The expression "elector" means any person whose name is for the time being on the register roll or book containing the names of the persons entitled to vote at the election with reference to which the expression is used:

The expression "register of electors" means the said register roll or book:

35 & 36 Vict. c. 33. The expression "polling agent" means an agent of the candidate appointed to attend at a polling station in pursuance of the Ballot Act, 1872, or of the Acts therein referred to or amending the same:

The expression "person" includes an association or body of persons, corporate or unincorporate, and where any act is done by any such association or body, the members of such association or body who have taken part in the commission of such act shall be liable to any fine or punishment imposed for the same by this Act:

The expression "committee room" shall not include any house or room occupied by a candidate at an election as a dwelling, by reason only of the candidate there transacting business with his agents in relation to such election; nor shall any room or building be deemed to be a committee room for the purposes of this Act by reason only of the candidate or any agent of the candidate addressing therein electors, committeemen, or others:

The expression "public office" means any office under the Crown or under the charter of a city or municipal borough or under the Acts relating to Municipal Corporations or to the

Poor Law, or under the Elementary Education Act, 1870, or under the Public Health Act, 1875, or under any Acts amending the above-mentioned Acts, or under any other Acts for the time being in force (whether passed before or after the commencement of this Act) relating to local government, whether the office is that of mayor, chairman, alderman, councillor, guardian, member of a board, commission, or other local authority in any county, city, borough, union, sanitary district, or other area, or is the office of clerk of the peace, town clerk, clerk or other officer under a council, board, commission, or other authority, or is any other office, to which a person is elected or appointed under any such charter or Act as above-mentioned, and includes any other municipal or parochial office; and the expressions "election," "election petition," "election court," and "register of electors," shall, where expressed to refer to an election for any such public office, be construed accordingly:

33 & 34 Vict. c. 75.
38 & 39 Vict. c. 55.

The expression "judicial office" includes the office of justice of the peace and revising barrister:

The expression "personal expenses" as used with respect to the expenditure of any candidate in relation to any election includes the reasonable travelling expenses of such candidate, and the reasonable expenses of his living at hotels or elsewhere for the purposes of and in relation to such election:

The expression "indictment" includes information:

The expression "costs" includes costs, charges, and expenses:

The expression "payment" includes any pecuniary or other reward; and the expressions "pecuniary reward" and "money" shall be deemed to include any office, place, or employment, and any valuable security or other equivalent for money, and any valuable consideration, and expressions referring to money shall be construed accordingly:

The expression "Licensing Acts" means the Licensing Acts, 1872 to 1874:

Other expressions have the same meaning as in the Corrupt Practices Prevention Acts.

Short titles.

65. (1.) The enactments described in the Third Schedule to this Act are in this Act referred to as the Corrupt Practices Prevention Acts.

(2.) The Acts mentioned in the Fourth Schedule to this Act are in this Act referred to and may be cited respectively by the short titles in that behalf in that schedule mentioned.

(3.) This Act may be cited as the Corrupt and Illegal Practices Prevention Act, 1883.

(4.) This Act and the Corrupt Practices Prevention Acts may be cited together as the Corrupt Practices Prevention Acts, 1854 to 1883.

Repeal of Acts.

66. The Acts set forth in the Fifth Schedule to this Act are hereby repealed as from the commencement of this Act to the extent in the third column of that schedule mentioned, provided that this repeal or the expiration of any enactment not continued by this Act shall not revive any enactment which at the commencement of this Act is repealed, and shall not affect anything duly done or suffered before the commencement of this Act, or any right acquired or accrued or any incapacity incurred before the commencement of this Act, and any person subject to any incapacity under any enactment hereby repealed or not continued shall continue subject thereto, and this Act shall apply to him as if he had become so subject in pursuance of the provisions of this Act.

67. This Act shall come into operation on the fifteenth day of October one thousand eight hundred and eighty-three, which day is in this Act referred to as the commencement of this Act.

Commencement of Act.

Application of Act to Scotland.

68. This Act shall apply to Scotland, with the following modifications:

Application of Act to Scotland.

(1.) The following expressions shall mean as follows:

The expression "misdemeanour" shall mean crime and offence:

The expression "indictment" shall include criminal letters:

The expression "solicitor" shall mean enrolled law agent:

The expression "revising barrister" shall mean sheriff:

The expression "barrister" shall mean advocate:

The expression "petty sessional court" shall mean sheriff court:

The expression "quarter sessions" shall mean the Court of Justiciary:

The expression "registration officer" shall mean an assessor under the enactments relating to the registration of parliamentary voters:

The expression "municipal borough" shall include royal burgh and burgh of regality and burgh of barony:

The expression "Acts relating to municipal corporations" shall include the General Police and Improvement (Scotland) Act, 1862, and any other Act relating to the constitution and government of burghs in Scotland:

The expression "mayor" shall mean provost or chief magistrate:

The expression "alderman" shall mean baillie:

The expression "Summary Jurisdiction Acts" shall mean the Summary Jurisdiction (Scotland) Acts, 1864 and 1881, and any Acts amending the same.

(2.) The provisions of this Act with respect to polling districts and the expenses of dividing a county or borough into polling districts shall not apply to Scotland.

(3.) The provisions respecting the attendance at the trial of an election petition of a representative of the Director of Public Prosecutions shall not apply to Scotland, and in place thereof the following provisions shall have effect:

(a.) At the trial of every election petition in Scotland her Majesty's advocate shall be represented by one of his deputes or by the procurator-fiscal of the sheriff court of the district, who shall attend such trial as part of his official duty, and shall give all necessary assistance to the judge with respect to the citation of witnesses and recovery of documents:

(b.) If the judge shall grant a warrant for the apprehension, commitment, or citation of any person suspected of being guilty of a corrupt or illegal practice, the case shall be reported to her Majesty's advocate in order that such person may be brought to trial before the High Court of Justiciary or the sheriff, according to the nature of the case:

(c.) It shall be the duty of the advocate depute or, in his absence, the procurator-fiscal, if it appears to him that a corrupt or illegal practice within the meaning of this Act has been committed by any person who has not received a certificate of indemnity, to report the case to her Majesty's advocate in order to such person being brought to trial before the proper court, although no warrant may have been issued by the judge.

(4.) The jurisdiction of the High Court of Justice under this Act shall, in Scotland, be exercised by one of the Divisions of the Court of Session, or by a judge of the said court to whom the same may be remitted by such division, and subject to an appeal thereto, and the Court of Session shall have power to make acts of sederunt for the purposes of this Act.

(5.) Court of Oyer and Terminer shall mean a circuit Court of Justiciary, and the High Court of Justiciary shall have powers to make acts of adjournal regulating the procedure in appeals to the circuit court under this Act.

(6.) All offences under this Act punishable on summary conviction may be prosecuted in the sheriff court in manner provided by the Summary Jurisdiction Acts, and all necessary jurisdictions are hereby conferred on sheriffs.

(7.) The authority given by this Act to the Director of Public Prosecutions in England shall in Scotland be exercised by her Majesty's advocate, and the reference to the Prosecution of Offences Act, 1879, shall not apply.

(8.) The expression "Licensing Acts" shall
25 & 26 Vict. c. 35. mean "The Public Houses Acts Amendment
39 & 40 (Scotland) Act, 1862," and "The Publicans' Cer-
Vict. c. 26. tificates (Scotland) Act, 1876," and the Acts thereby amended and therein recited.

(9.) The expression "register of licences" shall mean the register kept in pursuance of section twelve of the Act of the ninth year of the reign of King George the Fourth, chapter fifty-eight.

(10.) The references to the Public Health Act, 1875, and to the Elementary Education Act, 1870, shall be construed to refer to the Public Health (Scotland) Act, 1867, and to the Elementary Education (Scotland) Act, 1872.

(11.) Any reference to the Parliamentary Elections Returning Officers Act, 1875, shall not apply.

(12.) The provision with respect to the registration officer sending the corrupt and illegal practices list to overseers and the dealing with such list by overseers shall not apply, and in lieu thereof it is hereby enacted that the assessor shall in counties include the names of such persons in the list of persons who have become disqualified, and in boroughs shall omit the names of such persons from the list of persons entitled to vote.

(13.) The power given by this Act to the Lord Chancellor in England shall in Scotland, except so far as relates to the justices of the peace, be exercised by the Lord Justice General.

(14.) Any reference to the Attorney-General shall refer to the Lord Advocate.

(15.) The provisions with respect to the removal of cases to the Central Criminal Court or to the trial of cases at the Royal Courts of Justice shall not apply.

(16.) Section thirty-eight of the County Voters Registration (Scotland) Act, 1861, shall be substituted for section ninety-seven of the Parliamentary Registration Act, 1843, where reference is made to that section in this Act. 24 & 25 Vict. c. 83.

(17.) The provision of this Act with regard to costs shall not apply to Scotland, and instead thereof the following provision shall have effect:

The costs of petitions and other proceedings under "The Parliamentary Elections Act, 1868," and under this Act, shall, subject to any regulations which the Court of Session may make by act of sederunt, be taxed as nearly as possible according to the same principles as costs between agent and client are taxed in a cause in that court, and the auditor shall not allow any costs, charges, or expenses on a higher scale.

Application of Act to Ireland.

Application of Act to Ireland.

69. This Act shall apply to Ireland, with the following modifications:

(1.) No person shall be tried for any offence against this Act under any of the provisions of "The Prevention of Crime (Ireland) Act, 1882." 45 & 46 Vict. c. 25.

(2.) The expression "Summary Jurisdiction Acts" means, with reference to the Dublin Metropolitan Police District, the Acts regulating the powers and duties of justices of the peace and of the police in such district; and with reference to other parts of Ireland means the Petty Sessions (Ireland) Act, 1851, and any Acts amending the said Act. 14 & 15 Vict. c. 93.

(3.) Section one hundred and three of the Act of the session of the thirteenth and fourteenth years of the reign of her present Majesty, chapter sixty-nine, shall be substituted for section ninety-seven of the Parliamentary Registration Act, 1843, where reference is made to that section in this Act.

(4.) The provision with respect to the registration officer sending the corrupt and illegal practices list to overseers and the dealing with such list by overseers shall not apply, and in lieu thereof it is hereby enacted that the registration officer shall, after making out such list, himself publish the same in the manner in which he publishes the lists referred to in the twenty-first and the thirty-third sections of the Act of the session of the thirteenth and fourteenth years of the reign of her present Majesty, chapter sixty-nine; and shall also in the case of every person in the corrupt and illegal practices list enter "objected to" against his name in the register and lists made out by such registration officer in like manner as he is by law required to do in other cases of disqualification.

(5.) The Supreme Court of Judicature in Ireland shall be substituted for the Supreme Court of Judicature.

(6.) The High Court of Justice in Ireland shall be substituted for the High Court of Justice in England.

(7.) The Lord High Chancellor of Ireland shall be substituted for the Lord High Chancellor of Great Britain.

(8.) The Attorney-General for Ireland shall be substituted for the Director of Public Prosecutions, and the reference to the Prosecution of Offences Act, 1879, shall not apply.

(9.) The provisions of this Act relative to polling districts shall not apply to Ireland, but in the county of the town of Galway there shall be a polling station at Barna, and at such other places within the parliamentary borough of Galway as the town commissioners may appoint.

(10.) Any reference to Part IV. of the Municipal Corporations Act, 1882, shall be construed to refer to the Corrupt Practices (Municipal Elections) Act, 1872.

(11.) Any reference to the Licensing Acts shall be construed to refer to the Licensing Acts (Ireland), 1872—1874.

41 & 42 Vict. c. 52. (12.) The Public Health (Ireland) Act, 1878, shall be substituted for the Public Health Act, 1875.

(13.) The provisions with respect to the removal of cases to the Central Criminal Court, or to the trial of cases at the Royal Courts of Justice, shall not apply to Ireland.

Continuance.

Continuance. **70.** This Act shall continue in force until the thirty-first day of December one thousand eight hundred and eighty-four, and no longer, unless continued by Parliament; and such of the Corrupt Practices Prevention Acts as are referred to in Part I. of the Third Schedule to this Act shall continue in force until the same day, and no longer, unless continued by Parliament.

SCHEDULES.

FIRST SCHEDULE.

PART I.

PERSONS LEGALLY EMPLOYED FOR PAYMENT.

(1.) One election agent and no more.

(2.) In counties one deputy election agent (in this Act referred to as a sub-agent) to act within each polling district and no more.

(3.) One polling agent in each polling station and no more.

(4.) In a borough one clerk and one messenger, or if the number of electors in the borough exceeds five hundred, a number of clerks and messengers not exceeding in number one clerk and one messenger for every complete five hundred electors in the borough, and if there is a number of electors over and above any complete five hundred or complete five hundreds of electors, then one clerk and one messenger may be employed for such number, although not amounting to a complete five hundred.

(5.) In a county for the central committee room one clerk and one messenger, or if the number of electors in the county exceeds five thousand, then a number of clerks and messengers not exceeding in number one clerk and one messenger for every complete five thousand electors in the county; and if there is a number of electors over and above any complete five thousand or complete five thousands of electors, then one clerk and one messenger may be employed for such number, although not amounting to a complete five thousand.

(6.) In a county a number of clerks and messengers not exceeding in number one clerk and one messenger for each polling district in the county, or where the number of electors in a polling district exceeds five hundred one clerk and one messenger for every complete five hundred electors in the polling district, and if there is a number of electors over and above any complete five hundred or complete five hundreds of electors, then one clerk and one messenger may be employed for such number, although not amounting to a complete five hundred: Provided always, that the number of clerks and messengers so allowed in any county may be employed in any polling district where their services may be required.

(7.) Any such paid election agent, sub-agent, polling agent, clerk, and messenger may or may not be an elector but may not vote.

(8.) In the case of the boroughs of East Retford, Shoreham, Cricklade, Much Wenlock, and Aylesbury, the provisions of this part of this schedule shall apply as if such borough were a county.

Part II.

Legal Expenses in Addition to Expenses under Part I.

(1.) Sums paid to the returning officer for his charges not exceeding the amount authorized by the Act 38 & 39 Vict. c. 84.

(2.) The personal expenses of the candidate.

(3.) The expenses of printing, the expenses of advertising, and the expenses of publishing, issuing, and distributing addresses and notices.

(4.) The expenses of stationery, messages, postage, and telegrams.

(5.) The expenses of holding public meetings.

(6.) In a borough the expenses of one committee room, and if the number of electors in the borough exceeds five hundred, then of a number of committee rooms not exceeding the number of one committee room for every complete five hundred electors in the borough, and if there is a number of electors over and above any complete five hundred or complete five hundreds of electors, then of one committee room for such number, although not amounting to a complete five hundred.

(7.) In a county the expenses of a central committee room, and in addition of a number of committee rooms not exceeding in number one committee room for each polling district in the county, and where the number of electors in a polling district exceeds five hundred one additional committee room may be hired for every complete five hundred electors in such polling district over and above the first five hundred.

Part III.

Maximum for Miscellaneous Matters.

Expenses in respect of miscellaneous matters other than those mentioned in Part I. and Part II. of this schedule not exceeding in the whole the maximum amount of two hundred pounds, so nevertheless that such expenses are not incurred in respect of any matter or in any manner constituting an offence under this or any other Act, or in respect of any matter or thing, payment for which is expressly prohibited by this or any other Act.

Part IV.

Maximum Scale.

(1.) In a borough the expenses mentioned above in Parts I., II., and III. of this schedule, other than personal expenses and sums paid to the returning officer for his charges, shall not exceed in the whole the maximum amount in the scale following:

If the number of electors on the register—

	The maximum amount shall be—
Does not exceed 2,000 . .	350*l.*
Exceeds 2,000	380*l.*, and an additional 30*l.* for every complete 1,000 electors above 2,000.

Provided that in Ireland if the number of electors on the register—

	The maximum amount shall be—
Does not exceed 500 . .	200*l.*
Exceeds 500, but does not exceed 1,000	250*l.*
Exceeds 1,000, but does not exceed 1,500	275*l.*

(2.) In a county the expenses mentioned above in Parts I., II. and III. of this schedule, other than personal expenses and sums paid to the returning officer for his charges, shall not exceed in the whole the maximum amount in the scale following:

If the number of electors on the register—

	The maximum amount shall be—
Does not exceed 2,000	650*l.* in England and Scotland, and 500*l.* in Ireland.
Exceeds 2,000	710*l.* in England and Scotland, and 540*l.* in Ireland; and an additional 60*l.* in England and Scotland, and 40*l.* in Ireland, for every complete 1,000 electors above 2,000.

Part V.

General.

(1.) In the case of the boroughs of East Retford, Shoreham, Cricklade, Much Wenlock and Aylesbury, the provisions of Parts II., III. and IV. of this schedule shall apply as if such borough were a county.

(2.) For the purposes of this schedule, the number of electors shall be taken according to the enumeration of the electors in the register of electors.

(3.) Where there are two or more joint candidates at an election the maximum amount of expenses mentioned in Parts III. and IV. of this schedule shall, for each of such joint candidates, be reduced by one-fourth, or if there are more than two joint candidates by one-third.

(4.) Where the same election agent is appointed by or on behalf of two or more candidates at an election, or where two or more candidates, by themselves or any agent or agents, hire or use the same committee rooms for such election, or employ or use the services of the same sub-agents, clerks, messengers, or polling agents at such election, or publish a joint address or joint circular or notice at such election, those candidates shall be deemed for the purposes of this enactment to be joint candidates at such election.

Provided that—

(a) The employment and use of the same committee room, sub-agent, clerk, messenger, or polling agent, if accidental or casual, or of a trivial and unimportant character, shall not be deemed of itself to constitute persons joint candidates.

(b) Nothing in this enactment shall prevent candidates from ceasing to be joint candidates.

(c) Where any excess of expenses above the maximum allowed for one of two or more joint candidates has arisen owing to his having ceased to be a joint candidate, or to his having become a joint candidate after having begun to conduct his election as a separate candidate, and such ceasing or beginning was in good faith, and such excess is not more than under the circumstances is reasonable, and the total expenses of such candidate do not exceed the maximum amount allowed for a separate candidate, such excess shall be deemed to have arisen from a reasonable cause within the meaning of the enactments respecting the allowance by the High Court or election court of an exception from the provisions of this Act which would otherwise make an act an illegal practice, and the candidate and his election agent may be relieved accordingly from the consequences of having incurred such excess of expenses.

SECOND SCHEDULE.

Part I.

Form of Declarations as to Expenses.

Form for Candidate.

I , having been a candidate at the election for the county [*or* borough] of on the day of , do hereby solemnly and sincerely declare that I have examined the return of election expenses [about to be] transmitted by my election agent [*or if the candidate is his own election agent*, "by me"] to the returning officer at the said election, a copy of which is now shown to me and marked , and to the best of my knowledge and belief that return is correct;

And I further solemnly and sincerely declare that, except as appears from that return, I have not, and to the best of my knowledge and belief no person, nor any club, society, or association, has, on my behalf, made any payment, or given, promised, or offered any reward, office, employment, or valuable consideration, or incurred any liability on account of or in respect of the conduct or management of the said election.

And I further solemnly and sincerely declare that I have paid to my election agent [*if the candidate is also his own election agent, leave out* "to my election agent"] the sum of pounds and no more for the purpose of the said election, and that, except as specified in the said return, no money, security, or equivalent for money has to my knowledge or belief been paid, advanced, given, or deposited by any one to or in the hands of my election agent [*or if the candidate is his own election agent*, "myself"] or any other person for the purpose of defraying any expenses incurred on my behalf on account of or in respect of the conduct or management of the said election;

And I further solemnly and sincerely declare that I will not, except so far as I may be permitted by law, at any future time make or be party to the making or giving of, any payment, reward, office, employment, or valuable consideration for the purpose of defraying any such expenses as last mentioned, or provide or be party to the providing of any money, security, or equivalent for money for the purpose of defraying any such expenses.

Signature of declarant *C. D.*

Signed and declared by the above-named declarant on the day of , before me.

(Signed) *E. F.*

Justice of the Peace for

Form for Election Agent.

I, , being election agent to , candidate at the election for the county [*or* borough] of , on the day of , do hereby solemnly and sincerely declare that I have examined the return of election expenses about to be transmitted by me to the returning officer at the said election, and now shown to me and marked , and to the best of my knowledge and belief that return is correct;

And I hereby further solemnly and sincerely declare that, except as appears from that return, I have not and to the best of my knowledge and belief no other person, nor any club, society, or association has on behalf of the said candidate made any payment, or given, promised, or offered any reward, office, employment, or valuable consideration, or incurred any liability on account of or in respect of the conduct or management of the said election;

And I further solemnly and sincerely declare that I have received from the said candidate pounds and no more [*or* nothing] for the purpose of the said election, and that, except as specified in the said return sent by me, no money, security, or equivalent for money has been paid, advanced, given, or deposited by any one to me or in my hands, or, to the best of my knowledge and belief, to or in the hands of any other person for the purpose of defraying any expenses incurred on behalf of the said candidate on account of, or in respect of the conduct or management of the said election.

Signature of declarant *A. B.*

Signed and declared by the above-named declarant on the day of before me.

(Signed) *E. F.*

Justice of the peace for

FORM OF RETURN OF ELECTION EXPENSES.

I, *A. B.*, being election agent to *C. D.*, candidate at the election for the county [*or* borough] of on the day of , make the following return respecting election expenses of the said candidate at the said election [*or where the candidate has named himself as election agent,* "I, *C. D.*, candidate at the "election for the county [*or* borough] of on "the day of , acting as my own election "agent, make the following return respecting my "election expenses at the said election"].

Receipts.

Received of [*the above-named candidate*] [*or where the candidate is his own election agent,* "Paid by me"]	£
Received of *J. K.*	£
[*Here set out the name and description of every person, club, society, or association, whether the candidate or not, from whom any money, securities, or equivalent of money was received in respect of expenses incurred on account of or in connection with or incidental to the above election, and the amount received from each person, club, society, or association separately.*]	

Expenditure.

Paid to *E. F.*, the returning officer for the said county [*or* borough] for his charges at the said election	£
Personal expenses of the said *C. D.*, paid by himself [*or if the candidate is his own election agent,* "Paid by me as candidate"]	£
Do. do. paid by me [*or if the candidate is his own election agent, add* "acting as election agent"]	£
Received by me for my services as election agent at the said election [*or if the candidate is his own election agent, leave out this item*]	£
Paid to *G. H.*, as sub-agent of the polling district of	£
[*The name and description of each sub-agent and the sum paid to him must be set out separately.*]	
Paid to as polling agent	£

Paid to as clerk for days' services £
Paid to as messenger for days' services £

[*The names and descriptions of every polling agent, clerk, and messenger, and the sum paid to each, must be set out separately either in the account or in a separate list annexed to and referred to in the account, thus,* "Paid to polling agent (*or as the case may be*) as per annexed list £ ."]

Paid to the following persons in respect of goods supplied or work and labour done:

To *P. Q.* (printing) .... £
To *M. N.* (advertising) .... £
To *R. S.* (stationery) .... £

[*The name and description of each person, and the nature of the goods supplied, or the work and labour done by each, must be set out separately either in the account or in a separate list annexed to and referred to in the account.*]

Paid for postage .... £
Paid for telegrams .... £
Paid for the hire of rooms as follows:

For holding public meetings .... £
For committee rooms .... £

[*A room hired for a public meeting or for a committee room must be named or described so as to identify it; and the name and description of every person to whom any payment was made for each such room, together with the amount paid, must be set out separately either in the account or in a separate list annexed to and referred to in the account.*]

Paid for miscellaneous matters, namely.... £

[*The name and description of each person to whom any sum is paid, and the reason for which it was paid to him, must be set out separately either in the account or in a separate list annexed to and referred to in the account.*]

In addition to the above, I am aware, as election agent for *C. D.*, [*or if the candidate is his own election agent, leave out* "as election agent for *C. D.*"] of the following disputed and unpaid claims; namely,—

Disputed claims.

By *T. U.* for .... £

[*Here set out the name and description of each person whose claim is disputed, the amount of the claim, and the goods, work, or other matter on the ground of which the claim is based.*]

Unpaid claims allowed by the High Court to be paid after the proper time or in respect of which application has been or is about to be made to the High Court.

By *M. O.* for .... £

[*Here state the name and description of each person to whom any such claim is due, and the amount of the claim, and the goods, work, and labour or other matter on account of which the claim is due.*]

(Signed) *A. B.*

PART II.

FORM OF DECLARATION AS TO EXPENSES.

Form for candidate where declared a candidate or nominated in his absence and taking no part in the election.

I, , having been nominated [*or* having been declared by others] in my absence [to be] a candidate at the election for the county or borough of held on the day of , do hereby solemnly and sincerely declare that I have taken no part whatever in the said election.

And I further solemnly and sincerely declare that [*or* with the exception of] I have not, and no person, club, society, or association at my expense has, made any payment or given, promised, or offered, any reward, office, employment, or valuable consideration, or incurred any liability on account of or in respect of the conduct or management of the said election.

And I further solemnly and sincerely declare that [*or* with the exception of] I have not paid any money or given any security or equivalent for money to the person acting as my election agent at the said election, or to any other person, club, society, or association on account of or in respect of the conduct or management of the said election, and that [*or* with the exception of] I am entirely ignorant of any money security or equivalent for money having been paid, advanced, given, or deposited by any one for the purpose of defraying any expenses incurred on account of or in respect of the conduct or management of the said election.

And I further solemnly and sincerely declare that I will not, except so far as I may be permitted by law, at any future time make or be party to the making or giving of any payment, reward, office, employment, or valuable consideration for the purpose of defraying any such expenses as last mentioned, or provide or be party to the providing of any money, security, or equivalent of money for the purpose of defraying any such expenses.

Signature of declarant C. D.

Signed and declared by the above-named declarant on the day of , before me,

(Signed) *E. F.*

Justice of the Peace for

THIRD SCHEDULE.

Corrupt Practices Prevention Acts.

Session and Chapter.	Title of Act.	Enactments referred to as being the Corrupt Practices Prevention Acts.
	Part One. *Temporary.*	
17 & 18 Vict. c. 102.	The Corrupt Practices Prevention Act, 1854.	The whole Act so far as unrepealed.
26 & 27 Vict. c. 29.	An Act to amend and continue the law relating to corrupt practices at elections of members of Parliament.	The whole Act so far as unrepealed.
31 & 32 Vict. c. 125.	The Parliamentary Elections Act, 1868.	The whole Act so far as unrepealed.
35 & 36 Vict. c. 33.	The Ballot Act, 1872..........	Part III. so far as unrepealed.
42 & 43 Vict. c. 75.	The Parliamentary Elections and Corrupt Practices Act, 1879.	The whole Act so far as unrepealed.

Session and Chapter.	Title of Act.	Enactments referred to as being the Corrupt Practices Prevention Acts.
	PART TWO. *Permanent.*	
30 & 31 Vict. c. 102.	The Representation of the People Act, 1867.	Sections eleven, forty-nine, and fifty.
31 & 32 Vict. c. 48.	The Representation of the People (Scotland) Act, 1868.	Sections eight and forty-nine.
31 & 32 Vict. c. 49.	The Representation of the People (Ireland) Act, 1868.	Sections eight and thirteen.
44 & 45 Vict. c. 40.	The Universities Elections Amendment (Scotland) Act, 1881.	Sub-section seventeen of section two.

PART THREE.

ENACTMENTS DEFINING THE OFFENCES OF BRIBERY AND PERSONATION.

The Corrupt Practices Prevention Act, 1854, 17 & 18 Vict. c. 102, ss. 2, 3.

Bribery defined.

Sect. 2. The following persons shall be deemed guilty of bribery, and shall be punishable accordingly:—

(1.) Every person who shall, directly or indirectly, by himself, or by any other person on his behalf, give, lend, or agree to give or lend, or shall offer, promise, or promise to procure or to endeavour to procure, any money or valuable consideration to or for any voter, or to or for any person on behalf of any voter, or to or for any other person in order to induce any voter to vote or refrain from voting, or shall corruptly do any such act as aforesaid on account of such voter having voted or refrained from voting at any election:

(2.) Every person who shall, directly or indirectly, by himself, or by any other person on his behalf, give or procure, or agree to give or procure, or offer, promise, or promise to procure or to endeavour to procure, any office, place, or employment to or for any voter, or to or for any person on behalf of any voter, or to or for any other person in order to induce such voter to vote or refrain from voting, or shall corruptly do any such act as aforesaid on account of any voter having voted or refrained from voting at any election:

(3.) Every person who shall, directly or indirectly, by himself, or by any other person on his behalf, make any such gift, loan, offer, promise, procurement, or agreement as aforesaid to or for any person, in order to induce such person to procure or endeavour to procure the return of any person to serve in Parliament, or the vote of any voter at any election:

(4.) Every person who shall, upon or in consequence of any such gift, loan, offer, promise, procurement, or agreement, procure or engage, promise, or endeavour to procure the return of any person to serve in Parliament, or the vote of any voter at any election:

(5.) Every person who shall advance or pay, or cause to be paid, any money to or to the use of any other person with the intent that such money or any part thereof shall be expended in bribery at any election, or who shall knowingly pay or cause to be paid any money to any person in discharge or repayment of any money wholly or in part expended in bribery at any election. Provided always, that the aforesaid enactment shall not extend or be construed to extend to any money paid or agreed to be paid for or on account of any legal expenses bonâ fide incurred at or concerning any election.

Bribery further defined.

Sect. 3. The following persons shall also be deemed guilty of bribery, and shall be punishable accordingly:

(1.) Every voter who shall, before or during any election, directly or indirectly, by himself or by any other person on his behalf, receive, agree, or contract for any money, gift, loan, or valuable consideration, office, place, or employment, for himself or for any other person, for voting or agreeing to vote, or for refraining or agreeing to refrain from voting at any election:

(2.) Every person who shall, after any election, directly or indirectly, by himself or by any other person on his behalf, receive any money or valuable consideration on account of any person having voted or refrained from voting, or having induced any other person to vote or refrain from voting at any election.

The Representation of the People Act, 1867, 30 & 31 Vict. c. 102, s. 49.

Corrupt payment of rates to be punishable as bribery.

Any person, either directly or indirectly, corruptly paying any rate on behalf of any ratepayer for the purpose of enabling him to be registered as a voter, thereby to influence his vote at any future election, and any candidate or other person, either directly or indirectly, paying any rate on behalf of any voter for the purpose of inducing him to vote or refrain from voting, shall be guilty of bribery, and be punishable accordingly; and any person on whose behalf and with whose privity any such payment as in this section is mentioned is made, shall also be guilty of bribery, and punishable accordingly.

The Representation of the People (Scotland) Act, 1868, 31 & 32 Vict. c. 48, s. 49.

Corrupt payment of rates to be punishable as bribery.

Any person, either directly or indirectly, corruptly paying any rate on behalf of any ratepayer for the purpose of enabling him to be registered as a voter, thereby to influence his vote at any future election, and any candidate or other person, either directly or indirectly, paying any rate on behalf of any voter for the purpose of inducing him to vote or refrain from voting, shall be guilty of bribery, and be punishable accordingly; and any person on whose behalf and with whose privity any such payment as in this sectioned mentioned is made shall also be guilty of bribery, and punishable accordingly.

The Universities Elections Amendment (Scotland) Act, 1881, 44 & 45 Vict. c. 40, s. 2.

Corrupt payment of registration fee to be punish-

17. Any person, either directly or indirectly, corruptly paying any fee for the purpose of enabling any person to be registered as a member of the general council, and thereby to influence his vote at

any future election, and any candidate or other person, either directly or indirectly, paying such fee on behalf of any person for the purpose of inducing him to vote or to refrain from voting, shall be guilty of bribery, and shall be punishable accordingly; and any person on whose behalf and with whose privity any such payment as in this section mentioned is made, shall also be guilty of bribery, and punishable accordingly. able as bribery.

The Ballot Act, 1872, 35 & 36 Vict. c. 33, s. 24.

A person shall, for all purposes of the laws relating to parliamentary and municipal elections, be deemed to be guilty of the offence of personation who, at an election for a county or borough, or at a municipal election, applies for a ballot paper in the name of some other person, whether that name be that of a person living or dead, or of a fictitious person, or who, having voted once at any such election, applies at the same election for a ballot paper in his own name. Personation defined.

FOURTH SCHEDULE.—Short Titles.

Session and Chapter.	Long Title.	Short Title.
15 & 16 Vict. c. 57.	An Act to provide for more effectual inquiry into the existence of corrupt practices at the election of members to serve in Parliament.	Election Commissioners Act, 1852.
26 & 27 Vict. c. 29.	An Act to amend and continue the law relating to corrupt practices at elections of members of Parliament.	The Corrupt Practices Prevention Act, 1863.

FIFTH SCHEDULE.—Enactments Repealed.

Note.—Portions of Acts which have already been specifically repealed are in some instances included in the repeal in this schedule in order to preclude henceforth the necessity of looking back to previous Acts.

A description or citation of a portion of an Act is inclusive of the words, section, or other part first or last mentioned, or otherwise referred to as forming the beginning or as forming the end of the portion comprised in the description or citation.

Session and Chapter.	Title or Short Title.	Extent of Repeal.
60 Geo. 3 and 1 Geo. 4, c. 11.	An Act for the better regulation of polls, and for making further provision touching the election of members to serve in Parliament for Ireland.	Section thirty-six.
1 & 2 Geo. 4, c. 58.	An Act to regulate the expenses of election of Members to serve in Parliament for Ireland.	The whole Act except section three.
4 Geo. 4, c. 55.	An Act to consolidate and amend the several Acts now in force so far as the same relate to the election and return of members to serve in Parliament for the counties of cities and counties of towns in Ireland.	Section eighty-two.
17 & 18 Vict. c. 102.	The Corrupt Practices Prevention Act, 1854.	Section one. Section two, from "and any person so offending" to "with full costs of suit." Section three, from "and any person so offending" to the end of the section. Section four. Section five. Section six. Section seven, from "and all payments" to the end of the section. Section nine, section fourteen, section twenty-three, section thirty-six, section thirty-eight, from "and the words personal expenses" to the end of the section, and section thirty-nine and Schedule A.

Session and Chapter.	Title or Short Title.	Extent of Repeal.
21 & 22 Vict. c. 87.	An Act to continue and amend the Corrupt Practices Prevention Act, 1854.	The whole Act.
26 & 27 Vict. c. 29.	An Act to amend and continue the law relating to corrupt practices at elections of members of Parliament.	The whole Act, except section six.
30 & 31 Vict. c. 102.	The Representation of the People Act, 1867.	Section thirty-four, from "and in other boroughs the justices" to "greater part thereof is situate" and section thirty-six.
31 & 32 Vict. c. 48.	The Representation of the People (Scotland) Act, 1868.	Section twenty-five.
31 & 32 Vict. c. 49.	The Representation of the People (Ireland) Act, 1868.	Section twelve.
31 & 32 Vict. c. 58.	The Parliamentary Electors Registration Act, 1868.	Section eighteen, from "the power of dividing their county" to the end of the section.
31 & 32 Vict. c. 125.	The Parliamentary Elections Act, 1868.	So much of section three as relates to the definitions of "candidate." Section sixteen. Section thirty-three. Section thirty-six. Section forty-one, from "but according to the same principles" to "the High Court of Chancery." Section forty-three. Section forty-five. Section forty-six. Section forty-seven. Section fifty-eight, from "The principles" down to "in the court of session," being subsection sixteen.

Session and Chapter.	Title or Short Title.	Extent of Repeal.
35 & 36 Vict. c. 33.	The Ballot Act, 1872............	Section five, from the beginning down to "one hundred registered electors." Section twenty-four, from "The offence of personation, or of aiding," to "hard labour," and from "The offence of personation shall be deemed to be" to the end of the section.
42 & 43 Vict. c. 75.	The Parliamentary Elections and Corrupt Practices Act, 1879.	Section three and schedule.
43 Vict. c. 18..	The Parliamentary Elections and Corrupt Practices Act, 1880.	The whole Act, except sections one and three.

APPENDIX.

THE REPRESENTATION OF THE PEOPLE ACT, 1867.

30 & 31 Vict. c. 102.

An Act further to amend the Laws relating to the Representation of the People in England and Wales. [15th August, 1867.]

Whereas it is expedient to amend the laws relating to the representation of the people in England and Wales:

Be it enacted by the Queen's most excellent Majesty, by and with the advice and consent of the lords spiritual and temporal, and commons, in this present parliament assembled, and by the authority of the same, as follows:

Short title.

1. This act shall be cited for all purposes as "The Representation of the People Act, 1867."

Application of act.

2. This act shall not apply to Scotland or Ireland, nor in anywise affect the election of members to serve in parliament for the universities of Oxford or Cambridge.

PART I.

Franchises.

Occupation franchise for voters in boroughs.

3. Every man shall, in and after the year 1868, be entitled to be registered as a voter, and, when registered, to vote for a member or members to serve in parliament for a borough, who is qualified as follows; (that is to say,)

1. Is of full age, and not subject to any legal incapacity: and
2. Is on the last day of July in any year, and has during the whole of the preceding twelve calendar months been, an inhabitant occupier, as owner or tenant, of any dwelling-house within the borough; and
3. Has during the time of such occupation been rated as an ordinary occupier in respect of the premises so occupied by him within the borough to all rates

(if any) made for the relief of the poor in respect of such premises; and

4. Has on or before the 20th day of July in the same year bonâ fide paid an equal amount in the pound to that payable by other ordinary occupiers in respect of all poor rates that have become payable by him in respect of the said premises up to the preceding 5th day of January:

Provided that no man shall under this section be entitled to be registered as a voter by reason of his being a joint occupier of any dwelling-house.

Lodger franchise for voters in boroughs.

4. Every man shall, in and after the year 1868, be entitled to be registered as a voter, and, when registered, to vote for a member or members to serve in parliament for a borough, who is qualified as follows; (that is to say,)

1. Is of full age and not subject to any legal incapacity; and
2. As a lodger has occupied in the same borough separately and as sole tenant for the twelve months preceding the last day of July in any year the same lodgings, such lodgings being part of one and the same dwelling-house, and of a clear yearly value, if let unfurnished, of 10*l*. or upwards; and
3. Has resided in such lodgings during the twelve months immediately preceding the last day of July, and has claimed to be registered as a voter at the next ensuing registration of voters.

Property franchise for voters in counties.

5. Every man shall, in and after the year 1868, be entitled to be registered as a voter, and, when registered, to vote for a member or members to serve in parliament for a county, who is qualified as follows; (that is to say,)

1. Is of full age, and not subject to any legal incapacity, and is seised at law or in equity of any lands or tenements of freehold, copyhold, or any other tenure whatever, for his own life, or for the life of another, or for any lives whatsoever, or for any larger estate of the clear yearly value of not less than 5*l*. over and above all rents and charges payable out of or in respect of the same, or who is entitled, either as lessee or assignee, to any lands or tenements of freehold or of any other tenure whatever for the unexpired residue, whatever it may be, of any term originally created for a period of not less than sixty years (whether determinable on a life or lives or not), of the clear yearly value of not less than 5*l*. over and above all rents and charges payable out of or in respect of the same:

Provided that no person shall be registered as a voter under this section unless he has complied with the provisions of the 26th section of the act of the 2nd year of the reign of his majesty William IV. chapter 45.

Occupation franchise for voters in counties.

6. Every man shall, in and after the year 1868, be entitled to be registered as a voter, and, when registered, to vote for a member or members to serve in parliament for a county, who is qualified as follows; (that is to say,)

1. Is of full age, and not subject to any legal incapacity; and
2. Is on the last day of July in any year, and has during the 12 months immediately preceding been, the occupier, as owner or tenant, of lands or tenements within the county of the rateable value of 12*l.* or upwards: and
3. Has during the time of such occupation been rated in respect to the premises so occupied by him to all rates (if any) made for the relief of the poor in respect of the said premises; and
4. Has on or before the 20th day of July in the same year paid all poor rates that have become payable by him in respect of the said premises up to the preceding 5th day of January.

Occupiers in boroughs to be rated, and not owners.

7. Where the owner is rated at the time of the passing of this act to the poor rate in respect of a dwelling-house or other tenement situate in a parish wholly or partly in a borough, instead of the occupier, his liability to be rated in any future poor rate shall cease, and the following enactments shall take effect with respect to rating in all boroughs:

1. After the passing of this act no owner of any dwelling-house or other tenement situate in a parish either wholly or partly within a borough shall be rated to the poor rate instead of the occupier, except as hereinafter mentioned:
2. The full rateable value of every dwelling-house or other separate tenement, and the full rate in the pound payable by the occupier and the name of the occupier, shall be entered in the rate book:

Where the dwelling-house or tenement shall be wholly let out in apartments or lodgings not separately rated, the owner of such dwelling-house or tenement shall be rated in respect thereof to the poor rate:

Provisoes as to compositions, &c.

Provided as follows:

(1.) That nothing in this act contained shall affect any composition existing at the time of the passing of this act, so nevertheless that no such composition shall remain in force beyond the 29th day of September next:

(2.) That nothing herein contained shall affect any rate

made previously to the passing of this act, and the powers conferred by any subsisting act for the purpose of collecting and recovering a poor rate, shall remain and continue in force for the collection and recovery of any such rate or composition:

(3.) That where the occupier under a tenancy subsisting at the time of the passing of this act of any dwelling-house or other tenement which has been let to him free from rates is rated and has paid rates in pursuance of this act, he may deduct from any rent due or accruing due from him in respect of the said dwelling-house or other tenement, any amount paid by him on account of the rates to which he may be rendered liable by this act.

First registration of occupiers of dwelling houses, &c.

8. Where any occupier of a dwelling-house or other tenement (for which the owner at the time of the passing of this act is rated or is liable to be rated), would be entitled to be registered as an occupier in pursuance of this act at the first registration of parliamentary voters to be made after the year 1867, if he had been rated to the poor rate for the whole of the required period, such occupier shall, notwithstanding he may not have been rated prior to the 29th day of September, 1867, as an ordinary occupier, be entitled to be registered, subject to the following conditions:

1. That he has been duly rated as an ordinary occupier to all poor rates in respect of the premises after the liability of the owner to be rated to the poor rate has ceased, under the provisions of this act:
2. That he has, on or before the 20th day of July, 1868, paid all poor rates, which have become payable by him as an ordinary occupier in respect of the premises, up to the preceding 5th day of January.

Restriction as to number of votes in certain counties and boroughs;

9. At a contested election for any county or borough represented by three members no person shall vote for more than two candidates.

and in the city of London.

10. At a contested election for the city of London no person shall vote for more than three candidates.

No elector who has been employed for reward within six months of an election to be entitled to vote.

11. No elector who, within six months before or during any election for any county or borough, shall have been retained, hired or employed for all or any of the purposes of the election for reward by or on behalf of any candidate at such election as agent, canvasser, clerk, messenger or in other like employment, shall be entitled to vote at such election, and if he shall so vote he shall be guilty of a misdemeanor.

12. Whereas, upon representations made to her Majesty in joint addresses of both houses of Parliament, to the effect that the Select Committees of the House of Commons appointed to try the petitions complaining of undue elections and returns for the boroughs of Totnes, Reigate, Great Yarmouth and Lancaster had reason to believe that corrupt practices had extensively prevailed at the last elections for the said boroughs, commissioners were appointed for the purpose of making inquiry into the existence of such corrupt practices, in pursuance of the act of parliament, passed in the 16th year of the reign of her present Majesty, chapter 57, intituled "An Act to provide for the more effectual inquiry into the existence of corrupt practices at elections for members to serve in parliament:" and whereas the commissioners so appointed reported to her Majesty as follows:—

Boroughs of Totnes, Reigate, Yarmouth, and Lancaster to cease to return members after end of present parliament.

15 & 16 Vict. c. 57.

1. As respects the said borough of Totnes, that at every election for the said borough since and including the election in the year 1857 corrupt practices had extensively prevailed:
2. As respects the said borough of Reigate, that bribery and treating had prevailed at the election in the year 1859, and had extensively prevailed at the two elections in the year 1858, and at the elections in the years 1863 and 1865:
3. As respects the said borough of Great Yarmouth, that corrupt and illegal practices had extensively prevailed at the elections in the years 1859 and 1865:
4. As respects the said borough of Lancaster, that corrupt practices had extensively prevailed at the election in the year 1865, and, with rare exceptions, had for a long time prevailed at contested elections for members to serve in parliament for that borough:

Be it enacted, that from and after the end of this present parliament the boroughs of Totnes, Reigate, Great Yarmouth and Lancaster shall respectively cease to return any member or members to serve in parliament.

Persons reported guilty of bribery in Totnes disqualified as voters for southern division of Devon in respect of qualification arising in said borough.

13. Whereas the commissioners appointed under a commission of her Majesty, dated the 16th day of June, 1866, for the purpose of making inquiry into the existence of corrupt practices in the borough of Totnes, have by their report, dated the 29th day of January, 1867, reported to her Majesty that the persons named in Schedules (I.) and (K.) to the said report annexed had been guilty of giving or receiving bribes: be it enacted, that none of the persons so named in the said schedules shall have the right of voting for the southern division of the county of Devon, in respect of a qualification situated within the said borough of Totnes.

Persons reported guilty of bribery in Great Yarmouth disqualified as voters for north-eastern division of Norfolk or eastern division of Suffolk in respect of qualification arising in said borough.

14. Whereas the commissioners appointed under a commission of her Majesty, dated the 16th day of June, 1866, for the purpose of making inquiry into the existence of corrupt practices in the borough of Great Yarmouth, have by their report, dated the 20th day of December, 1866, reported to her Majesty that the persons named in Schedules (A.) and (B.) to the said report annexed had been guilty of giving or receiving bribes: be it enacted, that none of the persons so named in the said schedules shall have the right of voting for the north-eastern division of the county of Norfolk, or the eastern division of the county of Suffolk, in respect of a qualification situated within the borough of Great Yarmouth.

Persons reported guilty of bribery in Lancaster disqualified as voters for northern division of Lancaster in respect of qualification arising in said borough.

15. Whereas the commissioners appointed under a commission of her Majesty, dated the 16th day of June, 1866, for the purpose of making inquiry into the existence of corrupt practices in the borough of Lancaster, have by their report reported to her Majesty that certain persons had been guilty of giving or receiving bribes: be it enacted, that none of the said persons appearing by the schedules marked (A.) and (B.) to the said report annexed to have been bribed, or as bribing and treating, shall have the right of voting for the northern division of the county of Lancaster in respect of a qualification situated within the said borough of Lancaster.

Persons reported guilty of bribery in Reigate disqualified as voters for division of Mid-Surrey in respect of qualification arising in said borough.

16. Whereas the commissioners appointed under a commission of her Majesty, dated the 16th day of June, 1866, for the purpose of making inquiry into the existence of corrupt practices in the borough of Reigate, by their report, dated the 2nd day of February, 1867, reported to her Majesty that the persons named in Schedules (A.), (B.), and (C.) had been guilty of giving or receiving bribes: be it enacted, that none of the said persons so named in the said schedules, and appearing thereby to have been so guilty in the election which took place in the year 1865, shall have the right of voting for the division of Mid-Surrey in respect of a qualification situated within the borough of Reigate.

PART II.

Distribution of Seats.

Boroughs, as in Schedule (A.), to return one member each.

17. From and after the end of this present parliament, no borough which had a less population than ten thousand at the census of 1861 shall return more than one member to serve in parliament, such boroughs being enumerated in Schedule (A.) to this act annexed.

Boroughs herein named to

18. From and after the end of this present parliament, the city of Manchester, and the boroughs of Liverpool,

Birmingham, and Leeds, shall each respectively return three members to serve in parliament.

return three members each.

19. Each of the places named in Schedule (B.) to this act annexed shall be a borough, and, until otherwise directed by parliament, each such borough shall comprise such places as are specified and described in connection with the name of each such borough in the said Schedule (B.); and in all future parliaments the borough of Chelsea, named in the said schedule, shall return two members, and each of the other boroughs named in the said schedule shall return one member to serve in parliament.

New boroughs as in Schedule (B.), to return one member each, except Chelsea, which shall return two.

20. Registers of voters shall be formed in and after the year 1868, notwithstanding the continuance of this present parliament, for or in respect of the boroughs constituted by this act, in like manner as if before the passing of this act they respectively had been boroughs returning members to serve in parliament.

Registers of voters to be formed for new boroughs.

21. From and after the end of the present parliament, the boroughs of Merthyr Tydfil and Salford shall each return two members instead of one to serve in future parliaments; and the borough of the Tower Hamlets shall be divided into two divisions, and each division shall in all future parliaments be a separate borough returning two members to serve in parliament.

Merthyr Tydfil and Salford to return two members each.

The said divisions shall be known by the name of the borough of Hackney and the borough of the Tower Hamlets, and, until otherwise directed by parliament, shall comprise the places mentioned in connection with each such borough in Schedule (C.) hereto annexed.

Tower Hamlets to be divided into two divisions, each division to return two members.

22. Registers of voters shall be formed in and after the year 1868, notwithstanding the continuance of this present parliament, in respect of the said boroughs of Hackney and of the Tower Hamlets constituted under this act in like manner as if such divisions had previously to the passing of this act been separate boroughs returning members to serve in parliament.

Registers of voters to be formed for the boroughs of Hackney and the Tower Hamlets.

23. From and after the end of the present parliament, each county named in the first column of Schedule (D.) to this act annexed shall be divided into the divisions named in the second column of the said schedule, and, until otherwise directed by parliament, each of such divisions shall consist of the hundreds, lathes, wapentakes, and places mentioned in the third column of the said schedule.

Division of certain counties as in Schedule (D.).

In all future parliaments there shall be two members to serve for each of the divisions specified in the said second column, and such members shall be chosen in the same manner, and by the same description of voters, and in respect of the same rights of voting, as if each such division were a separate county.

All enactments relating to divisions of counties returning members to serve in parliament shall be deemed to apply to the divisions constituted as aforesaid.

Registers of voters shall be formed in and after the year 1868, notwithstanding the continuance of this present parliament, for or in respect of the divisions of counties constituted by this act, in like manner as if before the passing of this act they had respectively been counties returning members to serve in parliament.

University of London to return one member.

24. In all future parliaments the university of London shall return one member to serve in parliament.

Electors for members of the university of London.

25. Every man whose name is for the time being on the register of graduates constituting the convocation of the university of London shall, if of full age, and not subject to any legal incapacity, be entitled to vote in the election of a member to serve in any future parliament for the said university.

PART III.

Supplemental Provision.

Incidents of Franchise.

As to successive occupations.

26. Different premises occupied in immediate succession by any person as owner or tenant during the twelve calendar months next previous to the last day of July in any year shall, unless and except as herein is otherwise provided, have the same effect in qualifying such person to vote for a county or borough as a continued occupation of the same premises in the manner herein provided.

As to joint occupations in counties.

27. In a county where premises are in the joint occupation of several persons as owners or tenants, and the aggregate rateable value of such premises is such as would, if divided amongst the several occupiers, so far as the value is concerned, confer on each of them a vote, then each of such joint occupiers shall, if otherwise qualified, and subject to the conditions of this act, be entitled to be registered as a voter, and when registered to vote at an election for the county: provided always, that not more than two persons, being such joint occupiers, shall be entitled to be registered in respect of such premises, unless they shall have derived the same by descent, succession, marriage, marriage settlement, or devise, or unless they shall be bonâ fide engaged as partners carrying on trade or business thereon.

Notice of rate in arrear to be given

28. Where any poor rate due on the 5th day of January in any year from an occupier in respect of premises capable of conferring the franchise for a borough remains unpaid on the 1st day of June following, the overseers whose duty it may be to collect such rate shall, on or before the 20th of the same month of June, unless such rate has previously been paid, or has been duly demanded by a demand note, to be served in like manner as the notice in this section referred to, give or cause to be given a notice in the form set forth in Schedule (E.) to this act to every such occupier. The notice shall be deemed to be duly given if delivered to the occupier or left at his last or usual place of abode, or with some person on the premises in respect of which the rate is payable. Any overseer who shall wilfully withhold such notice, with intent to keep such occupier off the list or register of voters for the said borough, shall be deemed guilty of a breach of duty in the execution of the registration acts.

by overseers to voters, in form as in Schedule (E.)

Penalty for wilfully withholding notice.

29. The overseers of every parish wholly or partly within a borough shall, on or before the 22nd day of July in every year make out a list containing the name and place of abode of every person who shall not have paid, on or before the 20th day of the same month, all poor rates which shall have become payable from him in respect of any premises within the said parish before the 5th day of January then last past, and the overseers shall keep the said list, to be perused by any person, without payment of any fee, at any time between the hours of ten of the clock in the forenoon and four of the clock in the afternoon of any day except Sunday during the first fourteen days after the said 22nd day of July; any overseer wilfully neglecting or refusing to make out such list, or to allow the same to be perused as aforesaid, shall be deemed guilty of a breach of duty in the execution of the registration acts.

Overseers to make out a list of persons in arrear of rates, which shall be open to perusal without fee.

Penalty on overseer for neglect.

Registration of Voters.

30. The following regulations shall in and after the year one thousand eight hundred and sixty-eight be observed with respect to the registration of voters:

Regulation to be observed as to registration of voters.

1. The overseers of every parish or township shall make out or cause to be made out a list of all persons on whom a right to vote for a county in respect of the occupation of premises is conferred by this act, in the same manner, and subject to the same regulations, as nearly as circumstances admit, in and subject to which the overseers of parishes and townships in boroughs are required by the registration acts to make out or cause to be made out a list of all persons entitled to vote for a member or members for a borough in respect of the occupation of premises of a clear yearly value of not less than 10*l*.

2. The claim of every person desirous of being registered as a voter for a member or members to serve for any borough in respect of the occupation of lodgings shall be in the Form numbered 1 in Schedule (G.), or to the like effect, and shall have annexed thereto a declaration in the form and be certified in the manner in the said schedule mentioned, or as near thereto as circumstances admit; and every such claim shall after the last day of July and on or before the 25th day of August in any year be delivered to the overseers of the parish in which such lodgings shall be situate, and the particulars of such claim shall be duly published by such overseers on or before the 1st day of September next ensuing in a separate list, according to the Form numbered 2 in the said Schedule (G.):

So much of sect. 18 of the act of the session of the 6th year of the reign of her present Majesty, chapter 18, as relates to the manner of publishing lists of claimants, and to the delivery of copies thereof to persons requiring the same, shall apply to every such claim and list; and all the provisions of the 38th and 39th sections of the same act with respect to the proof of the claims of persons omitted from the lists of voters, and to objections thereto, and to the hearing thereof, shall, so far as the same are applicable, apply to claims and objections, and to the hearing thereof, under this section.

Definition of "expenses of registration."

31. The word "expenses" contained in the sects. 54 and 55 of the said Registration Act of the session of the 6th year of the reign of her present Majesty, chapter 18, shall be deemed to and shall include and apply to all proper and reasonable fees and charges of any clerk of the peace of any county, or of any town clerk of any city or borough, to be hereafter made or charged by him in any year for his trouble, care, and attention in the performance of the services and duties imposed upon him by the same act or by this act, in addition to any money actually paid or disbursed by him for or in respect of any such services or duties as aforesaid.

Provision as to duties of clerks of peace in parts of Lincolnshire.

32. Whereas several of the hundreds mentioned in the third column of the said Schedule (D.), and therein assigned to Mid-Lincolnshire, are situate in the parts of Lindsey, and others are situate in the parts of Kesteven, and the liberty of Lincoln consisting of the city and the county of the city of Lincoln is situate partly in the parts of Lindsey and partly in the parts of Kesteven, and there are separate clerks of the peace for the said parts of Lindsey and Kesteven: in forming the register for the said division of

Mid-Lincolnshire the clerk of the peace of the parts of Lindsey shall do and perform all such duties as are by law required to be done by clerks of the peace in regard to such of the hundreds assigned to Mid-Lincolnshire as aforesaid as are situate within the said parts of Lindsey, and in regard to so much of the liberty of Lincoln aforesaid as is situate within the said parts of Lindsey; and the clerk of the peace of the parts of Kesteven shall do and perform all such duties as are by law required to be done by clerks of the peace in regard to such of the said hundreds assigned to Mid-Lincolnshire as aforesaid as are situate within the said parts of Kesteven, and in regard to so much of the liberty of Lincoln aforesaid as is situate within the said parts of Kesteven.

Places for Election, and Polling Places.

Courts for the election of members for counties as in Schedule (D.).

33. The court for the election of members for each of the divisions mentioned in the second column of the said Schedule (D.) shall be holden at the places named for that purpose in the fourth column of the same schedule.

Provision for increased polling places in counties, &c.

34. In every county the justices of the peace having jurisdiction therein or in the larger part thereof, assembled at some court of general or quarter sessions, or at some adjournment thereof, held after the passing of this act, may, if they think convenience requires it, divide such county into polling districts, and assign to each district a polling place, in such manner as to enable each voter, so far as practicable, to have a polling place within a convenient distance of his residence; and the justices shall advertise, in such manner as they think fit a description of the polling districts so constituted by them, and the name of the polling place assigned to each district, and shall name the polling places at which the revising barristers are to hold their courts, and no revising barrister shall be obliged to hold his courts at any polling places not so named: Provided that the justices of the peace for the Isle of Ely, assembled as aforesaid, shall carry into effect the provisions of this section so far as regards the said Isle of Ely; but nothing herein contained shall affect the powers conferred by any other act of parliament of altering polling places or polling districts, or of creating additional polling places or districts:

Proviso as to Isle of Ely.

The local authority of every borough shall, if they think convenience requires it, as soon as may be after the passing of this act, divide such borough into polling districts, and the returning officer shall in the case of a contested election provide at least one booth or room for taking the poll in each polling district; and in cases where a parliamentary borough is constituted of two or more towns the distance between two of which shall exceed two miles, there shall be provided a booth or room for taking the poll in each of such towns:

Where any parish in a borough is divided into or forms part of more than one polling district, the overseers shall, so far as practicable, make out the lists of voters in such manner as to divide the names in conformity with each polling district:

The town clerk, as defined by the act of the 6th Victoria, chapter 18, shall cause the lists of voters for each borough to be copied, printed, arranged, and signed, and delivered in the manner directed by the said act, so as to correspond with the division of the borough into polling districts:

A description of the polling districts made or altered in pursuance of this act shall be advertised by the local authority in such manner as they think fit, and notice of the situation, division, and allotment of the polling booth or place for each district shall be given in manner now required by law:

The local authority shall mean in every municipal borough, and in every borough any part of which forms a municipal borough, the town council of such borough, *and in other boroughs the justices of the peace acting for such borough, or if there be no such justices then the justices acting for the division of the county in which such borough or the greater part thereof is situate;* and in cases where a parliamentary borough is constituted by the combination of two or more municipal boroughs, then the local authority shall mean the town council of that municipal borough in which the nomination takes place:

The local authority may from time to time alter any districts made by them under this act.

When polling places altered, &c., publication in London Gazette not required, but justices to advertise as they think fit.

35. When by virtue of the powers conferred by any other act of parliament polling places or polling districts are altered, or additional polling places or districts are created, it shall not be necessary that any declaration, direction, or order made as therein provided be published in the London Gazette, but the same shall be advertised by the justices in such manner as they shall think fit, and when so advertised shall have the same force and effect as if the same had been published in the London Gazette.

Payment of expenses of conveying voters in

36. *It shall not be lawful for any candidate, or any one on his behalf, at any election for any borough, except the several boroughs of East Retford, Shoreham, Cricklade, Much Wenlock, and Aylesbury, to pay any money on account of the conveyance of any voter to the poll, either to the voter himself* *or to any other person; and if any such candidate, or any person on his behalf, shall pay any money on account of the conveyance of any voter to the poll, such payment shall be deemed to be an illegal payment within the meaning of "The Corrupt Practices Prevention Act, 1854."* *boroughs to the poll illegal, except as herein named.*

37. At every contested election for any county or borough, unless some building or place belonging to the county or borough is provided for that purpose, the returning officer shall, whenever it is practicable so to do, instead of erecting a booth, hire a building or room for the purpose of taking the poll: **Rooms to be hired for taking polls wherever they can be obtained.**

Where in any place there is any room the expense of maintaining which is payable out of any rates levied in such place, such room may, with the consent of the person or corporation having the control over the same, be used for the purpose of taking the poll at such place.

38. The 47th and 48th sections of the act of the 6th year of the reign of her present Majesty, chapter 18, relating to the transmission and delivery of the book or books containing the lists of voters to the sheriff and returning officer, shall be construed as if the word "December" were substituted in those sections for the word "November," and the said book or books shall be the register of persons entitled to vote for the county or borough to which such register relates at any election which takes place during the year commencing on the 1st day of January next after such register is made, and the register of electors in force at the time of the passing of this act shall be the register in force until the 1st day of January, 1868. **Alteration as to time for delivery of lists and commencement of register of voters.**

39. The oath to be taken by a poll clerk shall hereafter be in the following form: **Oath or affirmation, &c. to be taken by poll clerks.**

"I A.B. do hereby swear, that I will truly and indifferently take the poll at the election of members to serve in parliament for the [borough *or* county] of

"So help me GOD."

Every person for the time being by law permitted to make a solemn affirmation or declaration instead of taking an oath may, instead of taking the oath hereby appointed, make a solemn affirmation in the form of the oath hereby appointed, substituting the words "solemnly, sincerely, and truly declare and affirm" for the word "swear," and omitting the words "So help me God."

40. The 36th section of the act of the 2nd year of King William the Fourth, chapter 45, disqualifying persons in receipt of parochial relief from being registered as voters for a borough, shall apply to a county also, and the said section shall be construed as if the word "county" were inserted therein before the word "city;" **Receipt of parochial relief to apply to counties as well as boroughs.**

and the overseers of every parish shall omit from the lists made out by them of persons entitled to vote for the borough and county in which such parish is situate the names of all persons who have received parochial relief within twelve calendar months next previous to the last day of July in the year in which the list is made out.

Election in University of London.

Vice-chancellor of university of London to be the returning officer.

41. The vice-chancellor of the university of London shall be the returning officer for such university, and the writ for any election of a member to serve in parliament for such university shall be directed to such vice-chancellor.

Elections for university of London to be within six days after receipt of writ, three clear days notice being given.

42. The vice-chancellor of the university of London shall proceed to election, in pursuance of any writ to be directed to him as hereinbefore mentioned, within six days after the receipt of such writ, giving three clear days notice of the day and place of election, exclusive of the day of proclamation and the day of election; and the vice-chancellor shall after such election certify the same, together with such writ, according to the directions thereof.

Polling at university of London may continue five days.

43. At every contested election of a member or members to serve in parliament for the university of London the polling shall commence at eight o'clock in the morning of the day next following the day fixed for the election, and may continue for not more than five days (Sunday, Christmas Day, Ascension Day, and Good Friday being excluded), but no poll shall be kept open later than four o'clock in the afternoon.

Power to vice-chancellor to appoint polling place, pro-vice-chancellors, and poll clerks, to conduct the poll in the university of London.

44. At every election of a member to serve in parliament for the university of London the vice-chancellor shall appoint the polling place, and also shall have power to appoint two or more pro-vice-chancellors, any one of whom may receive the votes and decide upon all questions during the absence of such vice-chancellor; and such vice-chancellor shall have power to appoint poll clerks and other officers, by one or more of whom the votes may be entered in the poll book, or such number of poll books as may be judged necessary by such vice-chancellor; and such vice-chancellor shall, not later than two o'clock in the afternoon of the day next following the close of the poll, openly declare the state of the poll and make proclamation of the member chosen.

Provisions of 24 & 25 Vict. c. 53, as to voting papers to apply to university of London.

45. All the provisions of an act passed in the 24th and 25th years of her present Majesty, entitled "An Act to provide that votes at elections for the universities may be recorded by means of voting papers," shall apply to every election of a member for the university of London.

46. So much of the 27th and 32nd sections of the act of the 2nd year of the reign of King William the Fourth, chapter 45, and of the 79th section of the act of the 6th year of the reign of her present Majesty, chapter 18, as relates to the residence of electors within seven miles of any city or borough, shall be repealed in respect to electors otherwise qualified to be registered and to vote for members to serve in parliament for the city of London: Provided always, that no person shall be registered as an elector for the said city unless he shall have resided for six calendar months next previous to the last day of July in any year, nor be entitled to vote at any election for the said city unless he shall have ever since the last day of July in the year in which his name was inserted in the register then in force have resided, and at the time of voting shall have continued to reside, within the said city, or within twenty-five miles thereof or any part thereof.

Residence of electors for the city of London extended to twenty-five miles.

Miscellaneous.

47. In any borough named in Schedules (B.) and (C.) to this act annexed, which is or includes a municipal borough, the mayor of such municipal borough shall be the returning officer, and in the other cases the returning officer shall be appointed in the same manner as if such places were included amongst the boroughs mentioned in Schedules (C.) and (D.) of the act of the 2nd year of his late Majesty William the Fourth, chapter 45, for which no persons are mentioned in such schedules as returning officers.

As to returning officers in new boroughs.

48. The following persons, that is to say, the right honourable Lord Viscount Eversley, the right honourable Russell Gurney, Sir John Thomas Buller Duckworth, baronet, Sir Francis Crossley, baronet, and John Walter, esquire, of whom not less than three shall be a quorum, shall be appointed boundary commissioners for England and Wales, and they shall, immediately after the passing of this act, proceed, by themselves or by assistant commissioners appointed by them, to inquire into the temporary boundaries of every borough constituted by this act, with power to suggest such alterations therein as they may deem expedient.

They shall also inquire into the boundaries of every other borough in England and Wales, except such boroughs as are wholly disfranchised by this act, with a view to ascertain whether the boundaries should be enlarged, so as to include within the limits of the borough all premises which ought, due regard being had to situation or other local circumstances, to be included therein for the purpose

Appointment of boundary commissioners, who may appoint assistant commissioners, to examine boundaries of boroughs constituted by this act, and all other boroughs, and divisions of counties as constituted by this act, and report if enlargement necessary.

of conferring upon the occupiers thereof the parliamentary franchise for such borough.

They shall also inquire into the divisions of counties as constituted by this act, and as to the places appointed for holding courts for the election of members for such divisions, with a view to ascertain whether, having regard to the natural and legal divisions of each county, and the distribution of the population therein, any and what alterations should be made in such divisions or places.

The said commissioners shall, with all practicable despatch, report to one of her majesty's principal secretaries of state upon the several matters in this section referred to them, and their report shall be laid before parliament.

The commissioners and assistant commissioners so appointed shall give notice, by public advertisement, of their intention to visit such counties and boroughs, and shall appoint a time for receiving the statements of any persons who may be desirous of giving information as to the boundaries or other local circumstances of such counties and boroughs, and the said commissioners or assistant commissioners shall by personal inspection, and such other means as the commissioners shall think necessary, possess themselves of such information as will enable the commissioners to make such report as herein mentioned.

Corrupt payment of rates to be punishable as bribery.

49. Any person, either directly or indirectly, corruptly paying any rate on behalf of any ratepayer for the purpose of enabling him to be registered as a voter, thereby to influence his vote at any future election, and any candidate or other person, either directly or indirectly, paying any rate on behalf of any voter for the purpose of inducing him to vote or refrain from voting, shall be guilty of bribery, and be punishable accordingly; and any person on whose behalf and with whose privity any such payment as in this section is mentioned is made shall also be guilty of bribery, and punishable accordingly.

Returning officer, &c. acting as agent guilty of misdemeanor.

50. No returning officer for any county or borough, nor his deputy, nor any partner or clerk of either of them, shall act as agent for any candidate in the management or conduct of his election as a member to serve in parliament for such county or borough; and if any returning officer, his deputy, the partner or clerk of either of them, shall so act, he shall be guilty of a misdemeanor.

Not necessary to dissolve parliament on any future demise of the crown.

51. Whereas great inconvenience may arise from the enactments now in force limiting the duration of the parliament in being at the demise of the crown: Be it therefore enacted, that the parliament in being at any future demise of the crown shall not be determined or dissolved by such demise, but shall continue so long as it would have continued but for such demise, unless it should be sooner prorogued or dissolved by the crown, anything in the act passed in the 6th year of her late Majesty Queen Anne, chapter 7, in any way notwithstanding.

52. Whereas it is expedient to amend the law relating to offices of profit the acceptance of which from the crown vacates the seats of members accepting the same, but does not render them incapable of being re-elected: Be it enacted, that where a person has been returned as a member to serve in parliament since the acceptance by him from the crown of any office described in Schedule (H.) to this act annexed, the subsequent acceptance by him from the crown of any other office or offices described in such schedule in lieu of and in immediate succession the one to the other shall not vacate his seat.

Members holding offices of profit from the crown, as in Schedule (H.), not required to vacate their seats on acceptance of another office.

53. Any copy of any of the said reports by the said commissioners appointed for the purpose of making inquiry into the existence of corrupt practices in any of the said boroughs of Totnes, Great Yarmouth, Lancaster, or Reigate, with the schedules thereof annexed, and purporting to be printed by the queen's printer, shall for the purposes of this act be deemed to be sufficient evidence of any such report of the said commissioners, and of the schedules annexed thereto.

Copy of reports of commissioners as to boroughs herein named, and printed by Queen's printer to be evidence.

54. Where separate registers of voters have been directed to be made in respect of the divisions of the borough and counties divided by this act into two divisions only, if a vacancy take place in the representation of the said county or borough before the summoning of a future parliament, and after the completion of such separate registers, such last-mentioned registers shall, for the purpose of any election to fill up such vacancy, be deemed together to form the register for the borough or county; and in the case of a county divided into more than two divisions, the clerk of the peace shall, from the separate registers, make out a register of voters for the county or original division of the county in which the election may be about to take place, in the same manner as if no new division or divisions of such county had been made by this act.

Provision in case of separate registers.

55. Nothing in this act contained shall affect the rights of persons whose names are for the time being on the register of voters for any county in which the boroughs constituted by this act are situate to vote in any election for such county in respect of any vacancy that may take place before the summoning of a future parliament, but

Temporary provisions consequent on formation of new boroughs.

after such summoning no person shall be entitled to be registered as a voter, or to vote in any election for any such county, who would not be entitled to be so registered, or to vote in case the qualifications held by him were situate in a borough other than one constituted by this act.

In the case of a parish wholly or partly situate within the limits of a borough constituted by this act, the revising barrister, in revising at any time before the summoning of a future parliament the list of voters for the county in which such parish is situate, shall write the word "borough" opposite to the name of each voter whose qualification in respect of the premises described in the list would not, after the summoning of a future parliament, entitle such voter to vote for the county; and at any election taking place after the summoning of a future parliament the vote of every person against whose name the word "borough" is written, if tendered in respect of such qualification, shall be rejected by the returning officer.

General saving.

56. The franchises conferred by this act shall be in addition to and not in substitution for any existing franchises, but so that no person shall be entitled to vote for the same place in respect of more than one qualification; and, subject to the provisions of this act, all laws, customs and enactments now in force conferring any right to vote, or otherwise relating to the representation of the people in England and Wales, and the registration of persons entitled to vote, shall remain in full force, and shall apply, as nearly as circumstances admit, to any person hereby authorized to vote, and shall also apply to any constituency hereby authorized to return a member or members to parliament, as if it had heretofore returned such members to parliament and to the franchises hereby conferred; and to the registers of voters hereby required to be formed.

As to issue of writs to county palatine of Lancaster.

57. From and after the passing of this act, the county palatine of Lancaster shall cease to be a county palatine, in so far as respects the issue, direction and transmission of writs for the election of members to serve in parliament for any division of the said county, or for any borough situate in the said county; and such writs may be issued under the same seal, be directed to the like officer, and transmitted in the like manner, under, to, and in which writs may be issued, directed and transmitted in the case of divisions of counties and boroughs not forming part of or situate in a county palatine; and any writ issued, directed and transmitted in manner directed by this section shall be valid accordingly.

58. All writs to be issued for the election of members to serve in parliament, and all mandates, precepts, instruments, proceedings and notices consequent upon such writs, or relating to the registration of voters, shall be framed and expressed in such manner and form as may be necessary for the carrying the provisions of this act into effect.

Writs, &c. to be made conformable to this act.

59. This act, so far as is consistent with the tenor thereof, shall be construed as one with the enactments for the time being in force relating to the representation of the people and with the registration acts; and in construing the provisions of the 24th and 25th sections of the act of the 2nd year of King William the Fourth, chapter 45, the expressions "the provisions hereinafter contained," and "as aforesaid," shall be deemed to refer to the provisions of this act conferring rights to vote as well as to the provisions of the said act.

This act, as far as consistent, to be construed with enactments now in force.

60. Notwithstanding anything in this act contained, in the event of a vacancy in the representation of any constituency, or of a dissolution of parliament taking place, and a writ or writs being issued before the 1st day of January, 1869, for the election of members to serve in the present or any new parliament, each election shall take place in the same manner in all respects as if no alteration had been made by this act in the franchises of electors, or in the places authorized to return a member or members to serve in parliament, with this exception, that the boroughs by this act disfranchised shall not be entitled to return members to serve in any such new parliament.

In event of dissolution of Parliament before Jan. 1, 1869, elections to take place as heretofore, except as to boroughs disfranchised.

61. The following terms shall in this act have the meanings hereinafter assigned to them, unless there is something in the context repugnant to such construction; (that is to say,)

Interpretation of terms:

"Month" shall mean calendar month: "Month:"

"Member" shall include a knight of the shire: "Member:"

"Election" shall mean an election of a member or members to serve in parliament: "Election:"

"County" shall not include a county of a city or county of a town, but shall mean any county, riding, parts or divisions of a county returning a member or members to serve in parliament: "County:"

"Borough" shall mean any borough, city, place, or combination of places, not being a county as hereinbefore defined, returning a member or members to serve in parliament: "Borough:"

"Dwelling-house:" "Dwelling-house" shall include any part of a house occupied as a separate dwelling, and separately rated to the relief of the poor:

"The Registration Acts." "The registration acts" shall mean the act of the 6th year of the reign of her present Majesty, chapter 18, and the act of the 28th year of the reign of her present Majesty, chapter 36, and any other acts or parts of acts relating to the registration of persons entitled to vote at and proceedings in the election of members to serve in parliament for England and Wales.

SCHEDULES.

SCHEDULE (A.)

Boroughs to return One Member only in future Parliaments.

Honiton.
Thetford.
Wells.
Evesham.
Marlborough.
Harwich.
Richmond.
Lymington.
Chippenham.
Bridport.
Stamford.
Chipping Wycombe.
Poole.
Knaresborough.
Andover.
Leominster.
Tewkesbury.
Ludlow.
Ripon.
Huntingdon.
Maldon.
Buckingham.
Newport (Isle of Wight).
New Malton.
Tavistock.
Lewes.
Cirencester.
Bodmin.
Great Marlow.
Devizes.
Hertford.
Dorchester.
Lichfield.
Cockermouth.
Bridgnorth.
Guildford.
Chichester.
Windsor.

SCHEDULE (B.)

New Boroughs.

County.	Places to be Boroughs.	Temporary Contents or Boundaries.
MIDDLESEX	Chelsea....	Parishes of Chelsea, Fulham, Hammersmith, Kensington.
DURHAM	Darlington.	Townships of Darlington, Haughton-le-Skerne, Cockerton.
	The Hartlepools.	Municipal Borough of Hartlepool. Townships of Throston, Stranton, Seaton Carew.
	Stockton ..	Municipal Borough of Stockton, and the Township of Thornaby.
KENT	Gravesend .	Parishes of Gravesend, Milton, Northfleet.
LANCASHIRE ..	Burnley ..	Townships of Burnley, Habergham Eaves.
LANCASHIRE AND CHESHIRE.	Staleybridge	Municipal Borough of Staleybridge. Remaining Portion of Township of Dukinfield. Township of Stalley. The District of the Local Board of Health of Mossley.
STAFFORDSHIRE .	Wednesbury	Parishes of Wednesbury, West Bromwich, Tipton.
YORKSHIRE, NORTH RIDING	Middlesborough.	Township of Linthorpe, and so much of the Townships of Middlesborough, Ormesby, and Eston as lie to the north of the road leading from Eston towards Yarm.
DO. WEST RIDING.	Dewsbury .	The Townships of Dewsbury, Batley, Soothill.

SCHEDULE (C).

New Boroughs formed by Division of the Borough of the Tower Hamlets.

Name of Borough.	Places comprised in the Borough.
BOROUGH OF TOWER HAMLETS........	The Parish of St. George's-in-the-East. The Hamlet of Mile End Old Town. The Poplar Union. The Stepney Union. The Whitechapel Union. The Tower of London.
BOROUGH OF HACKNEY	The Parish of St. John, Hackney. The Parish of St. Matthew, Bethnal Green. The Parish of St. Leonard, Shoreditch.

SCHEDULE (D.)

Counties to be divided.

Name of County to be divided.	Division.	Parts temporarily comprised in such Division.	Places temporarily appointed for holding Courts for Election of Members.
CHESHIRE ..	North Cheshire.	The Hundred of Macclesfield.	Macclesfield.
	Mid Cheshire.	The Hundreds of Bucklow, and Northwich.	Knutsford.
	South Cheshire.	The Hundreds of Broxton, Eddisbury, Nantwich, and Wirrall, and also the City and County of the City of Chester.	Chester.
DERBYSHIRE	North Derbyshire.	The Hundred of High Peak, and the Wapentake of Worksworth.	Bakewell.
	South Derbyshire.	The Hundreds of Repton and Gresley, Morleston and Litchurch, and Appletree.	Derby.
	East Derbyshire.	The Hundred of Scarsdale.	Chesterfield.
DEVONSHIRE	North Devonshire.	The Hundreds of Bampton, Braunton, Crediton, Fremington, Halberton, Hartland, Hayridge, Hemyock, North Tawton, Shebbear, Sherwill, South Molton, Tiverton, Winkleigh, Witheridge, and West Budleigh.	South Molton.
	East Devonshire.	The Hundreds of Axminster, Cliston, Colyton, East Budleigh, Exminster, Ottery St. Mary, Haytor, Teignbridge, and also the Castle of Exeter and the Hundred of Wonford, except such parts of the Hundred as are included in the Limits of the City and County of Exeter by the 2 & 3 Will. 4, c. 64.	Castle of Exeter.
	South Devonshire.	The Hundreds of Black Torrington, Ermington, Lifton, Plympton, Roborough, Stanborough and Coleridge, and Tavistock.	Plymouth.

Name of County to be divided.	Division.	Parts temporarily comprised in such Division.	Places temporarily appointed for holding Courts for Election of Members.
ESSEX......	North West Essex.	The Hundreds of Freshwell, Uttlesford, Clavering, Dunmow, Harlow, Waltham, Ongar, and Chelmsford.	Chelmsford.
	North East Essex.	The Hundreds of Hinckford, Lexden, Tendring, Winstree, Witham, Thurstable, and Dengie.	Braintree.
	South Essex..	The Hundreds of Becontree, Chafford, Barstable, and Rochford, with the Liberty of Havering.	Brentwood.
WEST KENT.	West Kent ..	The Lathe of Sutton at Hone.	Blackheath.
	Mid Kent....	Remainder of the Division.	Maidstone.
NORTH LANCASHIRE.	North Lancashire.	The Hundreds of Lonsdale, Amounderness, and Leyland.	Lancaster.
	North East Lancashire.	The Hundred of Blackburn	Blackburn.
SOUTH LANCASHIRE.	South East Lancashire.	The Hundred of Salford ..	Manchester.
	South West Lancashire.	The Hundred of West Derby	Liverpool.
LINCOLN....	North Lincolnshire.	The Wapentakes, Hundreds, or Sokes of Manley, Yarborough, Bradley Haverstoe, Ludborough, Walshcroft, Aslacoe, Corringham, Louth Eske, and Calceworth, so much as lies within Louth Eske.	Glanford Brigg.
	Mid Lincolnshire.	The Wapentakes, Hundreds, or Sokes of Well, Lawress, Wraggoe, Gartree, Candleshoe, Calceworth, except so much as lies within the Hundred of Louth Eske, Hill, Bolingbroke, Horncastle, Boothby Graffoe, and Langoe and Lincoln Liberty.	Lincoln.

Name of County to be divided.	Division.	Parts temporarily comprised in such Division.	Places temporarily appointed for holding Courts for Election of Members.
LINCOLN—*continued.*	South Lincolnshire.	The Wapentakes, Hundreds, or Sokes of Loveden, Flaxwell, Aswardhurn, Winnibriggs and Threo, Aveland, Beltisloe, Ness, Grantham Soke, Skirbeck, Kirton, and Holland Elloe.	Sleaford.
NORFOLK ..	West Norfolk	The Hundreds of Wayland, Launditch, South Greenhoe, Gallow, Brothercross, Smithdon, Freebridge Lynn, Freebridge Marshland, Clackclose, and Grimshoe.	Swaffham.
	North East Norfolk.	The Hundreds of East Flegg, West Flegg, Happing, Tunstead, Erpingham (North), Erpingham (South), Eynsford, Holt, and North Greenhoe.	Aylsham.
	South East Norfolk.	The Hundreds of Walsham, Blofield, Henstead, Humbleyard, Loddon, Clavering, Diss, Deepwade, Earsham, Guiltcross, Shropham, Taverham, Forehoe, and Mitford.	Norwich.
SOMERSETSHIRE.	East Somerset	The existing Sessional Divisions of Long Ashton, Keynsham, Weston, Axbridge and Temple Cloud, as established by virtue of the Order of Her Majesty's Justices of the Peace for the County of Somerset, and also all such other places in the said County as are locally situated within or are surrounded by the said Sessional Divisions, or any of them, and are not mentioned in the said Order.	Bath.

Name of County to be divided.	Division.	Parts temporarily comprised in such Division.	Places temporarily appointed for holding Courts for Election of Members.
SOMERSETSHIRE—*cont.*	Mid Somerset	The existing Sessional Divisions of Crewkerne, Yeovil, Somerton, Shepton Mallet, Wincanton, Wells, Frome, and Kilmersdon, as established by virtue of the Order of Her Majesty's Justices of the Peace for the said County of Somerset, and also all such other Places in the said County as are locally situated within or are surrounded by the said Sessional Divisions, or any of them, and are not mentioned in the said Order.	Wells.
	West Somerset.	The existing Sessional Divisions of Dunster, Dulverton, Williton, Wiveliscombe, Bishop's Lydeard, Wellington, Taunton, Bridgwater, and Ilminster, as established by virtue of the Order of Her Majesty's Justices of the Peace for the said County of Somerset, and also all such other Places as are locally situated within or are surrounded by the said Sessional Divisions, or any of them, and are not mentioned in the said Order.	Taunton.
STAFFORDSHIRE.	North Staffordshire.	The Hundreds of Totmonslow and Pirehill, North.	Stoke-upon-Trent.
	West Staffordshire.	The Hundreds of Pirehill, South Cuttlestone, and Seisdon.	Stafford.
	East Staffordshire.	The Hundreds of Offlow (North), Offlow (South).	Lichfield.

Name of County to be divided.	Division.	Parts temporarily comprised in such Division.	Places temporarily appointed for holding Courts for Election of Members.
EAST SURREY.	East Surrey -	The Hundred of Tandridge, and so much of the Hundred of Wallington as includes and lies to the East of the Parishes of Croydon and Sanderstead, and so much of the Hundred of Brixton as includes and lies to the East of the Parishes of Streatham, Clapham, and Lambeth.	Croydon.
	Mid Surrey -	The Remainder of the present Division.	Kingston-upon-Thames.
YORKSHIRE, WEST RIDING	Northern Division.	The Hundreds of Ewecross and Staincliffe, Claro, Skyrack, Barkstone Ash, and Osgoldcross.	Leeds.
	Mid-Division.	The Hundred of Morley.	Bradford.
	Southern Division.	The Hundreds of Agbrigg, Strafforth and Tickhill, and Staincross.	Wakefield.

SCHEDULE (E.)

To A. B.

City [*or* borough of] .

Take notice, that you will not be entitled to have your name inserted in the list of voters for this city [*or* borough] now about to be made in respect of the premises in your occupation in [*street or place*] unless you pay on or before the 20th day of July next all the poor rates which have become due from you in respect of such premises up to the 5th day of January last, amounting to £ , and if you omit to make such payment you will be incapable of being on the next register of voters for this city [*or* borough].

Dated the day of June, 18 .

C. D. } Overseers,
E. F. }
or
G. H. { Assistant Overseer,
or
I. K. Collector.

SCHEDULE (G.)

Form No. 1.

Claim of Lodger.

Borough of

To the overseers of the parish of .

I hereby claim to be inserted in the list of voters in respect of the occupation of the undermentioned lodgings, and the particulars of my qualification are stated in the columns below:

Christian Name and Surname at full length.	Profession, Trade, or Calling.	Description of Lodgings.	Description of House in which Lodgings situate, with Number, if any, and Name of Street.	Name, Description, and Residence of Landlord or other Person to whom Rent paid.

I, the above-named , hereby declare that I have been during the twelve months immediately preceding the last day of July in this year, the occupier as sole tenant of the above-mentioned lodgings, and that I have resided therein during the twelve months immediately preceding the said last day of July, and that such lodgings are of a clear yearly value, if let unfurnished, of ten pounds or upwards.

Dated the day of .

Signature of claimant .

Witness to the signature of the said , and I certify my belief in the accuracy of the above claim

Name of witness .

Residence and calling .

This claim must bear date the 1st day of August, or some day subsequent thereto, and must be delivered to the overseers after the last day of July, and on or before the 25th day of August.

Form No. 2.

List of Claimants in respect of Lodgings to be published by the Overseers.

The following persons claim to have their names inserted in the list of persons entitled to vote in the election of a member [*or* members] for the city [*or* borough] of :

Christian Name and Surname of each Claimant at full length.	Profession, Trade, or Calling.	Description of Lodgings.	Description of House in which Lodgings situate, with Number, if any, and Name of Street.	Name, Description, and Residence of Landlord or other Person to whom Rent paid.

(Signed) A. B. } Overseers
C. D. } of,
E. F. } *&c.*

SCHEDULE (II.)

Offices of Profit referred to in this Act.

Lord High Treasurer; Commissioner for executing the offices of Treasurer of the Exchequer of Great Britain and Lord High Treasurer of Ireland; President of the Privy Council; Vice-President of the Committee of Council for Education; Comptroller of her Majesty's Household; Treasurer of her Majesty's Household; Vice-Chamberlain of her Majesty's Household; Equerry or Groom in Waiting on her Majesty; Any principal Secretary of State; Chancellor and Under Treasurer of her Majesty's Exchequer; Paymaster General; Postmaster General; Lord High Admiral; Commissioner for executing the office of Lord High Admiral; Commissioner of her Majesty's Works and Public Buildings; President of the Committee of Privy Council for Trade and Plantations; Chief Secretary for Ireland; Commissioner for administering the Laws for the Relief of the Poor in England; Chancellor of the Duchy of Lancaster; Judge Advocate General; Attorney General for England; Solicitor General for England; Lord Advocate for Scotland; Solicitor General for Scotland; Attorney General for Ireland; Solicitor General for Ireland.

THE REPRESENTATION OF THE PEOPLE (SCOTLAND) ACT, 1868.

31 & 32 Vict. c. 48.

An Act for the Amendment of the Representation of the People in Scotland. [13th July, 1868.]

Whereas it is expedient to amend the laws relating to the representation of the people in Scotland:

Be it enacted by the Queen's most excellent Majesty, by and with the advice and consent of the lords spiritual and temporal, and commons, in this present parliament assembled, and by the authority of the same, as follows:

1. This act shall be cited for all purposes as "The Representation of the People (Scotland) Act, 1868." Short title.

2. This act shall apply to Scotland only, except in so far as it provides that certain boroughs in England shall cease to return members to serve in parliament. Application of act.

PART I.

Franchises.

3. Every man shall, in and after the year 1868, be entitled to be registered as a voter, and, when registered, to vote at elections for a member or members to serve in parliament for a burgh, who, when the sheriff proceeds to consider his right to be inserted or retained in the register of voters, is qualified as follows; that is to say, Occupation franchise for voters in burghs.

1. Is of full age, and not subject to any legal incapacity; and
2. Is, and has been for a period of not less than twelve calendar months next preceding the last day of July, an inhabitant occupier as owner or tenant of any dwelling house within the burgh:

Provided that no man shall under this section be entitled to be registered as a voter who, at any time during the said period of twelve calendar months, shall have been exempted from payment of poor rates on the ground of inability to pay; or who shall have failed to pay, on or before the 1st day of August in the present or the 20th day of June in any subsequent year, all poor rates (if any) that have become payable by him, in respect of said dwelling house or as an inhabitant of any parish in said burgh, up to the preceding 15th day of May; or who shall have been in the receipt of parochial relief within the twelve calendar months next preceding the said last day of July: Provided also, that no man shall under this section be entitled to be registered as a voter by reason of his being a joint occupier of any dwelling house.

Lodger franchise for voters in burghs.

4. Every man shall in and after the year 1868 be entitled to be registered as a voter, and, when registered, to vote for a member or members to serve in parliament for a burgh, who is qualified as follows; (that is to say,)

1. Is of full age and not subject to any legal incapacity; and
2. As a lodger has occupied in the same burgh separately, and as sole tenant for the twelve months preceding the last day of July in any year, lodgings of a clear yearly value, if let unfurnished, of 10*l.* or upwards; and
3. Has resided in such lodgings during the twelve months immediately preceding the last day of July, and has claimed to be registered as a voter at the next ensuing registration of voters.

Ownership franchise for voters in counties.

5. Every man shall, in and after the year 1868, be entitled to be registered as a voter, and, when registered, to vote at the election of a member or members to serve in parliament for a county, who, when the sheriff proceeds to consider his right to be inserted or retained on the register of voters, is qualified as follows; that is to say,

1. Is of full age, and not subject to any legal incapacity; and
2. Is, and has been for a period of not less than six calendar months next preceding the last day of July, the proprietor (whether he has made up his titles, or is infeft, or not) of lands and heritages, the yearly value of which, as appearing from the valuation roll of the county, shall be 5*l.* or upwards, after deduction of any feu duty, ground annual, or other annual consideration which he may be bound to pay or give or account for as a condition of his right, and after deduction of any annuity, life-rent provision, or such other annual burden.

Occupation franchise for voters in counties.

6. Every man shall be entitled to be registered as a voter, and, when registered, to vote at elections for a member to serve in parliament for a county, who, when the sheriff proceeds to consider his right to be inserted or retained in the register of voters, is qualified as follows; that is to say,

1. Is of full age and not subject to any legal incapacity; and
2. Is, and has been during the twelve calendar months immediately preceding the last day of July, in the actual personal occupancy as tenant of lands and heritages within the county of the annual value of 14*l.* or upwards, as appearing on the valuation roll of such county:

Provided that no man shall under this section be entitled

to be registered who, at any time during the said period of twelve calendar months, shall have been exempted from payment of poor rates on the ground of inability to pay; or who shall have failed to pay, on or before the 1st day of August in the present or the 20th day of June in any subsequent year, all poor rates (if any) that have become payable by him in respect of said lands and heritages up to the preceding 15th day of May; or who shall have been in the receipt of parochial relief within twelve calendar months next preceding the said last day of July.

Restriction on number of votes in Glasgow.

7. At a contested election for the City of Glasgow no person shall vote for more than two candidates.

Electors employed for reward within six months of an election not to vote.

8. No elector who, within six months before or during any election for any county or burgh, shall have been retained, hired, or employed for all or any of the purposes of the election for reward by or on behalf of any candidate at such election as agent, canvasser, clerk, messenger, or in other like employment, shall be entitled to vote at such election; and if he shall so vote, he shall be guilty of a crime and offence.

PART II.

Distribution of Seats.

New seats for the universities of Glasgow and Dundee, and counties of Lanark, Ayr, and Aberdeen.

9. In all future parliaments the Universities of Scotland shall return two members to serve in parliament; the city of Glasgow shall return three members to serve in parliament; and the town of Dundee, and the counties of Lanark, Ayr, and Aberdeen, shall each return two members to serve in parliament; and one of the members for the universities of Scotland shall be returned jointly by the University of Edinburgh and the University of St. Andrews; and the other of such members shall be returned jointly by the University of Glasgow and the University of Aberdeen.

Counties of Selkirk and Peebles to be united, and new district of burghs to return one member.

10. From and after the end of the present parliament the county of Selkirk shall cease to return a member to serve in parliament, and the county of Peebles shall cease to return a member to serve in parliament, and the said counties shall jointly return one member to serve in parliament; and the burghs and towns of Hawick, Galashiels, and Selkirk, specified in Schedule (A.) hereto annexed, shall be constituted into a district of burghs, and such district shall return one member to serve in parliament.

Certain counties to be divided, and each division to return a member.

11. From and after the end of the present parliament each county named in the first column of Schedule (B.) to this act annexed shall be divided into two divisions named in the second column of the said schedule; and, until otherwise directed by parliament, each of such divisions shall consist of the parishes mentioned in the third column of the said schedule; and each of such divisions shall in all future parliaments return one member to serve in parliament, in the same manner as if each such division were a separate county.

Registers of voters to be formed for new burghs and divisions of counties.

12. Registers of voters shall be formed in and after the year 1868, notwithstanding the continuance of the present parliament, for and in respect of the divisions of counties constituted under this act, in like manner as if such divisions had previously to the passing of this act been separate counties returning members to serve in parliament; and also for and in respect of the burghs constituted by this act in like manner as if before the passing of this act they respectively had been burghs returning or contributing to return members to serve in parliament.

PART III.

Supplemental Provisions.

Incidents of Franchise.

Successive occupancy.

13. Different premises occupied in immediate succession by any person as owner or tenant during the twelve calendar months next previous to the last day of July in any year shall have the same effect in qualifying such person to vote for a burgh or county respectively as a continued occupancy of the same premises in the manner herein provided: and this provision shall apply to the successive occupancy of premises in counties of the annual value of 50*l.* and upwards, as well as to premises which for the first time under this act afford the qualification for the franchise.

Life-renters.

Joint owners and joint occupants.

14. In a county where two or more persons are interested as liferenter and as fiar in any lands and heritages to which a right of voting is for the first time attached by this act, the right to be registered and to vote shall be in the liferenter, and not in the fiar: and where any such lands and heritages shall be owned, held, or occupied by more persons than one as joint owners, whether in fee or in liferent, or as joint tenants and joint occupants of the same, as the case may be, each of such joint owners shall be entitled to be registered and to vote, provided his share or interest in the said lands and heritages is of the annual value of 5*l.* as before specified, but not otherwise; and each of such joint tenants and joint occupants shall in like manner be entitled to be registered and to vote, provided the annual value of the said lands and heritages, as appearing on the valuation roll, held and occupied by them shall be sufficient, when divided by the number of such joint tenants and joint occupants, to give to each of them a sum of not less than 14*l.*, but not otherwise: provided always, that no greater number of persons than two shall be entitled to be registered as joint owners or joint tenants of the same lands and heritages unless their shares or interests in the same shall have come to them by inheritance, marriage, marriage settlement, or *mortis causâ* conveyance, or unless such joint owners or joint tenants shall be *bonâ fide* engaged as partners carrying on trade or business in or on such lands and heritages: provided also, that husbands shall be entitled to be registered and to vote in respect of lands and heritages as aforesaid belonging whether in fee or in liferent, to their wives, or owned or possessed by such husbands after the death of their wives by the courtesy of Scotland.

Husbands in right of their wives.

Valuation Rolls.

15. In every future valuation roll to be made up in any burgh, under the provisions of the valuation acts in force for the time, or under the provisions of this act, the assessor shall be bound to specify separately each dwelling house, and to ascertain and enter the yearly rent or value of the same, and also to enter the name and designation of the proprietor or reputed proprietor thereof, and, where there are tenants or occupiers, the names and designations of all such tenants and occupiers.

Dwelling houses to be specially entered in valuation rolls.

16. In every future valuation roll to be made up in any county the assessor, in addition to the particulars which by the acts last mentioned are required to be ascertained by him, shall also ascertain and enter in such roll the amount of feu duty, ground annual, rent, or other yearly consideration payable as a condition of his right by every proprietor of any lands or heritages entered in such roll as of the yearly rent or value of 5*l.* or upwards, and the name of the person to whom the said consideration is payable; and in order to the ascertainment of the particulars hereinbefore specified, it shall be lawful for the assessor to call upon any proprietor or tenant for receipts or other written evidence of the amount of such feu duty, ground annual, or other consideration, and such proprietor or tenant shall be bound to furnish and deliver such evidence to the assessor under the same penalty in case of failure or of false statement as is provided in similar cases by the act 17th and 18th Victoria, chapter 91; and it shall also be lawful for the assessor to exercise all the powers which, under the said act, he may lawfully exercise for the purposes thereof.

Valuation rolls in counties to contain certain additional particulars.

Provision for claims by persons improperly or erroneously exempted from payment of poor rates.

17. Where the name of any person, otherwise entitled to the franchise for any burgh or county, has in any year been omitted from the list of voters prepared by the assessor for such burgh or county on the ground that he has during the twelve calendar months preceding the last day of July in such year been exempted from payment of poor rates on account of inability to pay, it shall be competent for such person to give notice to such assessor of his claim to have his name entered in the register of voters for such burgh or county in the manner provided in the registration acts, and such claim shall be published and may be objected to in the manner provided in the said acts; and the sheriff shall dispose of the said claim, and if it shall be proved to his satisfaction that the person claiming has been improperly or erroneously exempted from payment of the said poor rates, and that he has on or before the 1st day of August in the present or the 20th day of June in any subsequent year paid or tendered payment of the amount of poor rates, from payment of which he was improperly or erroneously exempted as aforesaid, the sheriff shall insert the name of such person in the register of voters for the burgh or county, as the case may be; and the judgment of the sheriff sustaining or refusing the claim shall be liable to the appeal provided in the said registration acts, and generally the provisions of the said acts shall apply to the claims mentioned in this section and to all the proceedings following thereon.

Poor rate to be demanded.

Collector wilfully neglecting to do so punishable.

18. Where any poor rate due from an occupier of premises to which a right of voting is for the first time attached by this act remains unpaid on the 15th day of May in any year, the collector of poor rates for the parish in which such premises are situated shall, on or before the 25th day of July in the present or the 1st day of June in any subsequent year, unless such rate has previously been paid, or has been duly demanded by a demand note served in like manner as the notice in this section referred to, give or cause to be given a notice in the form set forth in Schedule (C.) to this act, to every such occupier. The notice shall be deemed to have been duly given if delivered to the occupier, or left at his last or usual place of abode, or with some person on the premises in respect of which the rate is payable. Any collector of poor rate who shall wilfully withhold such notice with intent to keep such occupier off the list or register of voters for the burgh or county, as the case may be, shall be deemed guilty of a crime and offence.

Registration of Voters.

Registration of voters.

19. The following regulations shall be observed with respect to the registration of voters:

1. The registration acts shall apply to the registration of all persons on whom a right to be registered and to vote is conferred for the first time by this act, in the same manner, and subject to the same regulations, as nearly as circumstances admit, in and subject to which they now apply to the registration of persons entitled at present to be registered and to vote; and the said acts, and also the valuation acts, shall apply to all burghs and divisions of counties on which the right of returning or contributing to return a member to serve in parliament is by this act conferred:
2. The collector of poor rates in each parish shall, on or before the 3rd day of August in the present and first day of July in any subsequent year, deliver or send to the assessor for the burgh or county, as the case may be, a list in the Form in the Schedule (D.) hereunto annexed, or as near thereto as circumstances admit, and in the order as nearly as may be in which the names appear in the valuation roll of such burgh or county, as the case may be, duly certified by him, of all occupiers of premises who have been, during the twelve calendar months preceding the last day of July in each year, exempted from payment of poor rates on the ground of inability to pay, or who have failed to pay, on or before the 1st day of August in the present or the 20th day of June in any subsequent year, all poor rates (if any) that have become payable by them up to the preceding 15th day of May, or who have been in the receipt of parochial relief within the twelve calendar months next preceding the last day of July in such year, and the assessor shall be guided by the said lists (which shall be *primâ facie* evidence of the correctness of the entries therein contained) in ascertaining the right of any person to be inserted or retained in the register of voters:
3. The claim of every person desirous of being registered as a voter for a member or members to serve for any burgh in respect of the occupation of lodgings shall be in the Form No. 1 in Schedule (I.), or to the like effect, and shall have annexed thereto a declaration in the form, and be certified in the manner, in the said schedule mentioned, or as near

thereto as circumstances admit; and every such claim shall, after the last day of July and on or before the 21st day of September in any year, be delivered to the assessor of the burgh in which such lodgings shall be situate, and the particulars of such claim shall be duly published by such assessor on or before the 25th day of September next ensuing in a separate list, according to the Form No. 2, in the said Schedule (I.):

4. The provisions of the registration acts relating to the manner of publishing lists of claimants in burghs, and to the delivery of copies thereof to persons requiring the same, shall apply to every such claim and list; and the provisions of the same acts with respect to the proof of the claims of persons omitted from the list of voters in burghs, and to objections thereto, and to the hearing thereof, shall, so far as the same are applicable, apply to claims and objections, and to the hearing thereof under this section:

5. Wherever any list or copy of a list other than a register for which payment is required and authorized by the act 19th and 20th Victoria, chapter 58, shall contain any number of persons names exceeding five thousand, the rate to be demanded and paid therefor shall be 5*s*., and for any such list or copy of such list containing any number of persons names exceeding ten thousand the rate to be demanded and paid therefor shall be 10*s*.

Alteration of dates respecting registration in burghs.

20. Whereas in consequence of the increase of the number of voters in burghs provided for by this act it is necessary to alter certain of the dates in the preparation of the register of voters in said burghs as provided for by the act 19 & 20 Vict. c. 58: Be it enacted as follows:

The 2nd section of the said recited act shall be read as if the words "15th day of September" were substituted for the words "15th day of August," and the words "from the 16th to the 21st days of September" were substituted for the words "from the 16th to the 25th days of August" therein:

The 3rd section of the said recited act shall be read as if the words "21st day of September" were substituted for the words "25th day of August" therein:

The 4th section of the said recited act shall be read as if the words "21st day of September" were substituted for the words "25th day of August" therein:

The 5th section of the said recited act shall be read as if the words "25th day of September" were substituted for the words "1st day of September," and the words "between the 25th day of September and the 1st day of October" were substituted for the words "during the first fourteen days of September" therein:

The 6th section of the said recited act shall be read as if the words "25th of September" were substituted for the words "1st of September" therein:

The 16th section of the said recited act shall be read as if the words "15th of September" were substituted for the words "16th day of August" therein:

The 18th section of the said recited act shall be read as if the words "25th day of September" were substituted for the words "1st day of September" therein:

The 19th section of the said recited act shall be read as if the words "25th day of September" were substituted for the words "1st day of September," and the words "the 16th day of October" were substituted for the words "the 1st day of October" therein:

The 25th section of the said recited act shall be read as if the words "15th day of October" were substituted for the words "30th day of September" therein:

The 26th section of the said recited act shall be read as if the words "16th day of October" were substituted for the words "1st day of October" therein:

The 29th section of the said recited act shall be read as if the words "15th day of October" were substituted for the words "30th day of September;" and the provision in the said section requiring the town clerk forthwith, after the 21st day of October in each year, to make all such corrections and alterations on the book therein mentioned as may be necessary to give effect to all decisions of the Court of Appeal, is hereby repealed.

Alteration of dates respecting registration in counties.

21. Whereas in consequence of the increase of the number of voters in counties provided for by this act it is necessary to alter certain of the dates in the preparation of the register of voters in counties, as provided for by the act of the 24th and 25th of Victoria, chapter 83:

Be it enacted as follows:

The 8th section of the said recited act shall be read as if the words "25th day of August" were substituted for the words "15th day of August," and the words "from the 26th day of August to the 4th day of September" were substituted for the words "from the 16th to the 25th days of August" therein:

The 9th section of the said recited act shall be read as if the words "4th day of September" were substituted for the words "25th day of August" therein:

The 10th section of the said recited act shall be read as if the words "11th day of September" were substituted for the words "1st day of September," and the words "from the 12th to the 24th days of September" were substituted for the words "from the 2nd to the 14th days of September" therein:

The 11th section of the said recited act shall be read as if the words "11th day of September" were substituted for the words "1st day of September" therein:

The 20th section of the said recited act shall be read as if the words "26th day of August and the 30th day of October" were substituted for the words "16th day of August and the 21st day of October" therein:

The 21st section of the said recited act shall be read as if the words "4th day of September" were substituted for the words "25th day of August" therein:

The 22nd section of the said recited act shall be read as if the words "11th day of September" were substituted for the words "1st day of September," and the words "4th day of September" were substituted for the words "25th day of August" therein:

The 23rd section of the said recited act shall be read as if the words "11th day of September and the 11th day of October" were substituted for the words "1st day of September and the 5th day of October" therein:

The 24th section of the said recited act shall be read as if the words "11th day of September" were substituted for the words "1st day of September" therein:

The 29th section of the said recited act shall be read as if the words "11th day of October" were substituted for the words "5th day of October" therein:

The 30th section of the said recited act shall be read as if the words "11th day of October" were substituted for the words "5th day of October" therein.

Appeals from decisions of sheriff in registration court.

22. All enactments at present in force regarding appeals from the judgments of sheriffs in registration courts for counties and burghs are hereby repealed, and in lieu thereof it is enacted as follows:

If any person whose name shall have been struck out of any register or list of voters by the sheriff, or who shall claim or object before the sheriff at any court, shall consider the decision of the sheriff on his case to be erroneous in point of law, he may, either himself or by some person on his behalf, in open court, require the sheriff to state the facts of the case, and such question of law, and his decision thereon, in a special case; and the sheriff shall prepare and sign and date such special case, and deliver the same in open court to the sheriff clerk or town clerk, as the case may be; and such person, or some person on his behalf, may thereupon in open court declare his intention to appeal against the said decision, and may, within ten days of the date of such special case, lay a certified copy thereof before the court of appeal hereinafter constituted, for their decision thereon; and the said court shall with all convenient speed hear parties and give their decision on such special case, and shall specify exactly every alteration or correction, if any, to be made upon the register in pursuance of such decision; and the register shall be as soon as may be after the 31st day of October in each year altered accordingly by or at the sight of the sheriff; and if it shall appear to the sheriff that his judgments respecting the qualifications of any two or more persons depend on the same question of law, he shall append to such special case the names of all such persons who have appealed against his judgment on their respective claims; and the decision of the said court on such special case shall extend and apply to the qualifications of all such persons, in like manner as if a separate appeal had been taken in the case of each of them; and the said court shall have power to award the costs of any appeal; and the decision of the said court shall be final, and not subject to review by any court, or in any manner whatsoever: provided always, that if the said court shall be of opinion that the statement of the matter of the appeal in any special case is not sufficient to enable them to give judgment in law, it shall be lawful for the said court to remit the said special case to the sheriff by whom it shall have been signed, in order that the same may be more fully stated.

Constitution of court of appeal.

23. The court for hearing appeals under the preceding section of this act shall consist of three judges of the court of session, to be named from time to time by act of sederunt of the said court, one judge to be named from each division of the inner house, and one from the lords ordinary in the outer house; and it shall be competent from time to time by act of sederunt to supply any vacancy which may occur in such court, and to regulate the sittings and forms of process therein so as to carry out the provisions of this act, and such acts of sederunt may be made, and such court may sit, either during the sitting of the court of session, or in vacation or recess; and the junior principal clerk of session shall be the clerk of such court.

Places for Election and Polling Places.

Places for election and returning

24. The writ for the election of the member for the district of burghs enumerated in Schedule (A.) to this act annexed shall be addressed to the sheriff mentioned in the

officers for new constituencies. fifth column of the said schedule, and, until otherwise directed by parliament, shall be proclaimed at the place named for that purpose in the third column thereof; and the writ for the election of the member for the counties of Peebles and Selkirk shall be addressed to the sheriff of the county of Peebles, and until otherwise directed by parliament shall be proclaimed at the burgh of Peebles; and in the case of a poll being demanded at any election for said counties the sheriff of the county of Peebles shall forthwith send a written notice to the sheriff of the county of Selkirk that a poll has been demanded, and also of the day on which it is to be taken; and the sheriffs of the said counties of Peebles and Selkirk respectively shall appoint such a number of substitutes and clerks as may be necessary at each of the polling places within their respective counties; and all the poll books shall at the final close thereof be sealed up and delivered or transmitted by the sheriff substitutes in charge of the polls to the said sheriff of the county of Peebles; and the writs for the election of members for the divisions of counties enumerated in Schedule (B.) to this act annexed shall be addressed to the sheriffs of such counties, and, until otherwise directed by parliament, shall be proclaimed at the places named for that purpose in the fourth column of the said schedule.

Payments for conveying voters in burghs to the poll illegal.

25. It shall not be lawful for any candidate, or any one on his behalf, at any election for any burgh to pay any money on account of the conveyance of any voter to the poll, either to the voter himself or to any other person; and if any such candidate, or any person on his behalf, shall pay any money on account of the conveyance of any voter to the poll, such payment shall be deemed to be an illegal payment within the meaning of the "Corrupt Practices Prevention Act, 1854."

Rooms to be hired for polling wherever they can be obtained.

26. At every contested election for any county or burgh, unless some building or place belonging to the county or burgh is provided for that purpose, the sheriff clerk in any county, and in any city or burgh the town clerk, shall, whenever it is practicable so to do, instead of erecting a booth, hire a building or room for the purpose of taking the poll at the places appointed for such county or burgh.

Where in any place there is any room, the expense of maintaining which is payable out of any rates levied in such place, or which is under the control of the town council or other local authority, such room may, with the consent of those having the control over the same, be used for the purpose of taking the poll at such place.

Where the town clerk incurs any expenses in erecting booths or hiring rooms for taking any poll under this act, he shall have the same right and means of recovering the same from the candidates which the sheriff clerk has by the present law and practice.

Elections in Universities.

27. The chancellor, the members of the university court, and the professors for the time being of each of the universities of Scotland, and also every person whose name is for the time being on the register, made up in terms of the provisions hereinafter set forth, of the general council of such university shall, if of full age, and not subject to any legal incapacity, be entitled to vote in the election of a member to serve in any future parliament for such university in terms of this act. **Franchise for universities.**

28. Under the conditions as to registration hereinafter mentioned, the following persons shall be members of general council of the respective universities, viz.: **Qualifications for members of general councils.**

1. All persons qualified under the 6th or 7th section of the act 21st and 22nd Victoria, chapter 83rd.
2. All persons on whom the university to which such general council belongs has after examination conferred the degree of doctor of medicine, or doctor of science, or bachelor of divinity, or bachelor of laws, or bachelor of medicine, or bachelor of science, or any other degree that may hereafter be instituted:
3. And whereas it was provided by the said 6th section of the last-mentioned act that in each university the general council should consist of, *inter alios*, "all persons who within three years from and "after the passing of this act shall establish, to "the satisfaction of the commissioners hereinafter "appointed, that they have as matriculated stu-"dents given regular attendance on the course of "study in the university for four complete ses-"sions, or such regular attendance for three com-"plete sessions in the university, and regular "attendance for one such complete session in any "other Scottish university, the attendance for at "least two of such sessions having been on the "course of study in the faculty of arts;" and whereas from various causes many persons omitted to establish their qualifications in terms of the provision just mentioned before the expiry of the time mentioned therein, and it is expedient to afford such persons the opportunity of becoming members of the general councils of their respective universities: be it enacted as follows: every person who may have omitted to establish his qualifica-

tion in terms of the recited provision of the sixth section of the act last mentioned, but who would have been entitled to have become a member of the general council of the university in terms of the said provision if his qualification had been established within the said period, and he had applied for registration in terms of said act, shall be a member of the general council of the university, provided that such person shall establish his qualification in terms of the recited provision to the satisfaction of the registrar and assistant registrars hereinafter mentioned, and shall farther comply with the conditions as to registration hereinafter mentioned:

Provided always, that no graduate of any university shall be disqualified from being a member of the general council of such university by reason of his being enrolled as a student in any class of the university: provided also, that the conditions as to registration hereinbefore mentioned shall not apply to the chancellor, the members of the university court, or the professors for the time being of each university, who shall be members of the general council of their respective universities, and entitled to vote as such, although their names are not inserted on the register hereinbefore mentioned.

Registration book to be kept.

29. The registrar of each university shall keep a registration book, which shall be in the form of Schedule (E.) to this act annexed, and in which, under the conditions hereinafter mentioned, shall be entered the names, designations, qualifications and ordinary places of residence of persons qualified to be members of general council, and from which the registers of general council hereinafter directed to be made up shall from time to time be prepared.

Registrar to enter names therein.

30. Within two months after the passing of this act the registrar shall transfer to the registration book from the presently existing register the names of all persons who before the passing of this act, and in virtue of the provisions of any ordinance of the commissioners under the act 21st and 22nd Victoria, chapter 83, have paid a composition in lieu of annual fees, and have been enrolled in such presently existing register in virtue of such payment; and he shall in like manner, from time to time after the passing of this act, on payment to the general university fund of a registration fee of 20*s*., enter in the registration book the name of every qualified person applying for registration, but who has not compounded under the provisions of any such ordinance as aforesaid: provided always, that an abatement shall be made from such fee equal to the sum that may already have been paid by the applicant in name of entrance money or annual fees: provided also, that after the passing of this act no person qualified to be a member of general council shall be required to pay any annual fee as the condition of having his name retained in the registration book, or inserted in the register to be from time to time made up from it, as hereinafter enacted.

31. On the 1st day of October, 1868, the registrar shall proceed to make up from the registration book an alphabetical register of members of general council, which register shall be in the form of Schedule (F.) to this act annexed, and shall be completed within fifteen days; but no names shall be included therein which have not been entered in the registration book before the said 1st day of October; and the said register, having been completed by the registrar as aforesaid, shall forthwith be revised and so far as necessary corrected by him, with the assistance of two members of the general council acting as assistant registrars, and who shall have been nominated and appointed for that purpose by the university court, at a meeting to be held of such court on or before the said 1st day of October; and the revision or correction shall be completed and a copy of the register, with the names numbered from one onwards in regular order, shall be signed by the registrar and assistant registrars on or before the 21st day of October following; and the copy so signed shall thereafter be submitted by the registrar to the vice-chancellor, and shall be authenticated by his signature on every page thereof, on or before the 25th day of October next ensuing; and the register so authenticated shall, so far as it remains unaltered by the university court as hereinafter provided, be conclusive of the right of persons to be members of the general council from the 26th day of October, 1868, to the 31st day of December, 1869, both days inclusive: provided always, that at any meeting of or election by the general council of any university appointed to take place on or before the said 26th day of October, 1868, the registration book for such university, as it stood on the 30th day of September immediately preceding, shall be conclusive evidence of the right of all persons whose names shall be entered therein to be members of such general council until the 5th day of November following.

Preparation of first register under this act.

Revision by registrar and assistant registrars.

Authentication by the vice-chancellor.

Register to be conclusive.

32. The registration book and also the register, authenticated as aforesaid, shall at all reasonable times be open to inspection, in the office of the registrar, by any person applying for inspection of the same, and copies thereof may be made on payment of a fee of 1s. for every 100

Appeal against undue insertion of names.

names, or fractional part thereof, copied; and if any member of the general council shall consider himself aggrieved by the insertion in the said register of the name of any person whom he considers not duly qualified, it shall be competent to him, within ten days after the day on or before which the register is hereby required to be authenticated, to appeal and apply to the university court to expunge the name complained of; and notice of such appeal shall immediately be given by the secretary of the court to the person against the insertion of whose name the appeal is taken, with an intimation of the day on which the appeal will be heard, and which shall be not sooner than twenty nor later than thirty days after the last day allowed for the authentication of the register; and it shall be in the power of such person to appear for his interest either personally or by substitute; and whether he appear or not, it shall be the duty of the registrar to attend and explain the reasons for the insertion of the name complained of; and the judgment of the court sustaining or dismissing the appeal shall be final, and not subject to any process of review, and the register shall, if necessary, be altered by or at the sight of the president of the said court in conformity with such judgment.

Appeal against omissions.

33. If any person whose name is not inserted in the register so authenticated as aforesaid shall consider himself aggrieved by its omission, it shall be competent to him, within the said period of ten days after the day on or before which the register is hereby required to be authenticated, to appeal and apply to the university court to have it so inserted; and the court shall meet to consider such appeal not later than thirty days after the last day allowed for the authentication of the register, and after hearing the appellant for his interest, either personally or by substitute, and the registrar in explanation of the reasons for the omission of the appellant's name, shall give judgment in the appeal; and such judgment shall be final, and not subject to any process of review, and the register shall, if necessary, be altered by or at the sight of the president of the said court in conformity with such judgment.

Quorum of university court for purposes of act.

34. For the purpose of performing any duty required by this act, the presence of a quorum of three shall be sufficient to constitute a meeting of the university court.

New registers to be made up annually.

35. On the 1st day of December, 1869, and on the 1st, or when the 1st is on a Sunday on the 2nd day of December in each succeeding year, the registrar shall proceed to prepare, in the form of schedule (F.) to this act annexed, a new alphabetical register for the year to commence on the 1st day of January next ensuing, which new register he shall make up by transferring to it from that in force at the time the names, designations, and addresses (with such corrections as he may consider necessary) of all members not known to be dead, and by transferring to it from the registration book the names, designations, qualifications, and ordinary places of residence of all persons who shall have paid the registration fee since the day of commencing to make up the register of the preceding year, and who are not known to have died since making payment; and such new register shall be completed within fifteen days, and shall thereafter be revised by the registrar with the assistance of two assistant registrars appointed by the university court, and shall then be authenticated by the vice-chancellor on or before the 31st day of December of the same year, and such revision and authentication shall be carried out in the same way as is provided in regard to the first register directed to be made up under this act; and the new register shall have the same effect for the year to which it applies as it is hereinbefore provided that the said first register shall have for the period between the 26th day of October, 1868, and the 31st day of December, 1869, and shall be subject in the same way as the said first register to alteration by the university court on appeal taken either against undue insertion or against undue omission of names.

Allowance to registrar and assistant registrars.

36. The registrar of each university shall be entitled to receive out of the general university fund a payment of one guinea and a half for every one hundred names, or fractional part thereof, that shall be entered in the first register prepared under this act, and of one guinea for every hundred names, or fractional part thereof, that shall be entered in the subsequent registers, and to a payment of half a guinea for every hour, or fractional part thereof, during which he shall be in attendance on the university court while considering and disposing of appeals under this act, as the same shall be certified by the president or secretary of the court; and each assistant registrar nominated and appointed by the university court under this act, and officiating in terms thereof, shall be entitled to receive from the same fund a payment of one guinea for every one hundred names, or fractional part thereof, that shall be entered in the first register prepared under this act, and of half a guinea for every hundred names, or fractional part thereof, entered in the subsequent registers.

Returning officers and intimation of election.

37. The vice-chanceller of the university of Edinburgh shall be the returning officer for the said university and the university of Saint Andrews; and the vice-chancellor of the university of Glasgow shall be the returning officer for the said university and the university of Aberdeen; and the writs for any election of a member to serve in parliament for such universities shall be directed to such returning officers respectively; and the vice-chancellor to whom a writ for any such election shall be directed shall endorse on the back thereof the day on which he received it, and shall, within three days thereafter, announce a day and hour (which day shall not be less than three or more than six clear days after that on which the writ was received), and a place within the city of Edinburgh, for an election for the universities of Edinburgh and Saint Andrews, or within the city of Glasgow for an election for the universities of Glasgow and Aberdeen, as the case may be, and shall give intimation thereof by advertisement in such newspapers as he shall deem expedient, and shall also, within the said first-mentioned three days, give intimation thereof in writing to the vice-chancellor of the university of Saint Andrews or of Aberdeen, as the case may be.

Proclamation of writs for universities.

38. On the day announced as aforesaid by the vice-chancellor for the election such vice-chancellor shall repair to the place named by him, to which place all persons entitled to vote in such election shall in the aforesaid advertisement be invited to repair on the day and at the hour named; and the said vice-chancellor shall then and there proclaim the writ by reading it; and if no more than one candidate shall be proposed for the choice of the electors, he shall, upon a show of hands, forthwith declare the person so put in nomination to be duly elected; it being always competent for any person entitled to vote in such election under this act to repair to the place where the writ is proclaimed, and to put any person in nomination; and if more than one candidate shall be proposed, and a poll shall be demanded, the proceedings shall be adjourned for the purpose of taking the poll for not less than six or more than ten clear days, exclusive of Saturdays and Sundays; and the vice-chancellor shall forthwith give public intimation of such adjournment, and of the names of the candidates who have been proposed, by advertisement in such newspapers as he shall deem expedient, and shall also give intimation thereof in writing to the vice-chancellor of the university of Saint Andrews or of Aberdeen, as the case may be.

Polling at university elections.

39. The following regulations shall be observed with respect to the polling:—

1. On the day to which the proceedings have been adjourned as aforesaid for the purpose of taking the poll the polling shall commence at each university at eight o'clock in the morning, and may continue for not more than five days (exclusive of Sundays), but no poll shall be kept open later than four o'clock in the afternoon.

2. The vice-chancellor of each university shall appoint the polling place at such university, and, if he shall think fit, shall advertise the same, and also shall have power to appoint one or more pro-vice-chancellors to take the poll at such university, and record the votes in poll books, and decide all questions with regard thereto, in the same manner as nearly as may be, and except as herein provided, as polls are now taken at elections for members to serve in parliament for burghs and counties in Scotland; and such vice-chancellor shall have power to appoint a poll clerk or poll clerks for the purpose of assisting the pro-vice-chancellor or pro-vice-chancellors in taking the poll as hereinbefore mentioned.

3. The poll books in which the votes have been recorded as hereinbefore provided shall be forthwith delivered by the pro-vice-chancellor to the vice-chancellor by whom he was appointed; and the vice-chancellors of the universities of Saint Andrews and Aberdeen respectively shall, on receiving such poll books, immediately transmit them to the vice-chancellor, who is the returning officer for such university; and such vice-chancellor, shall, within three days after such poll books have been received by him, in presence of the candidates or their agents, or of such of them as shall think proper to attend or to appoint such agent, cast up the number of votes as they appear on the several books, and shall forthwith publish in the Edinburgh Gazette a notice containing the name of the candidate for whom the largest number of votes has been given, and declaring such candidate to be duly elected, and shall make a return in the form of similar returns presently used (as nearly as may be) in terms of the writ, under his hand and seal, to the clerk of the crown in England, and if the votes be equal he shall make a double return.

4. All the provisions of an act passed in the 24th and 25th years of the reign of her present Majesty, intituled "An Act to provide that votes at elections for the universities may be recorded by means of voting papers," except so much of the said act as requires that the person delivering the voting paper shall make attestation of his personal acquaintance with the voter, shall apply to every election of a member for the universities of Edinburgh and Saint Andrews, and for the universities of Glasgow and Aberdeen, subject to the following provisions:

The words "recorded in the manner heretofore used," in the second section of the recited act, shall in this act mean "recorded in the manner hereinbefore directed."

The word "misdemeanor," in the fifth section of the recited act, shall include crime and offence.

A voting paper may be signed by a voter being in one of the Channel Islands in the presence of the following officers; that is to say,

1. In Jersey and Guernsey, of the bailiffs, or any lieutenant bailiff, jurat, or juge d'instruction:
2. In Alderney, of the judge of Alderney or any jurat:
3. In Sark, of the seneschal or deputy seneschal:

And for the purpose of certifying and attesting the signature of such voting paper, each of the said officers shall have all the powers of a justice of the peace under the recited act; and a statement of the official quality of such officer shall be a sufficient statement of quality in pursuance of the provisions of the said act.

In lieu of the schedule annexed to the recited act, the Schedule (G.) to this act annexed shall be substituted in elections for the universities of Edinburgh and Saint Andrews, and for the universities of Glasgow and Aberdeen.

University election expenses.

40. Every vice-chancellor to whom a writ for the election of a member to serve in parliament shall, under the provisions of this act, be directed, shall be allowed in Exchequer such payments for executing such writ as are allowed to sheriffs under the existing law in the case of elections for counties or burghs; and in all cases where a poll has been demanded the candidates shall be bound to pay and contribute among them to each pro-vice-chancellor appointed under this act, for superintending the poll, a fee of three guineas for the first, and of one guinea for each subsequent day in which he shall have been so engaged; and the candidates shall further be bound to pay and contribute among them to each poll clerk one guinea per day, and the candidates shall in like manner be bound to defray the necessary expenses incurred by the vice-chancellors in the transmission or receipt of poll books or other communications or in making any advertisements required or enjoined by this act; and if any person shall be proposed as a candidate without his consent, the person so proposing him shall be liable to pay his share of all such expenses in like manner as if he had been himself a candidate.

Provision for incapacity of

41. Where the vice-chancellor or registrar of any university is absent, or is incapacitated by illness for discharging any duty required of him by this act, or if the office of vice-chancellor or of registrar shall be vacant, the duties herein imposed on the vice-chancellor or registrar respectively shall be discharged by a person appointed for that purpose by the university court of such university; and such person shall in that respect, but in no other, act for the time as and be deemed to be vice-chancellor or registrar of such university.

vice-chancellor or registrar.

Miscellaneous.

42. Where any county has been divided for the purposes of this act, the commissioners of supply of such county are hereby empowered to appoint the same assessor to make up the register of voters in both divisions of such county, or, if they shall think proper, to appoint separate assessors to make up the said register for each such division; but, until they shall otherwise determine, the assessor appointed for the purpose of making up the register for the undivided county shall continue to act as assessor for both the divisions of such county, and shall, as hereinbefore provided, make up a separate register for each of such divisions: provided always, that such assessors shall in all respects be deemed to be assessors appointed in terms of the act 24th and 25th Victoria, chapter 83: provided also, that the expenses of registration shall be defrayed as at present by an assessment levied on the whole lands and heritages within the county, and not by an assessment levied separately on the lands and heritages within the divisions thereof respectively.

Registration where counties are divided.

43. Whereas, in order to provide for the seats hereinbefore distributed, it is expedient that certain boroughs in England having small populations should cease to return members to serve in parliament: be it therefore enacted, that from and after the end of this present parliament the boroughs of Arundel, Ashburton, Dartmouth, Honiton, Lyme Regis, Thetford, and Wells shall respectively cease to return any member to serve in parliament.

Certain boroughs in England to cease to return members.

44. Whereas it is expedient to shorten the period for proceeding to election in cities, burghs, and towns or districts of cities, burghs, and towns in Scotland, provided by the acts 5th and 6th William the Fourth, chapter 78, and 28 and 29 Victoria, chapter 92: be it enacted, that, except in the cases of the districts comprehending Kirkwall, Wick, Dornoch, Dingwall, Tain, and Cromarty, the day or days to be announced by the sheriff for the election or elections shall be not less than three and not more than six clear days after the day on which the writ was received by such sheriff.

Shortening of period for proceeding to elections in burghs.

45. In so far as regards the registration of voters, and generally for all purposes connected with the election of

Galashiels to be wholly in

Selkirkshire.

members to serve in parliament, the burgh of Galashiels shall be dealt with as if it were locally situated wholly within the county of Selkirk.

In burghs where there are no magistrates, police commissioners to appoint assessors.

46. In any burgh on which the right of contributing to return a member to serve in parliament is for the first time conferred by this act, and in which there are no magistrates elected in terms of the act 3rd and 4th William the Fourth, chapter 76, or the act 3rd and 4th William the Fourth, chapter 77, the commissioners of police acting in such burgh under any general or local police act shall appoint a suitable person to be the assessor in such burgh, and as such to make up a valuation roll of lands and heritages therein in terms of the Valuation Acts, and also to perform with reference to the registration of voters in such burgh all duties which by the registration acts can be imposed on assessors; and all appeals against valuations made by such assessor shall be heard and determined by such commissioners as the case may be, and the determination of such commissioners shall be dealt with in the same manner as the determinations of magistrates in existing royal or parliamentary burghs.

Where there is no town clerk, police commissioners or sheriff to appoint a person to act as such.

47. If in any such burgh there is no town clerk, it shall be the duty of the aforesaid commissioners of police, as soon as may be after the passing of this act, to nominate and appoint a fit and proper person to perform the duties of town clerk in so far as regards the registration of voters, and the election of members to serve in parliament; and on every occasion of the person so appointed ceasing to act, such commissioners shall in like manner, within the period of three weeks thereafter, make a similar appointment; and failing such appointment being duly made by the said commissioners, such appointment shall be made by the sheriff of the county; and every person so nominated and appointed shall, so long as he continues to act, be subject to the same disqualifications in regard to voting for or being elected a member of parliament, or acting as agent for any candidate, to which town clerks are now subject by law; and every such person shall be removable at the pleasure of the said commissioners or sheriff respectively by whom he was appointed.

Expenses of valuation, and registration of voters, and remuneration of person acting as assessor and town

48. In every such burgh on which the right of contributing to return a member to serve in parliament is for the first time conferred by this act, an account of the costs and expenses attending the preparation of the valuation roll under the Valuation Acts, and also of the costs and expenses attending the annual registration of voters, shall be made up annually at the sight of the person or persons by whom the assessor for such burgh was appointed; and such person or persons shall ascertain and fix the amount of such expenses, including therein the reasonable remuneration of the assessor, and of the town clerk, or of the person appointed to perform the duties of town clerk, where any such appointment has been made; and the amount of all such expenses and remuneration shall be assessed and levied on and recovered from the same description of persons and property as the police rate within such burgh; provided that no person shall be liable to such assessment who is not a proprietor or occupier of a dwelling-house or other lands and heritages within the burgh.

clerk, to be assessed on the burgh.

49. Any person, either directly or indirectly, corruptly paying any rate on behalf of any ratepayer for the purpose of enabling him to be registered as a voter, thereby to influence his vote at any future election, and any candidate or other person, either directly or indirectly, paying any rate on behalf of any voter for the purpose of inducing him to vote or refrain from voting, shall be guilty of bribery, and be punishable accordingly; and any person on whose behalf and with whose privity any such payment as in this section mentioned is made, shall also be guilty of bribery, and punishable accordingly.

Corrupt payment of rates to be punishable as bribery.

50. The provision of the 11th section of the act of the 2nd and 3rd years of King William the Fourth, cap. 65, disqualifying persons in receipt of parochial relief from being registered as voters, or voting for a burgh, shall apply to a county also; and the said provision of the said section shall be construed as if the word "county" were inserted therein before the word "city."

Receipt of parochial relief to disqualify for counties as well as burghs.

51. Whereas it is expedient to amend the law relating to offices of profit, the acceptance of which from the crown vacates the seats of members accepting the same, but does not render them incapable of being re-elected: be it enacted, that where a person has been returned as a member to serve in parliament since the acceptance by him from the crown of any office described in Schedule (H.) to this act annexed, the subsequent acceptance by him from the crown of any other office or offices described in such schedule, in lieu of and in immediate succession the one to the other, shall not vacate his seat.

Members holding offices of profit from the crown, as in Schedule (H.), not to vacate their seats on acceptance of another office.

52. Where separate registers of voters have been directed to be made in any county divided by this act, if a vacancy take place in the representation of the said county before the summoning of a future parliament, and after the completion of such separate registers, such last-mentioned registers shall, for the purpose of any election to fill up such vacancy, be deemed together to form the register for the county.

Provision in case of separate registers.

53. Nothing in this act contained shall affect the rights

Temporary provisions

consequent on formation of new burghs.

of persons whose names are for the time being on the register of voters for any county in which the burghs constituted by this act are situate to vote in any election for such county in respect of any vacancy that may take place before the summoning of a future parliament; but after such summoning no person shall be entitled to be registered as a voter or to vote in any election for any county in respect of any premises owned or occupied by him within any burgh.

In the case of a county within the limits of which is situate a burgh constituted by this act, the sheriff in revising at any time before the summoning of a future parliament the list of voters for such county shall write the word "burgh" opposite to the name of each voter whose qualification in respect of the premises described in the list would not, after the summoning of a future parliament, entitle such voter to vote for the county; and at any election for such county taking place after the summoning of a future parliament the vote of every person against whose name the word "burgh" is written, if tendered in respect of such qualification, shall be rejected by the polling sheriff.

Register to be conclusive evidence of qualification.

54. The 42nd section of the act passed in the 24th and 25th years of the reign of her present Majesty, chapter 83, is hereby repealed, and in lieu thereof it is enacted as follows: at every future election of a member to serve in parliament for any county or division of a county, the register of voters, made up in terms of the Registration Acts, shall be deemed and taken to be conclusive evidence that the persons therein named continue to have the qualifications which are annexed to their names respectively in the register in force at such election; and such persons shall not be required to take the oath of possession.

Right of voting not to be affected by dependance of appeal.

55. The right of voting at any election of a member or members to serve in parliament for any county, burgh, or university shall not be affected by any appeal depending at the time of issuing the writ for such election, and it shall be lawful for every person whose name has been entered on the register of voters to exercise the right of voting at such election as effectually, and every vote tendered thereat shall be as good, as if no such appeal were depending; and the subsequent decision in any appeal which shall be depending at the time of issuing the writ for any such election shall not in any way whatever alter or affect the poll taken at such election, or the return made thereat by the returning officers.

General saving clause.

56. The franchises conferred by this act shall be in addition to and not in substitution for any existing franchises, but so that no person shall be entitled to vote for the same place in respect of more than one qualification; and, subject to the provisions of this act, all laws, customs, and enactments now in force conferring any right to vote, or otherwise relating to the representation of the people in Scotland, and the registration of persons entitled to vote, shall remain in full force, and shall apply, as nearly as circumstances admit, to any person hereby authorized to vote, and shall also apply to any constituency hereby authorized to return or contribute to return a member or members to parliament, as if it had heretofore returned or contribute to return such members to parliament, and to the franchises hereby conferred and to the registers of voters hereby required to be formed.

Writs, &c., to be made conformable to this act.

57. All writs to be issued for the election of members to serve in parliament, and all mandates, precepts, instruments, proceedings, and notices consequent upon such writs, or relating to the registration of voters, shall be framed and expressed in such manner and form as may be necessary for the carrying the provisions of this act into effect.

Construction of act.

58. This act, so far as is consistent with the tenor thereof, shall be construed as one with the enactments for the time being in force relating to the representation of the people in Scotland, and with the Registration and Valuation Acts.

Interpretation of terms:

59. The following terms shall in this act have the meanings hereinafter assigned to them, unless there is something in the context repugnant to such construction; (that is to say,)

"Month:" "Month" shall mean calendar month:

"County:" "County" shall not include a county of a city, but shall mean any county or division of a county, or any combination of counties, or of counties and portions of counties, returning a member to serve in parliament:

"Burgh:" "Burgh" shall mean any city, town, burgh or district of cities, towns or burghs returning a member or members to serve in parliament:

"Dwelling house:" "Dwelling-house" shall include any part of a house occupied as a separate dwelling, and (in any parish in which poor rates are levied) the occupier of which is separately rated to the relief of the poor, either in respect thereof or as an inhabitant of such parish:

"Premises:" "Premises" shall, in regard to burghs, mean any dwelling-house; and in regard to counties, shall mean lands and heritages:

"The Registration Acts:" "The Registration Acts" shall mean the act of the 19th and 20th years of the reign of her present Majesty, chapter 58, and the act of the 24th and 25th years of the reign of her present Majesty, chapter 83, and any other acts or parts of acts relating to the registration of persons entitled to vote at, and proceedings in, the election of members to serve in parliament for Scotland:

"Proprietor" or "owner:" "Proprietor" or "owner" shall include any person who shall hold under a lease for a period of not less than fifty-seven years, exclusive of breaks.

"Valuation Acts:" "The Valuation Acts" shall mean the act of the 17th and 18th years of the reign of her present Majesty, chapter 91, the act of the 20th and 21st years of the said reign, chapter 58, the act of the 30th and 31st years of the said reign, chapter 80, and any other acts or parts of acts relating to the valuation of lands and heritages in Scotland:

"Assessor:" "Assessor" shall mean an assessor appointed under the Valuation Acts, or any of them, or under the Registration Acts, or any of them, or under this act, as the case may be:

"Oath of possession:" "Oath of possession" shall mean and include the words "that I am still proprietor (or occupant) of the property for which I am so registered, and hold the same for my own benefit, and not in trust for or at the pleasure of any other person."

SCHEDULES.

SCHEDULE (A.)

Hawick District.

Name of Burgh.	County in which Burgh is situated.	Place for proclaiming Writ.	Temporary Contents or Boundaries.	Sheriff to whom the Writ is to be addressed.
Hawick ..	Roxburgh	Hawick ..	The Boundaries of Hawick, as defined in "The Hawick Municipal Police and Improvement Act, 1861."	Sheriff of Roxburghshire.
Galashiels.	Selkirk ...	Ditto	The Limits of Galashiels, as fixed and defined under "The General Police and Improvement (Scotland) Act, 1862."	
Selkirk	Ditto	Ditto	The Boundaries of the Royal Burgh of Selkirk.	

SCHEDULE (B.)

Divisions of Counties.

Column 1. Name of County to be divided.	Column 2. Division.	Column 3. Parts temporarily comprised in such Division.	Column 4. Place for proclaiming Writ.
ABERDEENSHIRE.	East Aberdeenshire.	Parishes of Aberdour, Belhelvie, Bourtie, Crimond, Cruden, Daviot, Ellon, Fintray, Foveran, Fraserburgh, Fyvie, Keith-hall and Kinkell, King-Edward, Logie-Buchan, Longside, Lonmay, Methlie, Montquhitter, New Deer, New Machar, Old Deer, Old Meldrum, Peterhead, Pitsligo, Rathen, Slains, Strichen, Tarves, Turriff, Tyrie, Udny; together with so much of the Parish of Old Machar as is situated to the North and East of the River Don,—and the Parish of St. Fergus in Banffshire.	Peterhead.
	West Aberdeenshire.	Parishes of Aboyne and Glentanner, Alford, Auchindoir and Kearn, Auchterless, Birse, Chapel-of-Garioch, Clatt, Cluny, Coull, Crathie and Braemar, Culsamond, Drumblade, Dyce, Echt, Forgue, Glenbucket, Glenmuick, Tullich, and Glengairn, Huntly, Insch, Inverurie, Keig, Kemnay, Kildrummy, Kincardine O'Neil, Kinnellar, Kinnethmont, Kintore, Leochel-Cushnie, Leslie, Logie-Coldstone, Lumphanan, Midmar, Monymusk, Newhills, Oyne, Peter Culter, Premnay, Rayne, Rhynie, Skene,	Aberdeen.

Column 1. Name of County to be divided.	Column 2. Division.	Column 3. Parts temporarily comprised in such Division.	Column 4. Place for proclaiming Writ.
ABERDEENSHIRE—*con.*	West Aberdeenshire—*cont.*	Parishes of— Strathdon, Tarland and Migvie, Tough, Towie, Tullynessle and Forbes; together with so much of the Parish of Old Machar as is situated to the South and West of the River Don, and so much of the Parishes of Banchory-Devenick, Cabrach, Cairnie, Drumoak, and Glass as is situated within the County of Aberdeen, and the Parish of Gartly in the County of Banff.	Aberdeen.
AYRSHIRE ..	North Ayrshire	District of Cunningham, consisting of the parishes of Ardrossan, Dalry, Dreghorn, Fenwick, Irvine, Kilbirnie, Kilmarnock, Kilmaurs, Kilwinning, Largs, Loudoun, Stevenston, Stewartown, West Kilbride, and of Beith, and Dunlop, in so far as situated within the County of Ayr.	Kilmarnock.
	South Ayrshire.	Districts of Kyle and Carrick, consisting of the Parishes of Auchinleck, Ayr, Ballantrae, Barr, Colmonell, Coylton, Craigie, Dailly, Dalmellington, Dalrymple, Dundonald, Galston, Girvan, Kirkmichael, Kirkoswald, Mauchline, Maybole, Monkton and Prestwick, Muirkirk, New Cumnock, Newton-on-Ayr, Ochiltree, Old Cumnock, Riccarton, St. Quivox, Sorn, Stair, Straiton, Symington, Tarbolton.	Ayr.

Column 1. Name of County to be divided.	Column 2. Division.	Column 3. Parts temporarily comprised in such Division.	Column 4. Place for proclaiming Writ.
LANARKSHIRE	North Lanarkshire.	Parishes of Avondale, Barony, Blantyre, Bothwell, Cadder, Cambuslang, Carmunnock, City Parish of Glasgow, Dalziel, East Kilbride, Glassford, Hamilton, New Monkland, Old Monkland, Rutherglen, and so much of the Parishes of Govan and of Cathcart as is situated in Lanarkshire.	Hamilton.
	South Lanarkshire.	Parishes of Biggar, Cambusnethan, Carluke, Carmichael, Carnwath, Carstairs, Covington and Thankerton, Crawford, Crawfordjohn, Dalserf, Dolphington, Douglas, Dunsyre, Lanark, Leshmahagow, Libberton, Pitinain, Shotts, Stonehouse, Symington, Walston, Wandell and Lamington, Wiston and Roberton, and so much of the Parishes of Culter and Moffat as is situated within the County of Lanark.	Lanark.

SCHEDULE (C.)

To A. B., }
County [*or* Burgh] of }

Take notice, that you will not be entitled to have your name inserted in the list of voters for this county [*or* burgh] now about to be made in respect of the premises in your occupation in [*street or place*], unless you pay on or before the day of next all the poor rates which have become due from you in respect of such premises (*or as the case may be*) up to the 15th day of May last, amounting to £ ; and if you omit to make such payment you will be incapable of being entered on the next register of voters for this county [*or* burgh].

Dated the day of 18 .

C. D., Collector of Poor Rate for Parish of .

SCHEDULE (D.)

County [*or* burgh] of . Parish of .

I, collector of poor rates for the parish of do hereby certify that the following persons in the said parish have been exempted from poor rates therein during the twelve months preceding the 31st day of July on the ground of inability to pay; or have failed on or before the day of to pay all poor rates (if any) that have become payable by them up to the preceding 15th day of May; or have been in the receipt of parochial relief within the twelve calendar months next preceding the said 31st day of July.

Christian Name and Surname at full Length.	Profession, Trade, or Calling.	Place of Abode, with Number of House, Name of Street, &c. (if any).	State whether "Exempted," "Failed to pay," or "In Receipt of Relief."

Given under my hand this day of 18 .

SCHEDULE (E.)

Form of Registration Book of General Council.

Date.	Fee paid.	Name at full Length.	Designation (*i. e.*, Profession or Calling).	Residence and Post Town.	Qualification.
					Admitted by Commissioners; or M.D. of 1860; or M.A. of 1865; and so on.

SCHEDULE (F.)

UNIVERSITY OF .

Register of Members of the General Council for the [Fourteen Months] *or* Year commencing 1st .

Number.*	Name in full.	Designation.	Residence and Post Town.	Number in last Register.†	Number in Registration Book.‡

* The numbers to be consecutive.

† Reference to number of the member in the register of the preceding year. This reference will not occur in the first register prepared under this act.

‡ Reference to number of member in the registration book. This will be the only reference in the first register under the act. In subsequent years it will occur only when the member's name has not been in the previous year's register.

SCHEDULE (G.)

UNIVERSITY OF [*Name of University*].

Universities of [*name the universities*], Election 18 .

I, A. B. [*the christian and surnames of the elector in full, and his degree or other qualification to be here inserted*], do hereby declare that I have signed no other voting paper at this election, and I do hereby give my vote at this election for .

And I nominate

C. D.,
E. F.,
G. H.,

or one of them, to deliver this voting paper at the poll.

Witness my hand this day of 18 .

(Signed) A. B. of [*the elector's place of residence to be here inserted*].

Signed in my presence by the said A. B., who is personally known to me, on the above-mentioned day of 18 , the name of , as the candidate voted for, having been previously filled in.

(Signed) J. N., of [*the justice's or other officer's place of residence to be here inserted*], a justice of the peace for (*or as the case may be*).

SCHEDULE (H.)

Offices of Profit referred to in this Act.

Lord High Treasurer; Commissioner for executing offices of Treasurer of the Exchequer of Great Britain and Lord High Treasurer of Ireland; President of the Privy Council; Vice-President of the Committee of Council for Education; Comptroller of her Majesty's Household; Treasurer of her Majesty's Household; Vice-Chamberlain of her Majesty's Household; Equerry or Groom in Waiting on her Majesty; any principal Secretary of State; Chancellor and Under-Treasurer of her Majesty's Exchequer; Paymaster General; Postmaster General; Lord High Admiral; Commissioner for executing the office of Lord High Admiral; Commissioner of her Majesty's Works and Public Buildings; President of the Committee of Privy Council for Trade and Plantations; Chief Secretary for Ireland; Commissioner for administering the Laws for the Relief of the Poor in England; Chancellor of the Duchy of Lancaster; Judge Advocate General; Attorney General for England; Solicitor General for England; Lord Advocate for Scotland; Solicitor General for Scotland; Attorney General for Ireland; Solicitor General for Ireland.

SCHEDULE (I.)

Form No. 1.

Claim of Lodger.

Burgh of

To the assessor of the burgh of

I hereby claim to be inserted in the list of voters in respect of the occupation of the under-mentioned lodgings, and the particulars of my qualification are stated in the columns below.

Christian Name and Surname at full Length.	Profession, Trade, or Calling.	Description of Lodgings.	Description of House or Houses in which Lodgings situate, with Number, if any, and Name of Street.	Name, Description, and Residence of Persons or Person to whom Rent paid.

I, the above-named , hereby declare that I have been, during the twelve months immediately preceding the last day of July in this year, the occupier as sole tenant of the above-mentioned lodgings, and that I have resided therein during the twelve months immediately preceding the said last day of July, and that such lodgings are of a clear yearly value, if let unfurnished, of ten pounds or upwards.

Dated the day of .

Signature of claimant .

Witness to the signature of the said , and I certify my belief in the accuracy of the above claim.

Name of witness .

Residence and calling .

This claim must bear date the 1st day of August, or some day subsequent thereto, and must be delivered to the assessor after the last day of July, and on or before the 21st day of September.

Form No. 2.

List of Claimants in respect of Lodgings to be published by the Assessors.

The following persons claim to have their names inserted in the list of persons entitled to vote in the election of a member [*or* members] for the city or burgh of

Christian Name and Surname of each Claimant at full Length.	Profession, Trade or Calling.	Description of Lodgings.	Description of House in which Lodgings situate, with Number, if any, and Name of Street.	Name, Description, and Residence of Landlord or other Person to whom Rent paid.

(Signed) A. B., Assessor of

THE REPRESENTATION OF THE PEOPLE (IRELAND) ACT, 1868.

(31 & 32 VICT. c. 49.)

An Act to amend the Representation of the People in Ireland. [13th July, 1868.]

WHEREAS it is expedient to amend the laws relating to the representation of the people in Ireland:

Be it enacted by the Queen's most excellent Majesty, by and with the advice and consent of the lords spiritual and temporal, and commons, in this present parliament assembled, and by the authority of the same, as follows:

Preliminary.

Short title. **1.** This act may be cited for all purposes as "The Representation of the People (Ireland) Act, 1868."

Application of act. **2.** This act shall apply to Ireland only, but shall not in anywise affect the election of members to serve in parliament for the borough of the University of Dublin.

PART I.

FRANCHISES.

Occupation franchise in cities, towns and boroughs. **3.** From and after the passing of this act the 5th section of the act of the 13th and 14th years of the reign of her present Majesty, cap. 69, and all other sections or parts of the same act which relate to or affect the franchise conferred by the said 5th section, or the registration of voters upon whom it is conferred, and in which are the words "eight pounds" in reference to the said franchise, shall be read and construed as if the words "more than four pounds" had been used and were substituted in the said 5th and other sections instead of and for the words "eight pounds," so and in such manner that, subject to all the provisions of the said act, the occupation of lands, tenements, or hereditaments rated at the net annual value of more than four pounds shall be as effectual to qualify any man to be registered as a voter, and when registered to vote at any election of members to serve in parliament for any city, town, or borough in Ireland to be held after the passing of this act as the occupation of lands, tenements, and hereditaments rated at the net annual value of eight pounds and upwards was before the passing of this act; and in all provisions relating to such occupation, registration, or voting, and in all lists, returns, precepts, notices, or other forms made or issued in pursuance of the provisions of the registration acts, the words "more than four pounds" shall, when necessary, be substituted for the words "eight pounds."

4. Every man shall be entitled to be registered as a voter, and when registered to vote for a member or members to serve in parliament for a city, town, or borough, who is qualified as follows (that is to say,)

Lodger franchise for voters in cities, towns and boroughs.

1. Is of full age and not subject to any legal incapacity; and
2. As a lodger has occupied in such city, town, or borough, separately and as sole tenant for the twelve months preceding the 20th day of July in any year, the same lodgings, such lodgings being part of one and the same dwelling-house, and of a clear yearly value, if let unfurnished, of ten pounds or upwards; and
3. Has resided in such lodgings during the twelve months immediately preceding the 20th day of July, and has claimed to be registered as a voter at the next ensuing registration of voters.

5. The claim of every person desirous of being registered as a voter for a member or members to serve for any city, town, or borough, in respect of the occupation of lodgings shall be in the Form numbered 1, in Schedule (D.) to this act annexed, or to the like effect, and shall have annexed thereto a declaration in form and be certified in manner in the said schedule mentioned, or as near thereto as circumstances admit, and every such claim shall after the 20th day of July and on or before the 4th day of August in any year be delivered to the town clerk in the city, town or borough in which such lodgings shall be situate, and the particulars of such claim shall be duly published by such town clerk on or before the 11th day of August next ensuing, in a separate list, according to the form numbered 2, in the said Schedule (D.); and all the provisions of the registration acts with respect to the publishing of lists of claimants and to the delivery of copies thereof to persons requiring the same by the said town clerk shall apply to every such claim and list, and all the provisions of the same acts with respect to the proof of claims and to objections thereto and to the hearing thereof shall, so far as the same are applicable, apply to claims and objections and to the hearing thereof under this section.

Registration of persons occupying lodgings.

6. In a county where premises are in the joint occupation of several persons as owners or tenants, and the aggregate rateable value of such premises is such as would, if divided amongst the several occupiers, so far as the value is concerned, confer on each of them a vote, then each of such joint occupiers shall, if otherwise qualified, be entitled to be registered as a voter, and when registered to vote at an election for the county: Provided

As to joint occupation in counties.

always, that not more than two persons, being such joint occupiers, shall be entitled to be registered in respect of such premises, unless they shall have derived the same by descent, succession, marriage, marriage settlement, or devise, or unless they shall be *bonâ fide* engaged as partners carrying on trade or business thereon.

Provisions as to premises occupied in succession in counties.

7. The premises in respect of the occupation of which any person shall be entitled to be registered in any year, and to vote in the election for any county, shall not be required to be the same premises, but may be different premises, occupied in immediate succession by such person during the twelve calendar months next previous to the 20th day of July in such year, such person having paid on or before the 1st day of July in such year all the poor's rates which shall, previously to the 1st day of January in such year, have become payable from him in respect of all such premises so occupied by him in succession.

No elector who has been employed for reward within six months of an election to be entitled to vote.

8. No elector who, within six months before or during any election for any county, city, town or borough, shall have been retained, hired or employed for all or any of the purposes of the election for reward by or on behalf of any candidate at such election as agent, canvasser, clerk, messenger, or in any other like employment, shall be entitled to vote at such election, and if he shall so vote he shall be guilty of a misdemeanor.

PART II.

Boundaries of parliamentary boroughs.

9. Where at the time of the passing of this act the boundary of any municipal borough does not coincide with the parliamentary borough, all that part of such borough situate beyond the limits of the parliamentary borough, but within the municipal limits, shall form part of the borough for all purposes connected with the election of a member or members to serve in parliament for said borough.

PART III.

MISCELLANEOUS.

Rooms for taking polls to be hired wherever they can be obtained.

10. At every contested election for any county, city, town or borough, unless some building or place belonging to the county, city, town or borough is provided for that purpose, the returning officer shall, whenever it is practicable so to do, instead of erecting a booth, hire a building or room for the purpose of taking the poll:

Where in any place there is any room the expense of maintaining which is payable out of any rates levied in such place, such room may, with the consent of the person or corporation having the control over the same, be used for the purpose of taking the poll at such place.

Members holding offices of profit from the crown as in Schedule (E.), not to vacate their seats on acceptance of another office.

11. Whereas it is expedient to amend the law relating to offices of profit, the acceptance of which from the crown vacates the seats of members accepting the same, but does not render them incapable of being re-elected: Be it enacted, that where a person has been returned as a member to serve in parliament since the acceptance by him from the crown of any office described in Schedule (E.) to this act annexed, the subsequent acceptance by him from the crown of any other office or offices described in such schedule, in lieu of and in immediate succession the one to the other, shall not vacate his seat.

Payment of expenses of conveying voters in borough to the poll illegal.

12. It shall not be lawful for any candidate, or any one on his behalf, at any election for any city, town or borough, except the several boroughs of the county of the city of Cork, county of the town of Galway, and county of the city of Limerick, to pay any money on account of the conveyance of any voter to the poll, either to the voter himself or to any other person; and if any such candidate, or any person on his behalf, shall pay any money on account of the conveyance of any voter to the poll, such payment shall be deemed to be an illegal payment within the meaning of "The Corrupt Practices Prevention Act, 1854."

Returning officer, &c. acting as agent guilty of misdemeanor.

13. No returning officer for any county, city, town or borough, nor his deputy, nor any partner or clerk of either of them, shall act as agent for any candidate in the management or conduct of his election as a member to serve in parliament for such county, city, town, or borough; and if any returning officer, his deputy, the partner or clerk of either of them, shall so act, he shall be guilty of a misdemeanor.

Notice of claim to vote in cities, &c. to be signed by claimant.

14. Every notice of claim to be registered as a voter for any city, town, or borough in Ireland shall be signed by the person making such claim.

Sect. 72 of 1 & 2 Vict. c. 56, and sect. 5 of 6 & 7 Vict. c. 92, repealed.

15. From and after the passing of this act sect. 72 of the act of the 1st and 2nd years of the reign of her present Majesty, cap. 56, and sect. 5 of the act of the 6th and 7th years of the reign of her present Majesty, cap. 92, shall be and the same are hereby respectively repealed.

General saving.

16. The franchises conferred by this act shall be in addition to and not in substitution for any existing franchises, but so that no person shall be entitled to vote for the same place in respect of more than one qualification; and, subject to the provisions of this act, all laws, customs, and enactments now in force conferring any right to vote, or otherwise relating to the representation of the people in Ireland, and the registration of persons entitled to vote, shall remain in full force, and shall apply, as nearly as circumstances admit, to any person hereby authorized to vote, and to the franchises hereby conferred.

Precepts, &c. to be made conformable to this act.

17. All precepts, instruments, proceedings, and notices relating to the registration of voters shall be framed and expressed in such manner and form as may be necessary for the carrying the provisions of this act into effect.

Construction of act.

18. This act, so far as is consistent with the tenor thereof, shall be construed as one with the enactments for the time being in force relating to the representation of the people in Ireland, and with the registration acts.

Where value of premises in certain boroughs is not more than 4*l*., the rate is to be made on the immediate lessors.

19. From and after the passing of this act, sect. 116 of the said act of the 13th and 14th years of the reign of her present Majesty, cap. 69, and so far as regards poor rate in respect of lands, tenements, and hereditaments of which the net annual value shall be more than four pounds, the 63rd section of the act of the 12th and 13th years of the reign of her present Majesty, cap. 91, shall be and the same are hereby repealed; and whenever the net annual value of the whole of the rateable hereditaments in any electoral division situate wholly or in part in any of the boroughs of Dublin, Cork, Limerick, Belfast, or Waterford, occupied by any person or persons having no greater estate or interest therein than a tenancy from year to year, or holding under a lease or agreement, leases or agreements, made after the 24th day of August, 1843, shall not exceed four pounds, the poor rate in respect of such property shall, after the passing of this act, be made on the immediate lessor or lessors of such person or persons; and if at the time of making any such rate the name of the immediate lessor be not accurately known to the persons making the rate, it shall be sufficient to describe him therein as the "immediate lessor," with or without any name or further addition, and such rate shall be held to be duly made on him by such description, and shall be recoverable from him accordingly, notwithstanding any error or defect in his name or description, or the entire omission of his name therein.

In certain boroughs occupiers of lands, &c. where owners now rated shall be entitled to be registered.

20. In the boroughs of Dublin, Cork, Limerick, Belfast, and Waterford, every man who would be entitled to be registered at the next registration of parliamentary voters, under the provisions of this act, in respect of the occupation of lands, tenements, or hereditaments (for which the owner or immediate lessor at the time of the passing of this act is liable to be rated to the poor rate instead of the occupier), if he had been rated to the poor rate in respect of the said premises and had duly paid the said poor rate, shall, notwithstanding that he has not been so rated or paid any rate, be entitled to be registered at the next registration of parliamentary voters.

Collector general of rates to make lists of voters for the city of Dublin.

21. From and after the passing of this act the clerk of each Poor Law Union comprising any part or parts of the city of Dublin shall exclude from the list or lists to be made by him, in pursuance of the 32nd section of the said act of the 13th and 14th years of the reign of her present Majesty, cap. 69, every person who shall be rated as the occupier of any lands, tenements, or hereditaments situate within the municipal district of Dublin, as defined by an act passed in the 3rd year of the reign of her present Majesty, intituled "An Act for the Regulation of Municipal Corporations in Ireland," and the collector-general of rates for the city of Dublin shall, on or before the 8th day of July in every year, make out and transmit to the town clerk of the city of Dublin a list of every man of full age who shall be rated in the books of the said collector-general of rates for the said city in the then last rate made under the act of the 12th and 13th years of the reign of her present Majesty, intituled "An Act to provide for the Collection of Rates in the City of Dublin," as the occupier of any lands, tenements, or hereditaments situated within the municipal district of Dublin, as defined as aforesaid, of a net annual value of more than four pounds, and of every person who shall be rated in the said books in the then last rate made as aforesaid jointly with any other person or persons as the occupiers of any lands, tenements, or hereditaments situated within the said municipal district of a net annual value of such an amount as when divided by the number of occupiers would give to each such occupier a net annual value of more than four pounds; excluding nevertheless from such list every such occupier and every such joint occupier who shall not on or before the 1st day of July in such year have paid all poor rates (if any) which shall have become payable by him in respect of such premises previously to the 1st day of January then last; and such lists shall be in the form and shall contain the particulars mentioned on Form No. 6 in the Schedule (B.) annexed to the said act of the 13th and 14th years of the reign of her present Majesty, cap. 69; and such list shall be signed by the said collector-general, and shall be verified by him as true, according to the best of his belief, by an oath or declaration to be made by him before some justice of the peace acting in and for the city of Dublin, and which oath or declaration any such justice is hereby authorized and required to take.

Certain provisions of 13 & 14 Vict. c. 69,

22. The provisions of the 66th and 67th sections of the said act of the 13th and 14th years of the reign of her present Majesty, cap. 69, shall apply to the said

to apply to collector-general of rates.

collector-general of rates as fully as the same apply to the clerk of any union.

Remuneration of collector-general of rates.

23. The guardians of the poor of each union comprising any parts of the city of Dublin shall, by an order, make such annual allowance out of the rates to the said collector-general of rates as a compensation for the duty by this act imposed upon him as the said guardians shall think proper; but no such order shall be acted on, or any payment made thereunder, until the same shall be approved of by the poor law commissioners, and the payments sanctioned by them.

Town clerk.

24. For the purposes of the registration acts and of this act, in all towns under the Towns Improvement (Ireland) Act, 1854, the clerk of the town commissioners shall be the town clerk; and in all towns under the statute passed in the 9th year of the reign of King George the Fourth, cap. 82, the clerk of the paving, lighting and cleansing commissioners, and in towns under improvement or municipal commissioners the clerk to such commissioners, shall be the town clerk; and in towns under none of the authorities before mentioned, the collector of the grand jury cess shall act as town clerk.

Interpretation of terms:

25. The following terms shall in this act have the meanings hereinafter assigned to them, unless there is something in the context repugnant to such construction; (that is to say,)

"Month:" — "Month" shall mean calendar month:

"Member:" — "Member" shall include a knight of the shire:

"County:" — The word "county" shall include a riding or division of a county:

"County of a city:" "County of a town:" — The words "county of a city" or "county of a town," or "city" or "town" or "borough," respectively, shall include all places situate within the parliamentary boundaries of such city or town or borough, and none other:

"City:" "Town:" — The words "city" or "town" shall respectively include county of a city or county of a town:

"Registration Acts." — The "Registration Acts" shall mean the act of the 13th and 14th years of the reign of her present Majesty, cap. 69, and all other acts or parts of acts relating to the registration or qualification of persons entitled to vote at the election of members to serve in parliament for Ireland, as amended by this act.

SCHEDULES TO THIS ACT.

SCHEDULE (D.)

Form No. 1.

Claim of Lodger.

City, town, *or* borough of .

To the town clerk of the city, town, *or* borough of .

I hereby claim to be inserted in the list of voters in respect of the occupation of the under-mentioned lodgings, and the particulars of my qualification are stated in the columns below.

Christian Name and Surname at full Length.	Profession, Trade, or Calling.	Description of Lodgings.	Description of House in which Lodgings situate, with Number, if any, and name of Street.	Name, Description, and Residence of Landlord or other Person to whom Rent paid.

I, the above-named hereby declare that I have been during the twelve months immediately preceding the 20th day of July in this year the occupier as sole tenant of the above-mentioned lodgings, and that I have resided therein during the twelve months immediately preceding the said 20th day of July, and that such lodgings are of a clear yearly value, if let unfurnished, of 10*l*. or upwards.

Dated the day of .

Signature of claimant .

Witness to the signature of the said
And I certify my belief in the accuracy of the above claim.

Name of witness .

Residence and calling .

[This claim must bear date the 21st day of July, or some day subsequent thereto, and must be delivered to the town clerk on or before the 4th day of August.]

Form No. 2.

List of Claimants in respect of Lodgings to be published by the Town Clerk.

The following persons claim to have their names inserted in the list of persons entitled to vote in the election of a member [*or* members] for the city, town, *or* borough of .

Christian Name and Surname of each Claimant at full Length.	Profession, Trade, or Calling.	Description of Lodgings.	Description of House in which Lodgings situate, with Number, if any, and Name of Street.	Name, Description, and Residence of Landlord or other Person to whom Rent paid.

(Signed) A. B., town clerk.

SCHEDULE (E.)

Offices of Profit referred to in this Act.

Lord High Treasurer; Commissioner for executing the offices of Treasurer of the Exchequer of Great Britain and Lord High Treasurer of Ireland; President of the Privy Council; Vice-President of the Committee of Council for Education; Comptroller of her Majesty's Household; Treasurer of her Majesty's Household; Vice-Chamberlain of her Majesty's Household; Equerry or Groom in Waiting on her Majesty; any principal Secretary of State; Chancellor and Under-Treasurer of her Majesty's Exchequer; Paymaster-General; Postmaster-General; Lord High Admiral; Commissioner for executing the office of Lord High Admiral; Commissioner of her Majesty's Works and Public Buildings; President of the Committee of Privy Council for Trade and Plantations; Chief Secretary for Ireland; Commissioner for administering the Laws for the Relief of the Poor in England; Chancellor of the Duchy of Lancaster; Judge Advocate General; Attorney-General for Ireland; Solicitor-General for Ireland; Attorney-General for England; Solicitor-General for England; Lord Advocate for Scotland; Solicitor-General for Scotland.

THE PARLIAMENTARY ELECTIONS ACT, 1868.

(31 & 32 Vict. c. 125.)

An Act for amending the Laws relating to Election Petitions, and providing more effectually for the Prevention of Corrupt Practices at Parliamentary Elections. [31st July, 1868.]

Whereas it is expedient to amend the laws relating to election petitions, and to provide more effectually for the prevention of corrupt practices at parliamentary elections:

Be it enacted by the Queen's most excellent Majesty, by and with the advice and consent of the lords spiritual and temporal, and commons, in this present parliament assembled, and by the authority of the same, as follows:

Preliminary.

1. This act may be cited for all purposes as "The Parliamentary Elections Act, 1868." Short title of act.

2. The expression "the court" shall, for the purposes of this act, in its application to England mean the Court of Common Pleas at Westminster, and in its application to Ireland the Court of Common Pleas at Dublin, and such court shall, subject to the provisions of this act, have the same powers, jurisdiction, and authority with reference to an election petition and the proceedings thereon as it would have if such petition were an ordinary cause within their jurisdiction. Definition and jurisdiction of court.

3. The following terms shall in this act have the meanings hereinafter assigned to them, unless there is something in the context repugnant to such construction; (that is to say,) Interpretation of terms.

"Metropolitan district" shall mean the city of London and the liberties thereof, and any parish or place subject to the jurisdiction of the Metropolitan Board of Works: "Metropolitan district:"

"Election" shall mean an election of a member or members to serve in parliament: "Election:"

"County" shall not include a county of a city or county of a town, but shall mean any county, riding, parts, or division of a county returning a member or members to serve in parliament: "County:"

"Borough" shall mean any borough, university, city, place, or combination of places, not being a county as hereinbefore defined, returning a member or members to serve in parliament: "Borough:"

"*Candidate:*" [Repealed] "*Candidate*" *shall mean any person elected to serve in parliament at an election, and any person who has been nominated as or declared himself a candidate at an election:*

"Corrupt practices:" "Corrupt practices" or "corrupt practice" shall mean bribery, treating, and undue influence, or any of such offences, as defined by act of parliament, or recognized by the common law of parliament:

"Rules of court:" "Rules of court" shall mean rules to be made as hereinafter mentioned:

"Prescribed." "Prescribed" shall mean "prescribed by the rules of court."

Provision as to speaker. **4.** For the purposes of this act "speaker" shall be deemed to include deputy speaker; and when the office of speaker is vacant, the clerk of the House of Commons, or any other officer for the time being performing the duties of the clerk of the House of Commons, shall be deemed to be substituted for and to be included in the expression "the speaker."

Presentation and Service of Petition.

To whom and by whom election petition may be presented. **5.** From and after the next dissolution of parliament a petition complaining of an undue return or undue election of a member to serve in parliament for a county or borough may be presented to the Court of Common Pleas at Westminster, if such county or borough is situate in England, or to the Court of Common Pleas at Dublin, if such county or borough is situate in Ireland, by any one or more of the following persons:

1. Some person who voted or who had a right to vote at the election to which the petition relates; or,
2. Some person claiming to have had a right to be returned or elected at such election; or,
3. Some person alleging himself to have been a candidate at such election:

And such petition is hereinafter referred to as an election petition.

Regulations as to presentation of election petition. **6.** The following enactments shall be made with respect to the presentation of an election petition under this act:

1. The petition shall be signed by the petitioner, or all the petitioners if more than one:
2. The petition shall be presented within twenty-one days after the return has been made to the clerk of the crown in chancery in England, or to the clerk of the crown and hanaper in Ireland, as the case may be, of the member to whose election the petition relates, unless it question the return or election upon an allegation of corrupt practices, and specifically alleges a payment of money or other

reward to have been made by any member, or on his account, or with his privity, since the time of such return, in pursuance or in furtherance of such corrupt practices, in which case the petition may be presented at any time within twenty-eight days after the date of such payment:

3. Presentation of a petition shall be made by delivering it to the prescribed officer or otherwise dealing with the same in manner prescribed:

4. At the time of the presentation of the petition, or within three days afterwards, security for the payment of all costs, charges, and expenses that may become payable by the petitioner—
   (a) to any person summoned as a witness on his behalf, or,
   (b) to the member whose election or return is complained of (who is hereinafter referred to as the respondent),

   shall be given on behalf of the petitioner:

5. The security shall be to an amount of one thousand pounds; it shall be given either by recognizance to be entered into by any number of sureties not exceeding four, or by a deposit of money in manner prescribed, or partly in one way and partly in the other.

Copy of petition after presentation to be sent to returning officer.

7. On presentation of the petition the prescribed officer shall send a copy thereof to the returning officer of the county or borough to which the petition relates, who shall forthwith publish the same in the county or borough, as the case may be.

Recognizance may be objected to.

8. Notice of the presentation of a petition under this act, and of the nature of the proposed security, accompanied with a copy of the petition, shall, within the prescribed time, not exceeding five days after the presentation of the petition, be served by the petitioner on the respondent; and it shall be lawful for the respondent, where the security is given wholly or partially by recognizance, within a further prescribed time, not exceeding five days from the date of the service on him of the notice, to object in writing to such recognizance, on the ground that the sureties, or any of them, are insufficient, or that a surety is dead, or that he cannot be found or ascertained from the want of a sufficient description in the recognizance, or that a person named in the recognizance has not duly acknowledged the same.

Determination of objection to recognizance.

9. Any objection made to the security given shall be heard and decided on in the prescribed manner. If an objection to the security is allowed it shall be lawful for the petitioner, within a further prescribed time, not exceeding five days, to remove such objection, by a deposit in the prescribed manner of such sum of money as may be deemed by the court or officer having cognizance of the matter to make the security sufficient.

If on objection made the security is decided to be insufficient, and such objection is not removed in manner hereinbefore mentioned, no further proceedings shall be had on the petition; otherwise, on the expiration of the time limited for making objections, or, after objection made, on the sufficiency of the security being established, the petition shall be deemed to be at issue.

List of petitions at issue to be made.

10. The prescribed officer shall, as soon as may be, make out a list of all petitions under this act presented to the court of which he is such officer, and which are at issue, placing them in the order in which they were presented, and shall keep at his office a copy of such list, hereinafter referred to as the election list, open to the inspection in the prescribed manner of any person making application.

Such petitions, as far as conveniently may be, shall be tried in the order in which they stand in such list.

Trial of a Petition.

Mode of trial of election petitions.

11. The following enactments shall be made with respect to the trial of election petitions under this act:

1. The trial of every election petition shall be conducted before a puisne judge of one of her Majesty's superior courts of common law at Westminster or Dublin, according as the same shall have been presented to the court at Westminster or Dublin, to be selected from a rota to be formed as hereinafter mentioned.
2. The members of each of the Courts of Queen's Bench, Common Pleas, and Exchequer in England and Ireland shall respectively, on or before the third day of Michaelmas term in every year, select, by a majority of votes, one of the puisne judges of such court, not being a member of the House of Lords, to be placed on the rota for the trial of election petitions during the ensuing year.
3. If in any case the members of the said court are equally divided in their choice of a puisne judge to be placed on the rota, the chief justice of such court (including under that expression the chief baron of the Exchequer) shall have a second or casting vote.
4. Any judge placed on the rota shall be re-eligible in the succeeding or any subsequent year.
5. In the event of the death or the illness of any judge for the time being on the rota, or his inability to

act for any reasonable cause, the court to which he belongs shall fill up the vacancy by placing on the rota another puisne judge of the same court.

6. The judges for the time being on the rota shall, according to their seniority, respectively try the election petitions standing for trial under this act, unless they otherwise agree among themselves, in which case the trial of each election petition shall be taken in manner provided by such agreement.

7. Where it appears to the judges on the rota, after due consideration of the list of petitions under this act for the time being at issue, that the trial of such election petitions will be inconveniently delayed unless an additional judge or judges be appointed to assist the judges on the rota, each of the said courts (that is to say), the Court of Exchequer, the Court of Common Pleas, and Court of Queen's Bench, in the order named, shall, on and according to the requisition of such judges on the rota, select, in manner hereinbefore provided, one of the puisne judges of the court to try election petitions for the ensuing year; and any judge so selected shall, during that year, be deemed to be on the rota for the trial of election petitions.

8. Her Majesty may, in manner heretofore in use, appoint an additional puisne judge to each of the Courts of Queen's Bench, the Common Pleas, and the Exchequer in England.

9. Every election petition shall, except where it raises a question of law for the determination of the court, as hereinafter mentioned, be tried by one of the judges hereinbefore in that behalf mentioned, hereinafter referred to as the judge sitting in open court without a jury.

10. Notice of the time and place at which an election petition will be tried shall be given, not less than fourteen days before the day on which the trial is held, in the prescribed manner.

11. The trial of an election petition in the case of a petition relating to a borough election shall take place in the borough, and in the case of a petition relating to a county election in the county: provided always, that if it shall appear to the court that special circumstances exist which render it desirable that the petition should be tried elsewhere than in the borough or county, it shall be lawful for the court to appoint such other place for the trial as shall appear most convenient: provided also, that in the case of a petition relating to any

of the boroughs within the metropolitan district, the petition may be heard at such place within the district as the court may appoint.

12. The judge presiding at the trial may adjourn the same from time to time and from any one place to any other place within the county or borough, as to him may seem expedient.

13. At the conclusion of the trial the judge who tried the petition shall determine whether the member whose return or election is complained of, or any and what other person, was duly returned or elected, or whether the election was void, and shall forthwith certify in writing such determination to the speaker, and upon such certificate being given such determination shall be final to all intents and purposes.

14. Where any charge is made in an election petition of any corrupt practice having been committed at the election to which the petition refers, the judge shall, in addition to such certificate, and at the same time, report in writing to the speaker as follows:

    (a) Whether any corrupt practice has or has not been proved to have been committed by or with the knowledge and consent of any candidate at such election, and the nature of such corrupt practice:

    (b) The names of all persons (if any) who have been proved at the trial to have been guilty of any corrupt practice:

    (c) Whether corrupt practices have, or whether there is reason to believe that corrupt have, extensively prevailed at the election to which the petition relates.

15. The judge may at the same time make a special report to the speaker as to any matters arising in the course of the trial, an account of which, in his judgment, ought to be submitted to the House of Commons.

16. Where, upon the application of any party to a petition made in the prescribed manner to the court, it appears to the court that the case raised by the petition can be conveniently stated as a special case, the court may direct the same to be stated accordingly, and any such special case shall, as far as may be, be heard before the court, and the decision of the court shall be final; and the court shall certify to the speaker its determination in reference to such special case.

12. Provided always, that if it shall appear to the judge on the trial of the said petition that any question or questions of law as to the admissibility of evidence, or otherwise, require further consideration by the Court of Common Pleas, then it shall be lawful for the said judge to postpone the granting of the said certificate until the determination of such question or questions by the court, and for this purpose to reserve any such question or questions in like manner as questions are usually reserved by a judge on a trial at nisi prius.

Applications to the court respecting trials.

13. The House of Commons, on being informed by the speaker of such certificate and report or reports, if any, shall order the same to be entered in their journals, and shall give the necessary directions for confirming or altering the return, or for issuing a writ for a new election, or for carrying the determination into execution, as circumstances may require.

House of commons to carry out report.

14. Where the judge makes a special report, the House of Commons may make such order in respect of such special report as they think proper.

House of Commons may make order on special report.

15. If the judge states in his report on the trial of an election petition under this act that corrupt practices have, or that there is reason to believe that corrupt practices have, extensively prevailed in any county or borough at the election to which the petition relates, such statement shall, for all the purposes of the act of the session of the 15th and 16th years of the reign of her present Majesty, chapter 57, intituled "An Act to provide for more effectual inquiry into the existence of corrupt practices at elections of members to serve in parliament," have the same effect and may be dealt with in the same manner as if it were a report of a committee of the House of Commons appointed to try an election petition, and the expenses of any commission of inquiry which may be issued in accordance with the provisions of the said act shall be defrayed as if they were expenses incurred in the registration of voters for such county or borough.

Report of the judge as to corrupt practices.

16. *The report of the judge in respect of persons guilty of corrupt practices shall, for the purpose of the prosecution of such persons in pursuance of section 9 of the act of the 26th year of the reign of her present Majesty, chapter 29, have the same effect as the report of the election committee therein mentioned, that certain persons have been guilty of bribery and treating.*

Report of judge equivalent to report of election committee. [Repealed]

17. On the trial of an election petition under this act, unless the judge otherwise directs, any charge of a corrupt practice may be gone into and evidence in relation thereto received before any proof has been given of agency on the part of any candidate in respect of such corrupt practice.

Evidence of corrupt practices, how received.

Acceptance of office not to stop petition.

18. The trial of an election petition under this act shall be proceeded with, notwithstanding the acceptance by the respondent of an office of profit under the crown.

Prorogation of parliament.

19. The trial of an election petition under this act shall be proceeded with notwithstanding the prorogation of parliament.

Proceedings.

Form of petition.

20. An election petition under this act shall be in such form and state such matters as may be prescribed.

Service of petition.

21. An election petition under this act shall be served as nearly as may be in the manner in which a writ or summons is served, or in such other manner as may be prescribed.

Joint respondents to petition.

22. Two or more candidates may be made respondents to the same petition, and their case may, for the sake of convenience, be tried at the same time, but for all the purposes of this act such petition shall be deemed to be a separate petition against each respondent.

Provision in cases where more than one petition is presented.

23. Where, under this act, more petitions than one are presented relating to the same election or return, all such petitions shall in the election list be bracketed together, and shall be dealt with as one petition, but such petitions shall stand in the election list in the place where the last of such petitions would have stood if it had been the only petition presented, unless the court shall otherwise direct.

Shorthand writer to attend trial of election petition.

24. On the trial of an election petition under this act the shorthand writer of the House of Commons or his deputy shall attend and shall be sworn by the judge faithfully and truly to take down the evidence given at the trial, and from time to time as occasion requires to write or cause the same to be written in words at length; and it shall be the duty of such shorthand writer to take down such evidence, and from time to time to write or cause the same to be written at length, and a copy of such evidence shall accompany the certificate made by the judge to the speaker; and the expenses of the shorthand writer shall be deemed to be part of the expenses incurred in receiving the judge.

Jurisdiction and Rules of Court.

Rules to be made by court.

25. The judges for the time being on the rota for the trial of election petitions in England and Ireland may respectively from time to time make, and may from time to time revoke and alter, general rules and orders (in this act referred to as the rules of court), for the effectual execution of this act, and of the intention and object thereof, and the regulation of the practice, procedure, and costs of election petitions, and the trial thereof, and the certifying and reporting thereon.

Any general rules and orders made as aforesaid shall be deemed to be within the powers conferred by this act, and shall be of the same force as if they were enacted in the body of this act.

Any general rules and orders made in pursuance of this section shall be laid before parliament within three weeks after they are made, if parliament be then sitting, and if parliament be not then sitting, within three weeks after the beginning of the then next session of parliament.

Practice of House of Commons to be observed.

26. Until rules of court have been made in pursuance of this act, and so far as such rules do not extend, the principles, practice, and rules on which committees of the House of Commons have heretofore acted in dealing with election petitions shall be observed so far as may be by the court and judge in the case of election petitions under this act.

Performance of duties by prescribed officer.

27. The duties to be performed by the prescribed officer under this act shall be performed by such one or more of the masters of the Court of Common Pleas at Westminster as may be determined by the chief justice of the said Court of Common Pleas, and by the master of the Court of Common Pleas at Dublin, and there shall be awarded to such masters respectively, in addition to their existing salaries, such remuneration for the performance of the duties imposed on them in pursuance of this act as the chief justices of the said Courts of Common Pleas at Westminster and Dublin may respectively, with the consent of the commissioners of the treasury, determine.

Reception, Expenses, and Jurisdiction of Judge.

Reception of judge.

28. The judge shall be received at the place where he is about to try an election petition under this act with the same state, so far as circumstances admit, as a judge of assize is received at an assize town; he shall be received by the sheriff in the case of a petition relating to a county election, and in any other case by the mayor, in the case of a borough having a mayor, and in the case of a borough not having a mayor by the sheriff of the county in which the borough is situate, or by some person named by such sheriff.

The travelling and other expenses of the judge, and all expenses properly incurred by the sheriff or by such mayor or person named as aforesaid in receiving the judge and providing him with necessary accommodation and with a proper court, shall be defrayed by the commissioners of the treasury out of money to be provided by parliament.

Power of judge.

29. On the trial of an election petition under this act the judge shall, subject to the provisions of this act, have the same powers, jurisdiction, and authority as a judge of one of the superior courts and as a judge of assize and nisi prius, and the court held by him shall be a court of record.

Attendance on judge. **30.** The judge shall be attended on the trial of an election petition under this act in the same manner as if he were a judge sitting at nisi prius, and the expenses of such attendance shall be deemed to be part of the expenses of providing a court.

Witnesses.

Summons of witnesses. **31.** Witnesses shall be subpœnaed and sworn in the same manner as nearly as circumstances admit as in a trial at nisi prius, and shall be subject to the same penalties for perjury.

Judge may summon and examine witnesses. **32.** On the trial of an election petition under this act the judge may, by order under his hand, compel the attendance of any person as a witness who appears to him to have been concerned in the election to which the petition refers, and any person refusing to obey such order shall be guilty of contempt of court. The judge may examine any witness so compelled to attend or any person in court although such witness is not called and examined by any party to the petition. After the examination of a witness as aforesaid by a judge, such witness may be cross-examined by or on behalf of the petitioner and respondent, or either of them.

Indemnity to witnesses. [Repealed] **33.** *The provisions of the 7th section of the act of the session of the 26th and 27th years of the reign of her present Majesty, cap. 29, relating to the examination and indemnity of witnesses, shall apply to any witness appearing before a judge on the trial of an election petition under this act, in the same manner as in the case of a trial before a committee of the House of Commons before the passing of this act, and the certificate shall be given under the hand of the judge.*

Expenses of witnesses. **34.** The reasonable expenses incurred by any person in appearing to give evidence at the trial of an election petition under this act, according to the scale allowed to witnesses on the trial of civil actions at the assizes, may be allowed to such person by a certificate under the hand of the judge or of the prescribed officer, and such expenses if the witness was called and examined by the judge shall be deemed part of the expenses of providing a court, and in other cases shall be deemed to be costs of the petition.

Withdrawal and Abatement of Election Petitions.

Withdrawal of **35.** An election petition under this act shall not be withdrawn without the leave of the court or judge upon special application, to be made in and at the prescribed manner, time, and place.

petition and substitution of new petitioners.

No such application shall be made for the withdrawal of a petition until the prescribed notice has been given in the county or borough to which the petition relates of the intention of the petitioner to make an application for the withdrawal of his petition.

On the hearing of the application for withdrawal any person who might have been a petitioner in respect of the election to which the petition relates may apply to the court or judge to be substituted as a petitioner for the petitioner so desirous of withdrawing the petition.

The court or judge may, if it or he think fit, substitute as a petitioner any such applicant as aforesaid; and may further, if the proposed withdrawal is in the opinion of the court or judge induced by any corrupt bargain or consideration, by order direct that the security given on behalf of the original petitioner shall remain as security for any costs that may be incurred by the substituted petitioner, and that to the extent of the sum named in such security the original petitioner shall be liable to pay the costs of the substituted petitioner.

If no such order is made with respect to the security given on behalf of the original petitioner, security to the same amount as would be required in the case of a new petition, and subject to the like conditions, shall be given on behalf of the substituted petitioner before he proceeds with his petition, and within the prescribed time after the order of substitution.

Subject as aforesaid a substituted petitioner shall stand in the same position as nearly as may be, and be subject to the same liabilities as the original petitioner.

If a petition is withdrawn, the petitioner shall be liable to pay the costs of the respondent.

Where there are more petitioners than one, no application to withdraw a petition shall be made except with the consent of all the petitioners.

Court to report to the speaker circumstances of withdrawal.

36. *In every case of the withdrawal of an election petition under this act the court or judge shall report to the speaker whether in its or his opinion the withdrawal of such petition was the result of any corrupt arrangement, or in consideration of the withdrawal of any other petition, and if so, the circumstances attending the withdrawal.*

[Repealed]

Abatement of petition.

37. An election petition under this act shall be abated by the death of a sole petitioner or of the survivor of several petitioners.

The abatement of a petition shall not affect the liability of the petitioner to the payment of costs previously incurred.

On the abatement of a petition the prescribed notice of such abatement having taken place shall be given in the county or borough to which the petition relates, and within the prescribed time after the notice is given, any person who might have been a petitioner in respect of the election to which the petition relates may apply to the court or judge, in and at the prescribed manner, time, and place, to be substituted as a petitioner.

The court or judge may, if it or he think fit, substitute as a petitioner any such applicant who is desirous of being substituted, and on whose behalf security to the same amount is given as is required in the case of a new petition.

Admission in certain cases of voters to be respondents.

38. If before the trial of any election petition under this act any of the following events happen in the case of the respondent; (that is to say,)

(1.) If he dies:

(2.) If he is summoned to parliament as a peer of Great Britain by a writ issued under the great seal of Great Britain:

(3.) If the House of Commons have resolved that his seat is vacant:

(4.) If he gives in, and at the prescribed manner and time, notice to the court that he does not intend to oppose the petition.

Notice of such event having taken place shall be given in the county or borough to which the petition relates, and within the prescribed time after the notice is given any person who might have been a petitioner in respect of the election to which the petition relates may apply to the court or judge to be admitted as a respondent to oppose the petition, and such person shall on such application be admitted accordingly, either with the respondent, if there be a respondent, or in place of the respondent; and any number of persons not exceeding three may be so admitted.

Respondent not opposing not to appear as party or to sit.

39. A respondent who has given the prescribed notice that he does not intend to oppose the petition, shall not be allowed to appear or act as a party against such petition in any proceedings thereon, and shall not sit or vote in the House of Commons until the House of Commons has been informed of the report on the petition, and the court or judge shall in all cases in which such notice has been given in the prescribed time and manner report the same to the speaker of the House of Commons.

Provisions for cases of double return where the member com-

40. Where an election petition under this act complains of a double return, and the respondent has given notice to the prescribed officer that it is not his intention to oppose the petition, and no party has been admitted in pursuance of this act to defend such return, then the petitioner, if there be no petition complaining of the other member returned on such double return, may withdraw his petition by notice addressed to the prescribed officer, and upon the receipt of such notice the prescribed officer shall report the fact of the withdrawal of such petition to the speaker, and the House of Commons shall thereupon give the necessary directions for amending the said double return by taking off the file the indenture by which the respondent so declining to oppose the petition was returned, or otherwise as the case may require: Provided always, that this section shall not apply to Ireland.

plained of declines to defend his return.

Costs.

41. All costs, charges, and expenses of and incidental to the presentation of a petition under this act, and to the proceedings consequent thereon, with the exception of such costs, charges, and expenses as are by this act otherwise provided for, shall be defrayed by the parties to the petition, in such manner and in such proportions as the court or judge may determine, regard being had to the disallowance of any costs, charges, or expenses which may, in the opinion of the court or judge, have been caused by vexatious conduct, unfounded allegations, or unfounded objections on the part either of the petitioner or the respondent, and regard being had to the discouragement of any needless expense by throwing the burden of defraying the same on the parties by whom it has been caused, whether such parties are or not on the whole successful.

General costs of petition.

The costs may be taxed in the prescribed manner, *but according to the same principles as costs between attorney and client are taxed in a suit in the High Court of Chancery*, and such costs may be recovered in the same manner as the costs of an action at law, or in such other manner as may be prescribed.

[Repealed]

42. If any petitioner in an election petition presented under this act neglect or refuse for the space of six months after demand to pay to any person summoned as a witness on his behalf, or to the respondent, any sum certified to be due to him for his costs, charges, and expenses, and if such neglect or refusal be, within one year after such demand, proved to the satisfaction of the court of elections, in every such case every person who has entered into a recognizance relating to such petition under the provisions of this act shall be held to have made default in his said recognizance, and the prescribed officer shall thereupon certify such recognizance to be forfeited, and the same shall be dealt with in England in manner provided by the act of the 3rd year of the reign of King

Recognizance, when to be estreated, &c.

George the Fourth, chapter 46, and in Ireland in manner provided by "The Fines Act (Ireland), 1851."

Punishment of Corrupt Practices.

Punishment of candidate guilty of bribery.

[Repealed]

43. *Where it is found, by the report of the judge upon an election petition under this act that bribery has been committed by or with the knowledge and consent of any candidate at an election, such candidate shall be deemed to have been personally guilty of bribery at such election, and his election, if he has been elected, shall be void, and he shall be incapable of being elected to and of sitting in the House of Commons during the seven years next after the date of his being found guilty; and he shall further be incapable during the said period of seven years—*

(1.) *Of being registered as a voter and voting at any election in the United Kingdom; and*

(2.) *Of holding any office under the act of the session of the 5th and 6th years of the reign of his Majesty King William the Fourth, chapter 76, or of the session of the 3rd and 4th years of the reign of her present Majesty, chapter 108, or any municipal office; and*

(3.) *Of holding any judicial office, and of being appointed and of acting as a justice of the peace.*

Penalty for employing corrupt agent.

44. If on the trial of any election petition under this act any candidate is proved to have personally engaged at the election to which such petition relates as a canvasser or agent for the management of the election, any person knowing that such person has within seven years previous to such engagement been found guilty of any corrupt practice by any competent legal tribunal, or been reported guilty of any corrupt practice by a committee of the House of Commons, or by the report of the judge upon an election petition under this act, or by the report of commissioners appointed in pursuance of the act of the session of the 15th and 16th years of the reign of her present Majesty, chapter 57, the election of such candidate shall be void.

Disqualification of persons found guilty of bribery.

[Repealed]

45. *Any person, other than a candidate found guilty of bribery in any proceeding in which after notice of the charge he has had an opportunity of being heard, shall, during the seven years next after the time at which he is so found guilty, be incapable of being elected to and sitting in parliament; and also be incapable—*

(1.) *Of being registered as a voter and voting at any election in the United Kingdom; and*

(2.) *Of holding any office under the act of the session of the 5th and 6th years of the reign of his Majesty King William the Fourth, chapter 76, or of the session of the 3rd and 4th years of the reign of her present Majesty, chapter 108, or any municipal office; and*

(3.) *Of holding any judicial office and of being appointed and of acting as a justice of the peace.*

Amendment of the law relating to the disqualification of candidates for corrupt practices. [Repealed]

46. *For the purpose of disqualifying, in pursuance of the 36th section of "The Corrupt Practices Prevention Act, 1854," a member guilty of corrupt practices, other than personal bribery within the 43rd section of this act, the report of the judge on the trial of an election petition shall be deemed to be substituted for the declaration of an election committee, and the said section shall be construed as if the words "reported by a judge on the trial of an election petition" were inserted therein in the place of the words "declared by an election committee."*

Removal of disqualification on proof that disqualification was procured by perjury. [Repealed]

47. *If at any time after any person has become disqualified by virtue of this act, the witnesses, or any of them, on whose testimony such person shall have so become disqualified, shall, upon the prosecution of such person, be convicted of perjury in respect of such testimony, it shall be lawful for such person to move the court to order, and the court shall, upon being satisfied that such disqualification was procured by reason of perjury, order, that such disqualification shall thenceforth cease and determine, and the same shall cease and determine accordingly.*

Miscellaneous.

Returning officer may be sued for neglecting to return any person duly elected.

48. If any returning officer wilfully delays, neglects, or refuses duly to return any person who ought to be returned to serve in parliament for any county or borough, such person may, in case it has been determined on the hearing of an election petition under this act that such person was entitled to have been returned, sue the officer having so wilfully delayed, neglected, or refused duly to make such return at his election in any of her Majesty's courts of record at Westminster, and shall recover double the damages he has sustained by reason thereof, together with full costs of suit; provided such action be commenced within one year after the commission of the act on which it is grounded, or within six months after the conclusion of the trial relating to such election.

Calculation of time.

49. In reckoning time for the purposes of this act, Sunday, Christmas-day, Good Friday, and any day set apart for a public fast or public thanksgiving shall be excluded.

Controverted elections to be tried under act.

50. From and after the next dissolution of parliament no election or return to parliament shall be questioned except in accordance with the provisions of this act, but until such dissolution, elections and returns to parliament may be questioned in manner heretofore in use.

Returning

51. Where an election petition under this act complains

officer if complained of to be respondent. of the conduct of a returning officer, such returning officer shall for all the purposes of this act, except the admission of respondents in his place, be deemed to be a respondent.

Petition complaining of no return. **52.** A petition under this act complaining of no return may be presented to the court, and shall be deemed to be an election petition within the meaning of this act, and the court may make such order thereon as they think expedient for compelling a return to be made, or may allow such petition to be heard by the judge in manner hereinbefore provided with respect to ordinary election petitions.

Recrimination when petition for undue return. **53.** On the trial of a petition under this act, complaining of an undue return, and claiming the seat for some person, the respondent may give evidence to prove that the election of such person was undue in the same manner as if he had presented a petition complaining of such election.

Repeal of acts. **54.** From and after the next dissolution of parliament the acts contained in the schedule hereto are repealed, so far as relates to elections and petitions, to the extent therein mentioned; provided that such repeal shall not affect the validity or invalidity of anything already done or suffered, or any offence already committed, or any remedy or proceeding in respect thereof, or the proof of any past act or thing.

Provision as to payment of additional judges and remuneration of judges for duties to be performed under this act. **55.** The additional puisne judges appointed under this act to each of the Courts of Queen's Bench, the Common Pleas, and the Exchequer, in England, shall, as to rank, salary, pension, attendant officers, jurisdiction, and all other privileges and duties of a judge, stand in the same position as the other puisne judges of the court to which he is attached.

Any puisne judge of the said courts appointed in pursuance of or after the passing of this act shall be authorized to sit, and shall, when requested by the lord chancellor, sit as judge of the Court of Probate and Court of Marriage and Divorce, or of the Admiralty Court.

Commissions of inquiry into corrupt practices. **56.** If, upon a petition to the House of Commons, presented within twenty-one days after the return to the clerk of the crown in chancery in England, or to the clerk of the crown and hanaper in Ireland, of a member to serve in parliament for any borough or county, or within fourteen days after the meeting of parliament, and signed by any two or more electors of such borough or county, and alleging that corrupt practices have extensively prevailed at the then last election for such borough or county, or that there is reason to believe that corrupt practices have there so prevailed, an address be presented by both houses of parliament, praying that such allegation may be inquired into, the crown may appoint commissioners to inquire into the same; and if such commissioners in such case be appointed, they shall inquire in the same manner and with the same powers, and subject to all the provisions of the statute of the 15th and 16th of Victoria, chapter 57.

Rules as to agents practising in cases of election petitions.

57. Any person who, at the time of the passing of this act, was entitled to practise as agent, according to the principles, practice and rules of the House of Commons, in cases of election petitions, and matters relating to election of members of the House of Commons, shall be entitled to practise as an attorney or agent in cases of election petitions, and all matters relating to elections, before the court and judges prescribed by this act: provided that every such person so practising as aforesaid shall, in respect of such practice and everything relating thereto, be subject to the jurisdiction and orders of the court as if he were an attorney of the said court: and further provided that no such person shall practise as aforesaid until his name shall have been entered on a roll to be made and kept, and which is hereby authorized to be made and kept, by the prescribed officer in the prescribed manner.

Application of act to Scotland.

58. The provisions of this act shall apply to Scotland, subject to the following modifications:—

1. The expression "the court" shall mean either division of the inner house of the Court of Session, and either of such divisions shall have the same powers, jurisdiction and authority with reference to an election petition in Scotland, and the proceedings thereon, which by this act are conferred on the Court of Common Pleas at Westminster with respect to election petitions in England:
2. The expression "county" shall not include a county of a city, but shall mean any county or division of a county, or any combination of counties, or of counties and portions of counties, returning a member to serve in parliament:
3. The expression "borough" shall mean any university or universities, or any city, town, burgh, or district of cities, towns, or burghs returning a member or members to serve in parliament:
4. "Recognizance" shall mean a bond of caution, with usual and necessary clauses:
5. The trial of every election petition in Scotland shall be conducted before a judge of the Court of Session, to be selected from a rota to be formed as hereinafter mentioned:
6. The judges of the Court of Session shall, on or before the first day of the winter session in every year, select, by a majority of votes, two of the judges of

such court, not being members of the House of Lords, to be placed on the rota for the trial of election petitions during the ensuing year:

7. If in any case the judges of the said court are equally divided in their choice of a judge to be placed on the rota, the lord president shall have a second or casting vote:

8. Any judge placed on the rota shall be re-eligible in the succeeding or any subsequent year:

9. In the event of the death or illness of any judge for the time being on the rota, or his inability to act for any reasonable cause, the judges shall fill up the vacancy by placing on the rota another judge:

10. The judges for the time being on the rota shall, according to their seniority, respectively try the election petitions standing for trial under this act, unless they otherwise agree among themselves, in which case the trial of each election petition shall be taken in manner provided by such agreement:

11. Where it appears to the judges on the rota, after due consideration of the list of petitions under this act for the time being at issue, that the trial of such election petitions will be inconveniently delayed unless an additional judge or judges be appointed to assist the judges on the rota, the judges of the court of session shall, on and according to the requisition of such judges on the rota, select in manner hereinbefore provided, a judge to try election petitions for the ensuing year; and any judge so selected shall during that year be deemed to be on the rota for the trial of election petitions:

12. The duties to be performed by the prescribed officer under this act with reference to election petitions in Scotland shall be performed by such one or more of the principal clerks of session as may be determined by the lord president of the Court of Session; and there shall be awarded to such principal clerk or clerks, in addition to their existing salaries, such remuneration for the performance of the duties imposed on them in pursuance of this act as the said lord president may, with the consent of the commissioners of the treasury, determine:

13. The judge shall be received at the place where he is about to try an election petition under this act in the same manner and by the same authorities, as far as circumstances admit, as a judge of the Court of Justiciary is received at a circuit town, and he shall be attended by such officer or officers as shall be necessary:

14. The travelling and other expenses of the judge, and

of the officer or officers in attendance upon him, and all expenses properly incurred in providing the judge with a proper court, shall be defrayed by the commissioners of the treasury out of money to be provided by parliament:

15. On the trial of an election petition under this act, the judge shall, subject to the provisions of this act, have the same powers, jurisdictions, and authority as a judge of the Court of Session presiding at the trial of a civil cause without a jury:

16. *The principles of taxation of costs as between attorney and client in a suit in the High Court of Chancery shall in Scotland mean the principles of taxation of expenses as between agent and client in the Court of Session:* [Repealed]

17. Any of her Majesty's courts of record at Westminster shall in Scotland mean the Court of Session in Scotland:

18. In lieu of the provisions for the estreating of a recognizance under an election petition, the prescribed officer shall, when otherwise competent under the provisions of this act, certify that the conditions contained in the bond of caution have not been fulfilled, and it shall then be competent for the party or parties interested to register the said bond, and do diligence upon it as accords of law.

59. This act shall be in force until the expiration of three years from the passing of such act, and to the end of the then next session of parliament. Duration of act.

SCHEDULE.

Date of Act.	Title of Act.	Extent of Repeal.
4 & 5 Vict. c. 57 ..	An Act for the Prevention of Bribery at Elections.	The whole Act.
5 & 6 Vict. c. 102.	An Act for the better Discovery and Prevention of Bribery and Treating at the Election of Members of Parliament.	The whole Act.
11 & 12 Vict. c. 98	An Act to amend the Law for the Trial of Election Petitions.	The whole Act.
26 Vict. c. 29	An Act to amend and continue the Law relating to Corrupt Practices at Elections of Members of Parliament.	Section 8.
28 Vict. c. 8	An Act to amend "The Election Petitions Act, 1848," in certain particulars.	The whole Act.

THE CORRUPT PRACTICES PREVENTION ACT, 1854.

17 & 18 Vict. c. 102.

An Act to consolidate and amend the Laws relating to Bribery, Treating, and undue Influence at Elections of Members of Parliament.

[10th August, 1854.]

Whereas the laws now in force for preventing corrupt practices in the election of members to serve in parliament have been found insufficient: And whereas it is expedient to consolidate and amend such laws, and to make further provision for securing the freedom of such elections: Be it enacted, &c.

Repeal of acts in the schedule. [Repealed] 1. *The several acts of parliament mentioned in the schedule A. hereto annexed shall be repealed to the extent specified concerning the same acts respectively in the third column of the said schedule.*

Bribery defined. 2. The following persons shall be deemed guilty of bribery, and shall be punishable accordingly:

1. Every person who shall, directly or indirectly, by himself, or by any other person on his behalf, give, lend, or agree to give or lend, or shall offer, promise, or promise to procure or to endeavour to procure, any money or valuable consideration, to or for any voter, or to or for any person on behalf of any voter, or to or for any other person in order to induce any voter to vote, or refrain from voting, or shall corruptly do any such act as aforesaid, on account of such voter having voted or refrained from voting at any election:
2. Every person who shall, directly or indirectly, by himself or by any other person on his behalf, give or procure, or agree to give or procure, or offer, promise, or promise to procure or to endeavour to procure, any office, place, or employment to or for any voter, or to or for any person on behalf of any voter, or to or for any other person, in order to induce such voter to vote, or refrain from voting, or shall corruptly do any such act as aforesaid, on account of any voter having voted or refrained from voting at any election:
3. Every person who shall, directly or indirectly, by himself or by any other person on his behalf, make any such gift, loan, offer, promise, procurement, or agreement as aforesaid, to or for any person,

in order to induce such person to procure, or endeavour to procure, the return of any person to serve in parliament, or the vote of any voter at any election:

4. Every person who shall, upon or in consequence of any such gift, loan, offer, promise, procurement, or agreement, procure or engage, promise, or endeavour to procure the return of any person to serve in parliament, or the vote of any voter at any election:

5. Every person who shall advance or pay, or cause to be paid, any money to or to the use of any other person with the intent that such money or any part thereof shall be expended in bribery at any election, or who shall knowingly pay or cause to be paid any money to any person in discharge or repayment of any money wholly or in part expended in bribery at any election:

And any person so offending shall be guilty of a misdemeanor, and in Scotland of an offence punishable by fine and imprisonment, and shall also be liable to forfeit the sum of 100*l. to any person who shall sue for the same, together with full costs of suit:* Provided always, that the aforesaid enactment shall not extend or be construed to extend to any money paid or agreed to be paid for or on account of any legal expenses *bonâ fide* incurred at or concerning any election. [Repealed]

3. The following persons shall also be deemed guilty of bribery and shall be punishable accordingly: Bribery further defined.

1. Every voter who shall, before or during any election, directly or indirectly, by himself or by any other person on his behalf, receive, agree, or contract for any money, gift, loan, or valuable consideration, office, place, or employment, for himself or for any other person, for voting or agreeing to vote, or for refraining or agreeing to refrain from voting, at any election:

2. Every person who shall, after any election, directly or indirectly, by himself or by any other person on his behalf, receive any money or valuable consideration on account of any person having voted or refrained from voting, or having induced any other person to vote or to refrain from voting, at any election:

And any person so offending shall be guilty of a misdemeanor, and in Scotland of an offence punishable by fine and imprisonment, and shall also be liable to forfeit the sum of 10*l. to any person who shall sue for the same, together with full costs of suit.* [Repealed] *Penalty.*

Treating defined. [Repealed]

4. *Every candidate at an election, who shall corruptly by himself, or by or with any person, or by any other ways or means on his behalf, at any time, either before, during, or after any election, directly or indirectly, give or provide, or cause to be given or provided, or shall be accessory to the giving or providing, or shall pay, wholly or in part, any expenses incurred for any meat, drink, entertainment, or provision to or for any person, in order to be elected, or for being elected, or for the purpose of corruptly influencing such person or any other person to give or refrain from giving his vote at such election, or on account of such person having voted or refrained from voting, or being about to vote or refrain from voting, at such election, shall be deemed guilty of the offence of treating, and shall forfeit the sum of 50l. to any person who shall sue for the same, with full costs of suit; and every voter who shall corruptly accept or take any such meat, drink, entertainment, or provision, shall be incapable of voting at such election, and his vote, if given, shall be utterly void and of none effect.*

Penalty.

Undue influence defined. [Repealed]

5. *Every person who shall, directly or indirectly, by himself, or by any other person on his behalf, make use of, or threaten to make use of, any force, violence, or restraint, or inflict or threaten the infliction, by himself or by or through any other person, of any injury, damage, harm, or loss, or in any other manner practise intimidation upon or against any person in order to induce or compel such person to vote or refrain from voting, or on account of such person having voted or refrained from voting, at any election, or who shall, by abduction, duress, or any fraudulent device or contrivance, impede, prevent, or otherwise interfere with the free exercise of the franchise of any voter, or shall thereby compel, induce, or prevail upon any voter, either to give or to refrain from giving his vote at any election, shall be deemed to have committed the offence of undue influence, and shall be guilty of a misdemeanor, and in Scotland of an offence punishable by fine or imprisonment, and shall also be liable to forfeit the sum of 50l. to any person who shall sue for the same, together with full costs of suit.*

Penalty.

Names of offenders to be struck out of register, and inserted in separate list. [Repealed]

6. *Whenever it shall be proved before the revising barrister that any person who is or claims to be placed on the list or register of voters for any county, city, or borough has been convicted of bribery or undue influence at an election, or that judgment has been obtained against any such person for any penal sum hereby made recoverable in respect of the offences of bribery, treating, or undue influence, or either of them, then and in that case such revising barrister shall, in case the name of such person is in the list of voters, expunge the same therefrom, or shall, in case such person is claiming to have his name inserted therein, disallow such claim; and the*

names of all persons whose names shall be so expunged from the list of voters, and whose claims shall be so disallowed, shall be thereupon inserted in a separate list, to be entitled "The list of persons disqualified for bribery, treating, or undue influence," which last-mentioned list shall be appended to the list or register of voters, and shall be printed and published therewith, wherever the same shall be or is required to be printed or published.

No cockades, &c. to be given at elections.

7. No candidate before, during, or after any election shall in regard to such election, by himself or agent, directly or indirectly, give or provide to or for any person having a vote at such election, or to or for any inhabitant of the county, city, borough, or place for which such election is had, any cockade, ribbon, or other mark of distinction; and every person so giving or providing shall for every such offence forfeit the sum of 2*l.* to such person as shall sue for the same, together with full costs of suit; *and all payments made for or on account of any chairing, or any such cockade, ribbon, or mark of distinction as aforesaid, or of any bands of music or flags or banners, shall be deemed illegal payments within this act.*

Penalty.

[Repealed]

Voters not to serve as special constables during elections.

8. No person having a right to vote at the election for any county, city, borough, or other place shall be liable or compelled to serve as a special constable at or during any election for a member or members to serve in parliament for such county, city, borough, or other place, unless he shall consent so to act; and he shall not be liable to any fine, penalty, or punishment whatever for refusing so to act, any statute, law, or usage to the contrary notwithstanding.

Penalties how to be recovered.

[Repealed]

9. *The pecuniary penalties hereby imposed for the offences of bribery, treating, or undue influence respectively shall be recoverable by action or suit by any person who shall sue for the same in any of her Majesty's superior courts at Westminster, if the offence be committed in England or Wales, and in any of her Majesty's superior courts in Dublin if the offence be committed in Ireland, and in or before the Court of Session if the offence be committed in Scotland, and not otherwise.*

Costs and expenses of prosecutions.

10. It shall be lawful for any criminal court, before which any prosecution shall be instituted for any offence against the provisions of this act, to order payment to the prosecutor of such costs and expenses as to the said court shall appear to have been reasonably incurred in and about the conduct of such prosecution: Provided always, that no indictment for bribery or undue influence shall be triable before any court of quarter sessions.

Returning officer to

11. For the more effectual observance of this act, every returning officer to whom the execution of any writ or

give notice of election.

precept for electing any member or members to serve in parliament may appertain or belong shall, in lieu of the proclamation or notice of election heretofore used, publish or cause to be published such proclamation or notice of election as is mentioned in Schedule B. to this act, or to the like effect.

In cases of private prosecutions, if judgment be given for the defendant, he shall recover costs from the prosecutor.

12. In case of any indictment or information by a private prosecutor for any offence against the provisions of this act, if judgment shall be given for the defendant, he shall be entitled to recover from the prosecutor the costs sustained by the defendant by reason of such indictment or information, such costs to be taxed by the proper officer of the court in which such judgment shall be given.

Prosecutor not to be entitled to costs unless he shall have entered into a recognizance to conduct prosecution and pay costs.

13. It shall not be lawful for any court to order payment of the costs of a prosecution for any offence against the provisions of this act, unless the prosecutor shall, before or upon the finding of the indictment or the granting of the information, enter into a recognizance, with two sufficient sureties, in the sum of 200*l.* (to be acknowledged in like manner as is now required in cases of writs of certiorari awarded at the instance of a defendant in an indictment), with the conditions following; that is to say, that the prosecutor shall conduct the prosecution with effect, and shall pay to the defendant or defendants, in case he or they shall be acquitted, his or their costs.

Limitation of actions. [Repealed]

14. *No person shall be liable to any penalty or forfeiture hereby enacted or imposed, unless some prosecution, action, or suit for the offence committed shall be commenced against such person within the space of one year next after such offence against this act shall be committed, and unless such person shall be summoned or otherwise served with writ or process within the same space of time, so as such summons or service of writ or process shall not be prevented by such person absconding or withdrawing out of the jurisdiction of the court out of which such writ or other process shall have issued; and in case of any such prosecution, suit, or process as aforesaid, the same shall be proceeded with and carried on without any wilful delay.*

Power to returning officers to appoint election auditors.

15. Whereas it is expedient to make further provision for preventing the offences of bribery, treating, and undue influence, and also for diminishing the expenses of elections: Be it enacted, that within six days after the passing of this act the returning officers of the city of Canterbury, the boroughs of Cambridge, Kingston-upon-Hull, Maldon, and Barnstaple, and once in every year, in the month of August, the returning officer of every county, city, and borough shall appoint a fit and proper person to be an election officer, to be called "election auditor or auditor of election expenses," to act at any election or elections for and during the year then next ensuing, and until another appointment of election auditor shall be made; and such returning officer shall, in such way as he shall think best, give public notice of such appointment in such county, city, or borough; provided, that any person appointed an election auditor may be re-appointed as often as the returning officer for the time being shall think fit; and that every person who shall be an election auditor on the day appointed for any election shall continue to be the election auditor in respect of such election until the whole business of such election shall be concluded, notwithstanding the subsequent appointment of any other person as election auditor; and every election auditor upon his appointment shall make and sign before the returning officer the following declaration:

"I [*A. B.*] do solemnly and sincerely promise and declare, that I will well and truly and faithfully, to the best of my ability in all things, perform my duty as election auditor according to the provisions of 'The Corrupt Practices Prevention Act, 1854,'"

And every election auditor wilfully doing any act whatever contrary to the true intent and meaning of such declaration shall be deemed guilty of a misdemeanor and in Scotland of an offence punishable with fine and imprisonment.

Bills, &c. to be sent in within one month to candidate or right to recover barred.

16. All persons, as well agents as others, who shall have any bills, charges, or claims upon any candidate for or in respect of any election shall send in such bills, charges, or claims within one month from the day of the declaration of the election to such candidate, or to some authorized agent of such candidate acting on his behalf, otherwise such persons shall be barred of their right to recover such claims, and every or any part thereof: Provided always, that in case of the death within the said month of any person claiming the amount of such bill, charge, or claim, the legal representative of such person shall send in such bill, charge, or claim within one month after obtaining probate or letters of administration, or confirmation as executor, as the case may be, or the right to recover such claim shall be barred as aforesaid.

Bills, &c. received within one month to be sent in to election auditor.

17. Every candidate shall, by himself or his agent in that behalf, within three months after the day of the declaration of the election, or within two months after any bill, charge, or claim has been sent in by the legal representative of any deceased creditor, as hereinbefore provided, send in to the election auditor for payment all such bills, charges, or claims (except as hereinafter excepted) as have been sent in to such candidate within the one month hereinbefore specified from the day of the declaration of the election, or after the granting of probate or letters of administration, or confirmation as executor, as the case may be: Provided always, that the candidate shall, by himself or his agent as aforesaid, at the time of his sending in any such bill, charge, or claim, state to the election auditor whether he admits the whole amount of such bill, charge, or claim, or if not the whole, then how much thereof, if any, he admits to be correct: Provided also, that in case of the wilful default of the candidate, by himself or his agent as aforesaid, in sending in all such bills, charges, or claims, or in making such statement at the time of sending in such bills, charges, or claims, he shall be liable to a penalty of 20*l*., and to a further penalty of 10*l*. for every subsequent week of wilful default or neglect in sending in all such bills, charges, or claims, or in making such statement, to be recovered by any person who will sue for the same, together with full costs of suit: Provided always, that in case any such candidate shall be absent from the United Kingdom at the time of such election, he shall send in to the election auditor for payment any such bills, charges, or claims as aforesaid within one month after his return to the United Kingdom, which shall be of the same force and effect as if the same had been sent in as herein provided.

No payments to be made except through election auditor.

18. No payment of any bill, charge, or claim, or of any money whatever, for or in respect of any election, or the expenses thereof (except as herein excepted), shall be made by or by the authority of any candidate, except by or through such election auditor, and any payment made by or by the authority of any candidate otherwise than as herein provided shall be deemed and taken to be an illegal payment, and upon proof thereof such candidate shall forfeit the sum of 10*l*., with double the amount of such illegal payment, and full costs of suit, to any person who will sue for the same: Provided always, that it shall be lawful for any candidate, by himself or his agent, to name any banker through whom alone such bills, charges, or claims, or money, as aforesaid, shall be paid by the election auditor, and in that case the election auditor shall pay such bills, charges, and claims by cheques drawn on such banker, to be countersigned by the candidate or some person on his behalf specially appointed for that purpose.

Tender and payment into court by election auditor.

19. If the election auditor, by the authority of any candidate, tenders or offers to pay any sum in respect of any bill, charge, or claim sent in as hereinbefore provided, such tender shall be taken for all purposes to be the tender of such candidate, and may, in any action or other proceeding brought against such candidate to recover the amount of such bill, charge, or claim, be pleaded as such, or otherwise be made available according to the proceedings of the court in which such action or other proceeding is brought or carried on; and if such plea is pleaded, or if it shall be deemed advisable for any other reason to pay money into court in any action or other proceeding brought against a candidate in respect of any liability alleged to have been incurred by him at such election, the election auditor may, at the request of the candidate, and by leave of any one of the judges of the superior courts of common law at Westminster, or of any one of the judges of her Majesty's superior courts at Dublin, or of any one of the judges of the Court of Session in Scotland, as the case may be, pay into court the sum required; and such payment into court by the election auditor shall, for the purposes of such action, be deemed and taken to be and may be pleaded as payment into court by the candidate himself: Provided always, that on any issue or hearing in reference to any such tender or payment of money into court, it shall not be necessary to prove the appointment of the election auditor.

Copy of judgment and statement of payments made in satisfaction to be sent to auditor.

20. Nothing in this act contained (except as herein specially provided) shall be taken to limit the right of any creditor to bring any action or otherwise to proceed against a candidate for or in respect of any expenses connected with the election: and if in any such action or proceeding final judgment be obtained against the candidate, such candidate shall forthwith send to the election auditor a copy or certificate of such judgment; and when and as the monies recovered by the said judgments, or any part thereof, shall be paid or satisfied by such candidate, or shall be obtained under or by virtue of any execution, the said candidate shall thereupon forward to the election auditor a statement of the monies so paid or obtained in respect of such judgment.

Consent of auditor necessary before settling action.

21. No candidate shall be allowed to compound or settle any action or other proceeding brought against him in respect of any expenses alleged to have been incurred by him in or about the election, or to confess judgment in such action or proceeding, without the consent of the election auditor.

Candidate to pay personal expenses and expenses of advertising.

22. The personal expenses of any candidate, and the expenses of advertising in newspapers with reference to any election, shall be defrayed by the candidate himself, or by his authority, but a full and true account of the sums so paid in respect of the said advertisements shall, as soon as conveniently may be, be made out to the best of his ability, and rendered to such election auditor by such candidate, and the amount of such account shall be included in the general account of the expenses incurred at any election to be made out and kept by such election auditor as hereinafter provided.

Refreshments to voters on the days of nomination or polling declared illegal. [Repealed]

23. *And whereas doubts have also arisen as to whether the giving of refreshment to voters on the day of nomination or day of polling be or be not according to law, and it is expedient that such doubts should be removed: be it declared and enacted, that the giving or causing to be given to any voter on the day of nomination or day of polling, on account of such voter having polled or being about to poll, any meat, drink, or entertainment, by way of refreshment, or any money or ticket to enable such voter to obtain refreshment, shall be deemed an illegal act, and the person so offending shall forfeit the sum of forty shillings for each offence to any person who shall sue for the same, together with full costs of suit.*

No person to pay expenses of elections, except to candidate or election auditor.

24. No person shall pay or agree to pay any expenses of any election, or any sum of money whatever, in order or with a view to procure or promote the election of any person to serve in parliament, save to the candidate at such election, or to or under the authority of the election auditor, other than as excepted and allowed by this act; and every person who shall pay or agree to pay any such expenses or money as aforesaid, save as aforesaid, shall become liable to a penalty of 50*l*., and of double the money so paid or agreed to be paid, to be recovered in an action of debt by any one who shall sue for the same: provided, that if upon the trial of any action to recover any such penalty or penalties it shall appear to the judge who shall try the same that any such payment shall have been made or agreed to be made without any corrupt or improper intention, such judge may, if he shall think fit, reduce such penalty or penalties to any sum not less than 40*s*., and may also, if he shall think fit, direct that the plaintiff shall not be entitled to costs of such action: provided also, that no expenses of or relating to the registration of electors, and no subscriptions or contributions *bonâ fide* made to or for any public or charitable purpose, shall be deemed election expenses within the meaning of this act: provided also, that in any action to recover any penalty under this act it shall be lawful to the court in which such action shall be brought, or any judge thereof, if they or he shall think fit, to order that the plaintiff in such action shall give security for costs, or that all proceedings therein shall be stayed.

Candidates and agents may make

25. Any candidate, and his agents by him appointed in writing, according to the provisions of this act, may, at any time before the day of nomination, pay any lawful

and reasonable expenses in respect of the election which he or they shall *bonâ fide* believe fit and proper to be paid, in ready money, and the payment of which cannot conveniently be postponed; provided that the candidate and his agents shall, upon or before the day of nomination, make out to the best of his ability, and deliver to the election auditor, a full, true, and particular account of all such payments, with the names of the persons to whom they have been made, signed by such candidate or his agents respectively, and no payment so made shall be a legal payment within this act unless such account thereof shall be duly rendered to the election auditor.

payments before day of election.

Account of election expenses to be made out by election auditor.

26. The election auditor shall, as soon as he conveniently can, make out a full and true account of all the expenses incurred at the election, specifying therein every sum of money paid to him or paid by him or by his authority on behalf of each candidate, and of all sums claimed, although the same shall not have been allowed or paid, and every sum which has been paid into court as aforesaid or recovered by judgment against such candidate, and to whom by name, such payment was made, and for what particular debt or liability; and the election auditor shall include in such general account the amount of the sums paid by each candidate for advertisements, and he shall specify therein the total amount of expenses incurred by each candidate; and the account, when so made out, shall be duly signed by him; Provided always, that, if it shall be found necessary, the election auditor may from time to time make out a supplementary account or accounts, which shall be made and abstracted in the manner herein provided with reference to the first general account.

Election auditor to keep accounts in some convenient place which shall be open to inspection.

27. The election auditor shall keep all accounts which shall come to his hands in some fit and convenient place, and shall, at all reasonable and convenient times, submit the same to the inspection of the candidates and their agents, and permit them to take copies of the same or of any part thereof, upon request, and when such general account as aforesaid shall be so made out and signed by him, he shall keep the same in some fit and convenient place; and such general accounts shall be open to the inspection of any person, and copies thereof or of any part thereof shall be furnished to any person at all reasonable and convenient times, upon request, such person paying a fee, at the rate of 1*s.* for every 200 words, to a copying clerk for the same; and when the election auditor shall have concluded the business of any election he shall deliver over all accounts in his hands to the clerk of the peace in counties, and to the town clerk or other officer performing any of the duties of town clerk in cities and boroughs, and to the sheriff clerk in counties in Scotland, who shall allow them to be inspected by any person on the payment of 1*s*., and shall furnish copies of the same or of any part thereof on the payment of a fee at the rate of 1*s*. for every 200 words, to the copying clerk; provided always, that for any copy so furnished the fee shall in no instance be less than 1*s*., and shall deliver over to the candidates respectively the balance of all monies, if any, and all vouchers in his hands, except any vouchers appertaining personally to himself.

Election auditor to publish abstract of such accounts.

28. The election auditor shall also, as soon as he conveniently can, insert or cause to be inserted an abstract of such account, signed by him, in some newspaper published or circulating in the county or place where such election is held; and such abstract of account shall specify the amount of each of such bills, charges, or claims admitted to be correct, or claimed and objected to, and the names of the parties to whom the same shall have been paid or are due, or by whom the same have been claimed respectively.

Returning officer to appoint new election auditor in case of death, &c.

29. In case the person appointed to act as election auditor should, before his duties herein mentioned are completed, die, resign, or become incapable of acting as such election auditor, it shall be lawful for the returning officer for the time being to appoint some fit and proper person to act as such election auditor in the room of the person originally appointed as aforesaid for the remainder of the then current year of such appointment; and the returning officer shall give public notice of such appointment in the county, city, or borough.

Monies, &c. to be handed over to new election auditor.

30. All monies, bills, papers, and documents of and relating to the election which were in the hands or under the control of the election auditor going out of office, dying, resigning, or becoming incapable of acting as aforesaid, except receipts or vouchers for payments actually made by such election auditor, shall be handed over and transferred to the new election auditor appointed as hereinbefore mentioned; and such new election auditor shall in all respects, or as near thereto as may be, have the same powers and act in the same way as if he had been originally appointed previous to the election: Provided always, that it shall be lawful for such new election auditor, at all reasonable times, to have access to and take copies of or extracts from the receipts or vouchers above excepted.

Appointment and notification of agents.

31. Every candidate shall, before or at the nomination, or as soon after as conveniently may be, declare to the election auditor in writing the name or names of his agent or agents for election expenses, who shall be appointed in writing, and that he has not appointed and will not appoint any other agent without in like manner declaring the same to the election auditor, and no other than such agents shall have authority to expend any money or incur any expenses of or relating to the election, in the name or on the behalf of the candidate; and such agents may pay any of the current expenses of the election necessary to be paid in ready money, provided that such agents shall make out, to the best of their ability, and render from time to time, true and particular accounts to the election auditor of all such payments; and every such agent shall, as soon as conveniently may be after his appointment as aforesaid, make and sign the following declaration:

"I [*A. B.*], being appointed an agent, for election expenses by [*X. Y.*], a candidate at this election, do hereby solemnly and sincerely declare, that I have not knowingly made, authorized, or sanctioned, and that I will not knowingly make, authorize, or sanction, any payment on account of this election, otherwise than through the election auditor, save as excepted and allowed by 'The Corrupt Practices Prevention Act, 1854.'"

Nomination of absent candidates expenses.

32. In case any person shall be proposed and seconded at any election in his absence, and without his previous authority, it shall be lawful to the persons proposing and seconding such person to pay and agree to pay the lawful expenses of the election of such person; and such proposer and seconder having agreed to pay such lawful expenses shall become liable to pay the fees hereby made payable to the election auditor, and pay any of the lawful expenses of such election, in like manner and upon the same terms and conditions as herein provided concerning agents for election expenses appointed in writing by the candidates.

Payments before passing of act.

33. If any candidate at any election, or any member hereafter returned to serve in parliament, shall before the passing of this act have paid any money for or in respect of any election hereafter to be held, or any expenses thereof, such person shall, to the best of his ability, deliver a full, true, and particular account of such payment or payments to the election auditor.

Election auditor, how paid.

34. Every such election auditor shall be paid and be entitled to receive, by way of remuneration to him for his services in and about the election, the sum of 10*l.* from each candidate at the election, as and by way of first fee; and a further commission at the rate of 2*l.* per centum, from each candidate upon every payment made by him for or in respect of any bill, charge, or claim sent in to such election auditor as hereinbefore provided; and the reasonable expenses incurred by the election auditor in the business of the election and the performance of his duties pursuant to this act shall form part of the election expenses, and shall be paid rateably and proportionably by the candidates respectively.

In actions for penalties, parties, &c. to be competent witnesses.

35. On the trial of any action for recovery of any pecuniary penalty under this act, the parties to such action, and the husbands and wives of such parties respectively, shall be competent and compellable to give evidence in the same manner as parties, and their husbands and wives, are competent and compellable to give evidence in actions and suits under the act of the 14th and 15th Victoria, chapter 99, and "The Evidence Amendment Act, 1853," but subject to and with the exceptions contained in such several acts: provided always, that any such evidence shall not thereafter be used in any indictment or criminal proceeding under this act against the party giving it.

Candidate declared guilty of bribery incapable of being elected during parliament then in existence.

[Repealed]

36. *If any candidate at an election for any county, city, or borough shall be declared by any election committee guilty, by himself or his agents, of bribery, treating, or undue influence at such election, such candidate shall be incapable of being elected or sitting in parliament for such county, city, or borough during the parliament then in existence.*

Short title.

37. In citing this act in any instrument, document, or proceeding, or for any purpose whatsoever, it shall be sufficient to use the expression "The Corrupt Practices Prevention Act, 1854."

Interpretation of terms.

38. Throughout this act, in the construction thereof, except there be something in the subject or context repugnant to such construction, the word "county" shall extend to and mean any county, riding, parts, or division of a county, stewartry, or combined counties respectively returning a member or members to serve in parliament; and the words "city or borough" shall mean any university, city, borough, town corporate, county of a city, county of a town, cinque port, district of burghs, or other place or combination of places (not being a county as hereinbefore defined) returning a member or members to serve in parliament; and the word "election" shall mean the election of any member or members to serve in parliament; and the words "returning officer" shall apply to any person or persons to whom, by virtue of his or their office under any law, custom, or statute, the execution of any writ or precept doth or shall belong for the election of a member or members to serve in parliament, by whatever name or title such person or persons may be called; and the words "revising barrister" shall extend to and include an assistant barrister and chairman, presiding in any court held for the revision of the list of voters or his deputy in Ireland, and a sheriff or sheriff's court of appeal in Scotland, and every other person whose duty it may be to hold a court for the revision and correction of the list of registers of voters in any part of the United Kingdom; and the word "voter" shall mean any person who has or claims to have a right to vote in the election of a member or members to serve in parliament; and the words "candidate at an election" shall include all persons elected as members to serve in parliament at such election, and all persons nominated as candidates, or who shall have declared themselves candidates at or before such election; *and the words "personal expenses," as used herein with respect to the expenditure of any candidate in relation to any election, shall include the reasonable travelling expenses of such candidate, and the reasonable expenses of his living at hotels or elsewhere for the purposes of and in relation to such election.* [Repealed]

39. This act shall continue in force for one year next after the passing thereof, and thenceforth to the end of the then next session of parliament. **Duration of act.**

The SCHEDULE A. above referred to.

[Repealed.]

SCHEDULE B.

No. 1.—*Proclamation to be used in Counties.*

Election of knight, &c.

The sheriff of the county of will, at the day of now next ensuing, proceed to the election of a knight *or* knights, member *or* members [*as the case may be*] for the county *or* division of a county [*as the case may be*], at which time and place all persons entitled to vote at the said election are requested to give their attendance.

And take notice, that all persons who are guilty of bribery at the said election will, on conviction of such offence, be liable to the penalties mentioned in that behalf in "The Corrupt Practices Act, 1854."

And take notice, that all persons who are guilty of treating or undue influence at the said election will, on conviction of such offence, be liable to the penalties mentioned in that behalf in "The Corrupt Practices Prevention Act, 1854."

Signature of the proper officer.

No. 2.—*Notice of Election in Boroughs.*

City *or* borough of , day of .

In pursuance of a writ received by me for electing a burgess *or* burgesses [*as the case may be*] to serve in parliament for the city *or* borough [*as the case may be*], I do hereby give notice that I shall proceed to election accordingly on the day of , at o'clock in , when and where all persons concerned are to give their attendance.

And take notice, that all persons who are guilty of bribery at the said election will, on conviction of such offence, be liable to the penalties mentioned in that behalf in "The Corrupt Practices Prevention Act, 1854."

And take notice, that all persons who are guilty of treating or undue influence at the said election will, on conviction of such offence, be liable to the penalties mentioned in that behalf in "The Corrupt Practices Prevention Act."

Signature of the proper officer.

THE CORRUPT PRACTICES PREVENTION ACT, 1863.

26 Vict. c. 29.

An Act to amend and continue the Law relating to Corrupt Practices at Elections of Members of Parliament. [8th June, 1863.]

General allegations sufficient in indictments.

6. In any indictment or information for bribery or undue influence, and in any action or proceeding for any penalty for bribery, treating, or undue influence, it shall be sufficient to allege that the defendant was at the election at or in connection with which the offence is intended to be alleged to have been committed guilty of bribery, treating, or undue influence (as the case may require); and in any criminal or civil proceedings in relation to any such offence, the certificate of the returning officer in this behalf shall be sufficient evidence of the due holding of the election, and of any person therein named having been a candidate thereat.

This (sect. 6) is the only section of this act which has not been repealed.

THE PARLIAMENTARY ELECTIONS AND CORRUPT PRACTICES ACT, 1879.

42 & 43 Vict. c. 75.

An Act to amend and continue the Acts relating to Election Petitions, and to the prevention of Corrupt Practices at Parliamentary Elections.

[15th August, 1879.]

Be it enacted by the Queen's most excellent Majesty, by and with the advice and consent of the lords spiritual and temporal and commons, in this present parliament assembled, and by the authority of the same, as follows:

Short title.

1. This act may be cited as the Parliamentary Elections and Corrupt Practices Act, 1879.

Trial of election petition to be conducted before two judges.

2. The trial of every election petition, and the hearing of an application for the withdrawal of an election petition, shall be conducted before two judges instead of one, and the Parliamentary Elections Act, 1868, shall be construed as if for the purpose of hearing and determining the petition at the trial and of hearing and determining any application for the withdrawal of an election petition two judges were mentioned, and additional judges shall, if necessary, be placed on the rota accordingly.

Every certificate and every report sent to the speaker in pursuance of the said act shall be under the hands of both judges, and if the judges differ as to whether the member whose return or election is complained of was duly returned or elected they shall certify that difference, and the member shall be deemed to be duly elected or returned; and if the judges determine that such member was not duly elected or returned, but differ as to the rest of the determination, they shall certify that difference, and the election shall be deemed to be void; and if the judges differ as to the subject of a report to the speaker, they shall certify that difference, and make no report on the subject on which they so differ.

Save as aforesaid, any order, act, application, or thing for the purposes of the said act may continue to be made or done by, to, or before one judge. The expenses incident to the sitting of two judges shall be defrayed as the expenses of one judge are payable under the provisions of the said act.

Continuance of acts. [Repealed]

3. *This act and the acts mentioned in the schedule to this act, so far as they are unrepealed, shall continue in force until the 31st day of December, 1880, and any enactments*

amending or affecting the enactments continued by this act shall, in so far as they are temporary in their duration, be continued in like manner.

SCHEDULE.

ACTS REFERRED TO.

[Repealed.]

THE BALLOT ACT, 1872.

35 & 36 VICT. c. 33.

An Act to amend the Law relating to Procedure at Parliamentary and Municipal Elections.

[18th July, 1872.]

WHEREAS it is expedient to amend the law relating to procedure at parliamentary and municipal elections:

Be it enacted by the Queen's most Excellent Majesty, by and with the advice and consent of the Lords Spiritual and Temporal, and Commons, in this present Parliament assembled, and by the authority of the same, as follows:

PART I.

PARLIAMENTARY ELECTIONS.

Procedure at Elections.

Nomination of candidates for parliamentary elections.

1. A candidate for election to serve in parliament for a county or borough shall be nominated in writing. The writing shall be subscribed by two registered electors of such county or borough as proposer and seconder, and by eight other registered electors of the same county or borough as assenting to the nomination, and shall be delivered during the time appointed for the election to the returning officer by the candidate himself, or his proposer or seconder.

If at the expiration of one hour after the time appointed for the election no more candidates stand nominated than there are vacancies to be filled up, the returning officer shall forthwith declare the candidates who may stand nominated to be elected, and return their names to the clerk of the crown in Chancery; but if at the expiration of such hour more candidates stand nominated than there are vacancies to be filled up, the returning officer shall adjourn the election and shall take a poll in manner in this act mentioned.

A candidate may, during the time appointed for the election, but not afterwards, withdraw from his candidature by giving a notice to that effect, signed by him, to the returning officer: provided that the proposer of a candidate nominated in his absence out of the United Kingdom may withdraw such candidate by a written notice signed by him and delivered to the returning officer, together with a written declaration of such absence of the candidate.

If after the adjournment of an election by the returning officer for the purpose of taking a poll one of the candidates nominated shall die before the poll has commenced, the returning officer shall, upon being satisfied of the fact of such death, countermand notice of the poll, and all the proceedings with reference to the election shall be commenced afresh in all respects as if the writ had been received by the returning officer on the day on which proof was given to him of such death; provided that no fresh nomination shall be necessary in the case of a candidate who stood nominated at the time of the countermand of the poll.

Poll at elections.

2. In the case of a poll at an election the votes shall be given by ballot. The ballot of each voter shall consist of a paper (in this act called a ballot paper) showing the names and description of the candidates. Each ballot paper shall have a number printed on the back, and shall have attached a counterfoil with the same number printed on the face. At the time of voting, the ballot paper shall be marked on both sides with an official mark, and delivered to the voter within the polling station, and the number of such voter on the register of voters shall be marked on the counterfoil, and the voter having secretly marked his vote on the paper, and folded it up so as to conceal his vote, shall place it in a closed box in the presence of the officer presiding at the polling station (in this act called "the presiding officer") after having shown to him the official mark at the back.

Any ballot paper which has not on its back the official mark, or on which votes are given to more candidates than the voter is entitled to vote for, or on which anything, except the said number on the back, is written or marked by which the voter can be identified, shall be void and not counted.

After the close of the poll the ballot boxes shall be sealed up, so as to prevent the introduction of additional ballot papers, and shall be taken charge of by the returning officer, and that officer shall, in the presence of such agents, if any, of the candidates as may be in attendance, open the ballot boxes, and ascertain the result of the poll

the votes given to each candidate, and shall
eclare to be elected the candidates or candidate
ne majority of votes have been given, and
names to the clerk of the crown in Chancery.
n of the returning officer as to any question
espect of any ballot paper shall be final, subject
to [illegible] on petition questioning the election or return.

Where an equality of votes is found to exist between any candidates at an election for a county or borough, and the addition of a vote would entitle any of such candidates to be declared elected, the returning officer, if a registered elector of such county or borough, may give such additional vote, but shall not in any other case be entitled to vote at an election for which he is returning officer.

Offences at Elections.

Offences in respect of nomination papers, ballot papers, and ballot boxes.

3. Every person who—

(1.) Forges or fraudulently defaces or fraudulently destroys any nomination paper, or delivers to the returning officer any nomination paper knowing the same to be forged; or

(2.) Forges or counterfeits or fraudulently defaces or fraudulently destroys any ballot paper, or the official mark on any ballot paper; or

(3.) Without due authority supplies any ballot paper to any person; or

(4.) Fraudulently puts into any ballot box any paper other than the ballot paper which he is authorized by law to put in; or

(5.) Fraudulently takes out of the polling station any ballot paper; or

(6.) Without due authority destroys, takes, opens, or otherwise interferes with any ballot box or packet of ballot papers then in use for the purposes of the election;

shall be guilty of a misdemeanor, and be liable, if he is a returning officer or an officer or clerk in attendance at a polling station, to imprisonment for any term not exceeding two years, with or without hard labour, and if he is any other person, to imprisonment for any term not exceeding six months, with or without hard labour.

Any attempt to commit any offence specified in this section shall be punishable in the manner in which the offence itself is punishable.

In any indictment or other prosecution for an offence in relation to the nomination papers, ballot boxes, ballot papers, and marking instruments at an election, the property in such papers, boxes, and instruments may be stated to be in the returning officer at such election, as well as the property in the counterfoils.

4. Every officer, clerk, and agent in attendance at a polling station shall maintain and aid in maintaining the secrecy of the voting in such station, and shall not communicate, except for some purpose authorized by law, before the poll is closed, to any person any information as to the name or number on the register of voters of any elector who has or has not applied for a ballot paper or voted at that station, or as to the official mark, and no such officer, clerk, or agent, and no person whosoever, shall interfere with or attempt to interfere with a voter when marking his vote, or otherwise attempt to obtain in the polling station information as to the candidate for whom any voter in such station is about to vote or has voted, or communicate at any time to any person any information obtained in a polling station as to the candidate for whom any voter in such station is about to vote or has voted, or as to the number on the back of the ballot paper given to any voter at such station. Every officer, clerk, and agent in attendance at the counting of the votes shall maintain and aid in maintaining the secrecy of the voting, and shall not attempt to ascertain at such counting the number on the back of any ballot paper, or communicate any information obtained at such counting as to the candidate for whom any vote is given in any particular ballot paper. No person shall, directly or indirectly, induce any voter to display his ballot paper after he shall have marked the same, so as to make known to any person the name of the candidate for or against whom he has so marked his vote.

Infringement of secrecy.

Every person who acts in contravention of the provisions of this section shall be liable, on summary conviction before two justices of the peace, to imprisonment for any term not exceeding six months, with or without hard labour.

Amendment of Law.

5. *The local authority (as hereinafter defined) of every county shall by order, as soon as may be practicable after the passing of this act, divide such county into polling districts, and assign a polling place to each district, in such manner that, so far as is reasonably practicable, every elector resident in the county shall have a polling place within a distance not exceeding four miles from his residence, so, nevertheless, that a polling district need not in any case be constituted containing less than one hundred registered electors.*

Division of counties and boroughs into polling districts. [Repealed]

The local authority (as hereinafter defined) of every borough shall take into consideration the division of such borough into polling districts, and, if they think it desirable, by order, divide such borough into polling districts in such manner as they may think most convenient for taking the votes of the electors at a poll.

The local authority of every county and borough shall, on or before the 1st day of May, 1873, send to one of her Majesty's principal secretaries of state, to be laid by him before both houses of parliament, a copy of any order made by such authority in pursuance of this section, and a report, in such form as he may require, stating how far the provisions of this act with respect to polling districts have been complied with in their county or borough; and if they make any order after the 1st day of May, 1873, with respect to polling districts or polling places in their county or borough, they shall send a copy of such order to the said secretary of state, to be laid by him before both houses of parliament.

The local authority of a county or borough in this section means the authority having power to divide such county or borough into polling districts under sect. 34 of the Representation of the People Act, 1867, and any enactments amending that section; and such authority shall exercise the powers thereby given to them for the purposes of this section; and the provisions of the said section as to the local authority of a borough constituted by the combination of two or more municipal boroughs shall apply to a borough constituted by the combination of a municipal borough and other places, whether municipal boroughs or not; and in the case of a borough of which a town council is not the local authority and which is not wholly situate within one petty sessional division, the justices of the peace for the county in which such borough or the larger part thereof in area is situate, assembled at some court of general or quarter sessions, or at some adjournment thereof, shall be the local authority thereof, and shall for this purpose have jurisdiction over the whole of such borough; and in the case of such borough and of a county, a court of general sessions shall be assembled within twenty-one days after the passing of this act, and any such court may be assembled and adjourned from time to time for the purpose.

No election shall be questioned by reason of any non-compliance with this section or any informality relative to polling districts or polling places, and any order made by a local authority in relation to polling districts or polling places shall apply only to lists of voters made subsequently to its date, and to registers of voters formed out of such lists, and to elections held after the time at which a register of voters so formed has come into force: Provided that where any such order is made between the 1st day of July and the 1st day of November in any year, and does not create any new division between two or more polling districts of any parish for which a separate poor rate is or can be made, such order shall apply to the register of voters which comes into force next after such order is made, and to elections held after that register so comes into force; and the clerk of the peace or town clerk, as the case may be, shall copy, print, and arrange the lists of voters for the purpose of such register in accordance with such order.

Use of school and public room for poll.

6. The returning officer at a parliamentary election may use, free of charge, for the purpose of taking the poll at such election, any room in a school receiving a grant out of moneys provided by parliament, and any room the expense of maintaining which is payable out of any local rate, but he shall make good any damage done to such room, and defray any expense incurred by the person or body of persons, corporate or unincorporate, having control over the same on account of its being used for the purpose of taking the poll as aforesaid.

The use of any room in an unoccupied house for the purpose of taking the poll shall not render any person liable to be rated or to pay any rate for such house.

Conclusiveness of register of voters.

7. At any election for a county or borough, a person shall not be entitled to vote unless his name is on the register of voters for the time being in force for such county or borough, and every person whose name is on such register shall be entitled to demand and receive a ballot paper and to vote: Provided that nothing in this section shall entitle any person to vote who is prohibited from voting by any statute, or by the common law of parliament, or relieve such person from any penalties to which he may be liable for voting.

Duties of Returning and Election Officers.

General powers and duties of returning officer.

8. Subject to the provisions of this act, every returning officer shall provide such nomination papers, polling stations, ballot boxes, ballot papers, stamping instruments, copies of register of voters, and other things, appoint and pay such officers, and do such other acts and things as may be necessary for effectually conducting an election in manner provided by this act.

All expenses properly incurred by any returning officer in carrying into effect the provisions of this act, in the case of any parliamentary election, shall be payable in the same manner as expenses incurred in the erection of polling booths at such election are by law payable.

Where the sheriff is returning officer for more than one county as defined for the purposes of parliamentary elections, he may, without prejudice to any other power, by writing under his hand, appoint a fit person to be his deputy for all or any of the purposes relating to an election in any such county, and may, by himself or such deputy, exercise any powers and do any things which the returning officer is authorized or required to exercise or do in relation to such election. Every such deputy, and also any under sheriff shall, in so far as he acts as returning officer, be deemed to be included in the term returning officer in the provisions of this act relating to parliamentary elections, and the enactments with which this part of this act is to be construed as one.

Keeping of order in station.

9. If any person misconducts himself in the polling station, or fails to obey the lawful orders of the presiding officer, he may immediately, by order of the presiding officer, be removed from the polling station by any constable in or near that station, or any other person authorized in writing by the returning officer to remove him; and the person so removed shall not, unless with the permission of the presiding officer, again be allowed to enter the polling station during the day.

Any person so removed as aforesaid, if charged with the commission in such station of any offence, may be kept in custody until he can be brought before a justice of the peace.

Provided that the powers conferred by this section shall not be exercised so as to prevent any elector who is otherwise entitled to vote at any polling station from having an opportunity of voting at such station.

Powers of presiding officer and administration of oaths, &c.

10. For the purpose of the adjournment of the poll, and of every other enactment relating to the poll, a presiding officer shall have the power by law belonging to a deputy returning officer; and any presiding officer and any clerk appointed by the returning officer to attend at a polling station shall have the power of asking the questions and administering the oath authorized by law to be asked of and administered to voters, and any justice of the peace and any returning officer may take and receive any declaration authorized by this act to be taken before him.

Liability of officers for misconduct.

11. Every returning officer, presiding officer, and clerk who is guilty of any wilful misfeasance or any wilful act or omission in contravention of this act shall, in addition to any other penalty or liability to which he may be subject, forfeit to any person aggrieved by such misfeasance, act, or omission a penal sum not exceeding 100*l*.

30 & 31 Vict. c. 102.

Sect. 50 of the Representation of the People Act, 1867 (which relates to the acting of any returning officer, or his partner or clerk, as agent for a candidate), shall apply to any returning officer or officer appointed by him in pursuance of this act, and to his partner or clerk.

Miscellaneous.

Prohibition of disclosure of vote.

12. No person who has voted at an election shall, in any legal proceeding to question the election or return, be required to state for whom he has voted.

Non-compliance with rules.

13. No election shall be declared invalid by reason of a non-compliance with the rules contained in the first schedule to this act, or any mistake in the use of the forms in the second schedule to this act, if it appears to the tribunal having cognizance of the question that the election was conducted in accordance with the principles laid down in the body of this act, and that such non-compliance or mistake did not affect the result of the election.

Use of municipal ballot boxes, &c. for parliamentary election, and vice versâ.

14. Where a parliamentary borough and municipal borough occupy the whole or any part of the same area, any ballot boxes or fittings for polling stations and compartments provided for such parliamentary borough or such municipal borough may be used in any municipal or parliamentary election in such borough free of charge, and any damage other than reasonable wear and tear caused to the same shall be paid as part of the expenses of the election at which they are so used.

Construction of act.

15. This part of this act shall, so far as is consistent with the tenor thereof, be construed as one with the enactments for the time being in force relating to the representation of the people, and to the registration of persons entitled to vote at the election of members to serve in parliament, and with any enactments otherwise relating to the subject-matter of this part of this act, and terms used in this part of this act shall have the same meaning as in the said enactments; and in construing the said enactments relating to an election or to the poll or taking the votes by poll, the mode of election and of taking the poll established by this act shall for the purposes of the said enactments be deemed to be substituted for the mode of election or poll, or taking the votes by poll, referred to in the said enactments; and any person applying for a ballot paper under this act shall be deemed "to tender his vote," or "to assume to vote," within the meaning of the said enactments; and any application for a ballot paper under this act, or expressions relative thereto, shall be equivalent to "voting" in the said enactments and any expressions relative thereto; and the term "polling booth" as used in the said enactments shall be deemed to include a polling station; and the term "proclamation" as used in the said enactments shall be deemed to include a public notice given in pursuance of this act.

Application of Part of Act to Scotland.

Alterations for application of Part I. to Scotland.

16. This part of this act shall apply to Scotland, subject to the following provisions:—

(1.) The expression "crime and offence" shall be equivalent to the expression "misdemeanor," and shall be substituted therefor:

(2.) All offences under this act for which any person may be punished on summary conviction shall be prosecuted before the sheriff under the provisions of "The Summary Procedure Act, 1864;" and all jurisdictions, powers, and authorities necessary for that purpose are hereby conferred on sheriffs:

(3.) The expression "sheriff" shall include sheriff substitute:

(4.) The provisions of this act relating to the division of counties and boroughs into polling districts shall not apply to Scotland:

(5.) The ballot boxes, ballot papers, stamping instruments, and other requisites for a parliamentary election shall be provided and paid for in the same manner as polling rooms or booths under the fortieth section of the act of the 2nd and 3rd years of the reign of King William the Fourth, chapter 65, intituled "An Act to amend the Representation of the People in Scotland;" and the reasonable remuneration of presiding officers, assistants, and clerks employed by the returning officer at such an election, and all other expenses properly incurred by the returning officer, and by sheriff clerks and town clerks, in carrying into effect the provisions of this act, shall be paid by the candidates; provided always, that if any person shall be proposed as a candidate without his consent the person so proposing him shall be liable to defray his share of all those expenses in like manner as if he had been a candidate himself: provided also, that the fee to be paid to each presiding officer shall in no case exceed the sum of three guineas per day, and the fee to be paid to each assistant to the returning officer shall not exceed two guineas per day, and the fee to be paid to each clerk shall not exceed one guinea per day.

Application of Part of Act to Ireland.

Alterations for application of Part I. to Ireland.

17. This part of this act shall apply to Ireland, subject to the following modifications:—

(1.) The expression "clerk of the crown in chancery" shall mean the clerk of the crown and hanaper in Ireland:

(2.) The preceding provisions of this part of this act with respect to the division of counties and boroughs into polling districts shall not extend to Ireland:

(3.) In the construction of the preceding provisions of this part of this act as applying to Ireland, sect. 13 of "The Representation of the People (Ireland) Act, 1868," shall be substituted for sect. 50 of "The Representation of the People Act, 1867," wherever in such provisions the said last-mentioned section occurs. The provision contained in the 6th section of this act providing for the use of school rooms free of charge, for the purpose of taking the poll at elections, shall not apply to any school adjoining or adjacent to any church or other place of worship, nor to any school connected with a nunnery or other religious establishment:

(4.) No returning officer shall be entitled to claim, or be paid, any sum or sums of money for the erection of polling booths or stations and compartments other than the sum or sums actually and necessarily incurred and paid by him in reference to the same, any statute or statutes to the contrary now in force notwithstanding, nor shall the expenses of providing sufficient polling stations or booths and compartments at every polling place exceed the sum or sums now given and allowed by statute in Ireland.

Provisions as to polling districts and polling places in Ireland.

18. With respect to polling districts and polling places in Ireland, the following regulations shall have effect; that is to say,

(1.) The lord lieutenant, by and with the advice of the Privy Council in Ireland, shall appoint special sessions to be held by the chairman of quarter sessions and justices of the peace having jurisdiction in each county or riding of a county in Ireland, at such places and times before the 1st day of November next after the passing of this act as shall seem fit for the purpose of dividing such county or riding into polling districts and appointing polling places for such districts:

(2.) The clerk of the said Privy Council shall cause each such appointment to be notified to the clerk of the peace of the county to which the same relates, and shall cause notice of the same to be published twice in each of two consecutive weeks in one or more newspapers usually circulated in such county, and once in the Dublin Gazette:

(3.) The clerk of the peace of each county in Ireland shall, within five days after the receipt of such notification as aforesaid, send a written or printed notice of the same to the chairman, and to every justice of the peace having jurisdiction within the county or riding to which the same relates:

(4.) The chairman of quarter sessions and the justices of the peace having jurisdiction in any county or riding assembled at such special sessions appointed in manner aforesaid, or at any adjournment of the same before the 1st day of December next after the passing of this act, shall make an order dividing such county or riding of a county into polling districts, and appointing in each such polling district a place (in this section referred to as a "polling place") for taking the poll at contested elections of members to serve in parliament for such county:

(5.) Every such division shall be made in such manner so that, as far as practicable, every building or place in such county in which petty sessions are at the time of the passing of this act held shall be a polling place: provided always, that where it appears to the chairman and justices assembled at special sessions that, for the purpose of affording full facilities for taking the poll at contested elections, there should be polling places in addition to such buildings or places where petty sessions are held as aforesaid, they shall appoint so many polling places in addition to such buildings or places as they may think necessary, and constitute a polling district for each such polling place:

(6.) Every such order shall specify the barony or baronies, half barony or half baronies, townland or townlands, parish or parishes, and places constituting each such polling district:

(7.) A copy of every such order shall forthwith be sent by the clerk of the peace for such county to the clerk of the said Privy Council, who thereupon shall submit the same for confirmation by the lord lieutenant and Privy Council in Ireland, in the manner by this act provided, and such order shall not be of any validity until the same has been so confirmed:

(8.) Notice of the intended confirmation of any such

order shall be given by the clerk of the said Privy Council at least one month before the day fixed for such confirmation by the publication of such notice and order in one or more newspapers circulating within such county or riding to which the order has reference:

(9.) It shall be lawful for the lord lieutenant and Privy Council, on the day fixed for the intended confirmation of any such order, to confirm the same as it stands, or with such variation, alteration or modification as may seem fit: provided always, that where any person is dissatisfied with any such order, it shall be lawful for such person, within fourteen days after the publication of the notice of the intended confirmation of such order, to appeal against the same, and such appeal shall be in writing, stating the grounds thereof, and shall be signed by such person, and shall within such time be lodged with the clerk of the Privy Council; and it shall be lawful for the lord lieutenant and Privy Council, previous to the confirmation of any such order, to hear and determine such appeal against the same, and to make such order as to the costs of such appeal as may seem meet:

(10.) When any such order has been confirmed as aforesaid, the clerk of the said Privy Council shall transmit a copy of the same to the clerk of the peace of the county to which the same relates, and shall cause the same to be published once in the Dublin Gazette, and once in the newspaper in which the notice of intended confirmation was published:

(11.) The provisions of the act of the session of the 27th and 28th years of the reign of her present Majesty, chapter 22, for ascertaining the voters in the new or altered polling districts referred to in the 9th section of the said act, and for making separate lists of voters, and otherwise in relation thereto, shall extend and apply to every case in which any order in relation to any county has been confirmed under the authority of this section, in like manner as if such sections were herein re-enacted, and the polling districts to which the same refer or apply had been polling districts constituted under the authority of this section; and the register of voters in force in such county at the time of confirming such order as amended by the printed books given into the custody of the sheriff of such county in manner by the said act provided, and the said printed books shall be the register of persons entitled to vote at any election of a member or members to serve in parliament which shall take place in and for such county until the 1st day of January next after the giving of the said books as aforesaid: Provided always, that in the construction of the said provisions, the terms "the passing of this act" and the "said act" shall respectively be construed to mean the confirming of any order made under the authority of this section and this act.

(12.) At any election of a member or members to serve in parliament for any county to which any such order relates held after the confirming of any such order, and before the register of voters to be formed subsequently to the date of the confirming of such order under the provisions of this section shall be in force, the poll shall be taken as if no such order had been made:

(13.) All precepts, notices, and forms relating to the registration of voters shall be framed and expressed in such manner and form as may be necessary for the carrying the provisions of this act into effect:

(14.) When the chairman of quarter sessions and justices of the peace having jurisdiction in any county or riding in Ireland, assembled at any general or quarter sessions in any division of such county or riding, are of opinion that for the purpose of affording further facilities for polling at contested elections there should be within such district polling places in addition to the places appointed in manner aforesaid, they may by resolution determine that at the next general or quarter sessions in such division of such county the necessity for such additional polling places shall be considered by the chairman and justices assembled at the same:

(15.) The clerk of the peace of such county shall, within five days after the making of such resolution, send a written or printed copy of the same to the chairman and to every justice of the peace having jurisdiction within the county to which the same relates, and shall cause a copy of such resolution to be published twice in each of two consecutive weeks in some newspaper circulated in such county:

(16.) The said chairman and justices assembled at such general or quarter sessions holden next after the making of such resolution shall consider whether additional polling places are necessary, and if they are of such opinion they may, by an order to be made in like manner and subject to the same provisions as to the making, confirming, and taking effect of the same as are in this section contained in relation to orders to be made at special sessions under the authority of the same, appoint such other places to be polling places as they shall think fit, and shall constitute polling districts for such polling places:

(17.) No election shall be questioned by reason of any polling district not having been constituted in conformity with the provisions of this act, or by reason of any informality relative to any polling district:

(18.) When any day fixed for taking the poll at any election is the day fixed for the holding of the petty sessions court at any polling place, the court, shall stand *ipso facto* adjourned till the next day, which shall in that case be the legal day for holding said court, and if that day be a Sunday or legal holiday, till the next day:

(19.) The term "the lord lieutenant" in this section shall mean the lord lieutenant of Ireland and the lords justices or other chief governors or governor of Ireland for the time being, and the term "chairman of quarter sessions" in this section shall include any person duly appointed to do the duty of such chairman during his sickness or absence.

Amendment of law as to voting in wards in certain boroughs.

19. Where the name of any person is required to be inserted in any list of voters for any ward of any city, town, or borough under the provisions of sect. 7 of the act passed in the session of parliament held in the 13th and 14th years of the reign of her present Majesty, chapter 68, as qualified in respect of any property qualification, or as the occupier of any lands, tenements, or hereditaments situate in whole or in part beyond the limits of such ward, then and in every such case the names so required to be inserted shall be placed in alphabetical order in a separate part of such list to be styled "the list of rural or out voters of such ward," and the property, lands, tenements, and hereditaments in respect of which such person is qualified as aforesaid shall for the purposes of the said act and the acts amending the same, in relation to the providing of booths and compartments within each ward of any city, town, or borough, and the voting therein of persons entitled to vote in respect of any such qualifications aforesaid, be deemed to constitute a separate ward: provided always, that the name of any such person shall not be placed in such separate list if such person shall, in writing under his hand, object thereto, and if such objection is delivered to such clerk of the peace on or before the 25th day of August next preceding the making of such list under the provisions aforesaid, and in such case in relation to such person the provisions of this section shall not apply.

PART II.

Municipal Elections.

Application to municipal election of enactments relating to the poll at parliamentary elections.

20. The poll at every contested municipal election shall, so far as circumstances admit, be conducted in the manner in which the poll is by this act directed to be conducted at a contested parliamentary election, and, subject to the modifications expressed in the schedules annexed hereto, such provisions of this act and of the said schedules as relate to or are concerned with a poll at a parliamentary election shall apply to a poll at a contested municipal election: provided as follows:

(1.) The term "returning officer" shall mean the mayor or other officer who, under the law relating to municipal elections, presides at such elections:

(2.) The term "petition questioning the election or return" shall mean any proceeding in which a municipal election can be questioned:

(3.) The mayor shall provide everything which in the case of a parliamentary election is required to be provided by the returning officer for the purpose of a poll:

(4.) All expenses shall be defrayed in manner provided by law with respect to the expenses of a municipal election:

(5.) No return shall be made to the clerk of the crown in chancery:

(6.) Nothing in this act shall be deemed to authorize the appointment of any agents of a candidate in a municipal election, but if in the case of a municipal election any agent of a candidate is appointed, and a notice in writing of such appointment is given to the returning officer, the provisions of this act with respect to agents of candidates shall, so far as respects such agent, apply in the case of that election:

(7.) The provisions of this act with respect to—

(*a*) The voting of a returning officer; and

(*b*) The use of a room for taking a poll; and

(*c*) The right to vote of persons whose names are on the register of voters;

shall not apply in the case of a municipal election.

A municipal election shall, except in so far as relates to

the taking of the poll in the event of its being contested, be conducted in the manner in which it would have been conducted if this act had not passed.

21. Assessors shall not be elected in any ward of any municipal borough, and a municipal election need not be held before the assessors or their deputies, but may be held before the mayor, alderman, or other returning officer only.

Abolition of ward assessors.

Application of Part of Act to Scotland.

22. This part of this act shall apply to Scotland, subject to the following provisions:—

Alterations for application of Part II. to Scotland.

(1.) The term "mayor" shall mean the provost or other chief magistrate of a municipal borough, as defined by this act:

(2.) All municipal elections shall be conducted in the same manner in all respects in which elections of councillors in the royal burghs contained in Schedule C. to the act of the session of the 3rd and 4th years of the reign of King William the Fourth, chapter 76, intituled "An Act to alter and amend the laws for the election of the magistrates and councillors of the royal burghs in Scotland," are directed to be conducted by the acts in force at the time of the passing of this act as amended by this act; and all such acts shall apply to such elections accordingly.

Application of Part of Act to Ireland.

23. This part of this act shall apply to Ireland, with the following modifications:—

Alterations for application of Part II. to Ireland.

(1.) The term "mayor" shall include the chairman of commissioners, chairman of municipal commissioners, chairman of town commissioners, and chairman of township commissioners.

(2.) The provisions of "The Municipal Corporation Act, 1859," following; that is to say, section 5 and section 6, and section 7 except so much thereof as relates to the form of nomination papers, and Sect. 8 except so much thereof as relates to assessors, shall extend and apply to every municipal borough in Ireland, and shall be substituted for any provisions in force in relation to the nomination at municipal elections: Provided always, that the term "councillor" in these sections shall for the purposes of this section include alderman, commissioner, municipal commissioner, town commissioner, township commissioner, or assessor of any municipal borough.

22 Vict. c. 35.

Part III.

Personation.

Definition and punishment of personation.

24. The following enactments shall be made with respect to personation at parliamentary and municipal elections:

A person shall for all purposes of the laws relating to parliamentary and municipal elections be deemed to be guilty of the offence of personation who at an election for a county or borough, or at a municipal election, applies for a ballot paper in the name of some other person, whether that name be that of a person living or dead, or of a fictitious person, or who having voted once at any such election applies at the same election for a ballot paper in his own name.

[Repealed] *The offence of personation, or of aiding, abetting, counselling, or procuring the commission of the offence of personation by any person, shall be a felony, and any person convicted thereof shall be punished by imprisonment for a term not exceeding two years together with hard labour.* It shall be the duty of the returning officer to institute a prosecution against any person whom he may believe to have been guilty of personation, or of aiding, abetting, counselling, or procuring the commission of the offence of personation by any person, at the election for which he is returning officer, and the costs and expenses of the prosecutor and the witnesses in such case, together with compensation for their trouble and loss of time, shall be allowed by the court in the same manner in which courts are empowered to allow the same in cases of felony.

The provisions of the registration acts, specified in the third schedule to this act, shall in England and Ireland respectively apply to personation under this act in the same manner as they apply to a person who knowingly personates and falsely assumes to vote in the name of another person as mentioned in the said acts.

[Repealed] *The offence of personation shall be deemed to be a corrupt practice within the meaning of the Parliamentary Elections Act*, 1868.

If, on the trial of any election petition questioning the election or return for any county or borough, any candidate is found by the report of the judge by himself or his agents to have been guilty of personation, or by himself or his agents to have aided, abetted, counselled, or procured the commission at such election of the offence of personation by any person, such candidate shall be incapable of being elected or sitting in parliament for such county or borough during the parliament then in existence.

Vote to be struck off for bribery, treating, or undue influence.

25. Where a candidate, on the trial of an election petition claiming the seat for any person, is proved to have been guilty, by himself or by any person on his behalf, of bribery, treating, or undue influence in respect of any person who voted at such election, or where any person retained or employed for reward by or on behalf of such candidate for all or any or the purposes of such election, as agent, clerk, messenger, or in any other employment, is proved on such trial to have voted at such election, there shall, on a scrutiny, be struck off from the number of votes appearing to have been given to such candidate one vote for every person who voted at such election and is proved to have been so bribed, treated, or unduly influenced, or so retained or employed for reward as aforesaid.

Alterations in act as applying to Scotland.

26. This part of this act shall apply to Scotland, subject to the following provision:—

The offence of personation shall be deemed to be a crime and offence, and the rules of the law of Scotland with respect to apprehension, detention, precognition, commitment, and bail shall apply thereto. and any person accused thereof may be brought to trial in the court of justiciary, whether in Edinburgh or on circuit, at the instance of the Lord Advocate, or before the sheriff court at the instance of the procurator fiscal.

Construction of part of act.

27. This part of this act, so far as regards parliamentary elections, shall be construed as one with "The Parliamentary Elections Act, 1868," and shall apply to an election for a university or combination of universities.

PART IV.

MISCELLANEOUS.

Effect of schedules.

28. The schedules to this act, and the notes thereto, and directions therein, shall be construed and have effect as part of this act.

Definitions.

29. In this act—

"Municipal borough:"

The expression "municipal borough" means any place for the time being subject to the Municipal Corporation Acts, or any of them:

"Municipal Corporation Acts:"

The expression "Municipal Corporation Acts" means—

(a) As regards England, the act of the session of the 5th and 6th years of the reign of King William the Fourth, chapter 76, intituled "An Act to provide for the regulation of municipal corporations in England and Wales," and the acts amending the same:

(*b*) As regards Scotland, the act of the session of the 3rd and 4th years of the reign of King William the Fourth, chapter 76, intituled "An Act to alter and amend the laws for the election of magistrates and councillors of the Royal burghs in Scotland," and the act of the same session, chapter 77, intituled "An Act to provide for the appointment and election of magistrates and councillors for the several burghs and towns of Scotland which now return or contribute to return members to parliament, and are not royal burghs," and the act of the session of the 13th and 14th years of the reign of her present Majesty, chapter 33, intituled "An Act to make more effectual provision for regulating the police of towns and populous places in Scotland, and for paving, draining, cleansing, lighting, and improving the same;" and "The General Police and Improvement (Scotland) Act, 1862," and any acts amending the same:

(*c*) As regards Ireland, the act of the session of the 3rd and 4th years of the reign of her present Majesty, chapter 108, intituled "An Act for the regulation of municipal corporations in Ireland," the act of the 9th year of George the Fourth, chapter 82, The Towns Improvement (Ireland) Act, 1854, and every local and personal act providing for the election of commissioners in any towns or places for purposes similar to the purposes of the said acts.

"Municipal election."

The expression "municipal election" means—

(*a*) As regards England, an election of any person to serve the office of councillor, auditor, or assessor of any municipal borough, or of councillor for a ward of a municipal borough; and

(*b*) As regards Scotland, an election of any person to serve the office of councillor or commissioner of any municipal borough, or of a ward or district of any municipal borough:

(*c*) As regards Ireland, an election of any person to serve the office of alderman, councillor, commissioner, municipal commissioner, town commissioner, township commissioner, or assessor of any municipal borough.

Application of act.

30. This act shall apply to any parliamentary or municipal election which may be held after the passing thereof.

Saving.

31. Nothing in this act, except Part III. thereof, shall apply to any election for a university or combination of universities.

Repeal.

32. The acts specified in the 4th, 5th, and 6th schedules to this act, to the extent specified in the third column of those schedules, and all other enactments inconsistent with this act, are hereby repealed. Repeal of acts in schedules.

Provided that this repeal shall not affect—

(*a*) Anything duly done or suffered under any enactment hereby repealed; or

(*b*) Any right or liability acquired, accrued, or incurred under any enactment hereby repealed; or

(*c*) Any penalty, forfeiture, or punishment incurred in respect of any offence committed against any enactment hereby repealed; or

(*d*) Any investigation, legal proceeding, or remedy in respect of any such right, liability, penalty, forfeiture, or punishment as aforesaid; and any such investigation, legal proceeding, and remedy may be carried on as if this act had not passed.

33. This act may be cited as The Ballot Act, 1872, and shall continue in force till the 31st day of December, 1880, and no longer, unless parliament shall otherwise determine; and on the said day the acts in the 4th, 5th, and 6th Schedules shall be thereupon revived; provided that such revival shall not affect any act done, any rights acquired, any liability or penalty incurred, or any proceeding pending under this act, but such proceeding shall be carried on as if this act had continued in force. Short title.

SCHEDULES.

FIRST SCHEDULE.

Part I.

Rules for Parliamentary Elections.

Election.

1. The returning officer shall, in the case of a county election, within two days after the day on which he receives the writ, and in the case of a borough election, on the day on which he receives the writ or the following day, give public notice, between the hours of nine in the morning and four in the afternoon, of the day on which and the place at which he will proceed to an election, and of the time appointed for the election, and of the day on which the poll will be taken in case the election is contested, and of the time and place at which forms of nomination papers may be obtained, and in the case

of a county election shall send one of such notices by post under cover, to the postmaster of the principal post office of each polling place in the county, endorsed with the words "Notice of election," and the same shall be forwarded free of charge; and the postmaster receiving the same shall forthwith publish the same in the manner in which post office notices are usually published.

2. The day of election shall be fixed by the returning officer as follows; that is to say, in the case of an election for a county or a district borough not later than the ninth day after the day on which he receives the writ, with an interval of not less than three clear days between the day on which he gives the notice and the day of election; and in the case of an election for any borough other than a district borough not later than the fourth day after the day on which he receives the writ, with an interval of not less than two clear days between the day on which he gives the notice and the day of election.

3. The place of election shall be a convenient room situate in the town in which such election would have been held if this act had not passed, or where the election would not have been held in a town, then situate in such town in the county as the returning officer may from time to time determine as being in his opinion most convenient for the electors.

4. The time appointed for the election shall be such two hours between the hours of ten in the forenoon and three in the afternoon as may be appointed by the returning officer, and the returning officer shall attend during those two hours, and for one hour after.

5. Each candidate shall be nominated by a separate nomination paper, but the same electors or any of them may subscribe as many nomination papers as there are vacancies to be filled, but no more.

6. Each candidate shall be described in the nomination paper in such manner as in the opinion of the returning officer is calculated to sufficiently identify such candidate; the description shall include his names, his abode, and his rank, profession, or calling and his surname shall come first in the list of his names. No objection to a nomination paper on the ground of the description of the candidate therein being insufficient, or not being in compliance with this rule, shall be allowed or deemed valid, unless such objection is made by the returning officer, or by some other person, at or immediately after the time of the delivery of the nomination paper.

7. The returning officer shall supply a form of nomination paper to any registered elector requiring the same during such two hours as the returning officer may fix, between the hours of ten in the morning and two in the afternoon on each day intervening between the day on which notice of the election was given and the day of election, and during the time appointed for the election; but nothing in this act shall render obligatory the use of a nomination paper supplied by the returning officer, so, however, that the paper be in the form prescribed by this act.

8. The nomination papers shall be delivered to the returning officer at the place of election during the time appointed for the election; and the candidate nominated by each nomination paper, and his proposer and seconder, and one other person selected by the candidate, and no person other than aforesaid, shall, except for the purpose of assisting the returning officer, be entitled to attend the proceedings during the time appointed for the election.

9. If the election is contested the returning officer shall, as soon as practicable after adjourning the election, give public notice of the day on which the poll will be taken, and of the candidates described as in their respective nomination papers, and of the names of the persons who subscribed the nomination paper of each candidate, and of the order in which the names of the candidates will be printed in the ballot paper, and, in the case of an election for a county, deliver to the postmaster of the principal post office of the town in which is situate the place of election a paper, signed by himself, containing the names of the candidates nominated, and stating the day on which the poll is to be taken, and the postmaster shall forward the information contained in such paper by telegraph, free of charge, to the several postal telegraph offices situate in the county for which the election is to be held, and such information shall be published forthwith at each such office in the manner in which post office notices are usually published.

10. If any candidate nominated during the time appointed for the election is withdrawn in pursuance of this act, the returning officer shall give public notice of the name of such candidate, and the names of the persons who subscribed the nomination paper of such candidate, as well as of the candidates who stood nominated or were elected.

11. The returning officer shall, on the nomination paper being delivered to him, forthwith publish notice of the name of the person nominated as a candidate, and of the names of his proposer and seconder, by placarding or causing to be placarded the names of the candidate and his proposer and seconder in a conspicuous position outside the building in which the room is situate appointed for the election.

12. A person shall not be entitled to have his name inserted in any ballot paper as a candidate unless he has been nominated in manner provided by this act, and every person whose nomination paper has been delivered to the returning officer during the time appointed for the election shall be deemed to have been nominated in manner provided by this act, unless objection be made to his nomination paper by the returning officer or some other person before the expiration of the time appointed for the election or within one hour afterwards.

13. The returning officer shall decide on the validity of every objection made to a nomination paper, and his decision, if disallowing the objection, shall be final; but if allowing the same, shall be subject to reversal on petition questioning the election or return.

The Poll.

14. The poll shall take place on such day as the returning officer may appoint, not being in the case of an election for a county or a district borough less than two nor more than six clear days, and not being in the case of an election for a borough other than a district borough more than three clear days after the day fixed for the election.

15. At every polling place the returning officer shall provide a sufficient number of polling stations for the accommodation of the electors entitled to vote at such polling place, and shall distribute the polling stations amongst those electors in such manner as he thinks most convenient, provided that in a district borough there shall be at least one polling station at each contributory place of such borough.

16. Each polling station shall be furnished with such number of compartments, in which the voters can mark their votes screened from observation, as the returning officer thinks necessary, so that at least one compartment be provided for every one hundred and fifty electors entitled to vote at such polling station.

17. A separate room or separate booth may contain a separate polling station, or several polling stations may be constructed in the same room or booth.

18. No person shall be admitted to vote at any polling station except the one allotted to him.

19. The returning officer shall give public notice of the situation of polling stations and the description of voters entitled to vote at each station, and of the mode in which electors are to vote.

20. The returning officer shall provide each polling station with materials for voters to mark the ballot papers, with instruments for stamping thereon the official mark, and with copies of the register of voters, or such part thereof as contains the names of the voters allotted to vote at such station. He shall keep the official mark secret, and an interval of not less than seven years shall intervene between the use of the same official mark at elections for the same county or borough.

21. The returning officer shall appoint a presiding officer to preside at each station, and the officer so appointed shall keep order at his station, shall regulate the number of electors to be admitted at a time, and shall exclude all other persons except the clerks, the agents of the candidates, and the constables on duty.

22. Every ballot paper shall contain a list of the candidates described as in their respective nomination papers, and arranged alphabetically in the order of their surnames, and (if there are two or more candidates with the same surname) of their other names: it shall be in the form set forth in the Second Schedule to this act or as near thereto as circumstances admit, and shall be capable of being folded up.

23. Every ballot box shall be so constructed that the ballot papers can be introduced therein, but cannot be withdrawn

therefrom, without the box being unlocked. The presiding officer at any polling station, just before the commencement of the poll, shall show the ballot box empty to such persons, if any, as may be present in such station, so that they may see that it is empty, and shall then lock it up, and place his seal upon it in such manner as to prevent its being opened without breaking such seal, and shall place it in his view for the receipt of ballot papers, and keep it so locked and sealed.

24. Immediately before a ballot paper is delivered to an elector it shall be marked on both sides with the official mark, either stamped or perforated, and the number, name, and description of the elector as stated in the copy of the register shall be called out, and the number of such elector shall be marked on the counterfoil, and a mark shall be placed in the register against the number of the elector, to denote that he has received a ballot paper, but without showing the particular ballot paper which he has received.

25. The elector, on receiving the ballot paper, shall forthwith proceed into one of the compartments in the polling station and there mark his paper, and fold it up so as to conceal his vote, and shall then put his ballot paper, so folded up, into the ballot box; he shall vote without undue delay, and shall quit the polling station as soon as he has put his ballot paper into the ballot box.

26. The presiding officer, on the application of any voter who is incapacitated by blindness or other physical cause from voting in manner prescribed in this act, or (if the poll be taken on Saturday) of any voter who declares that he is of the Jewish persuasion, and objects on religious grounds to vote in manner prescribed by this act, or of any voter who makes such a declaration as hereinafter mentioned that he is unable to read, shall, in the presence of the agents of the candidates, cause the vote of such voter to be marked on a ballot paper in manner directed by such voter, and the ballot paper to be placed in the ballot box, and the name and number on the register of voters of every voter whose vote is marked in pursuance of this rule, and the reason why it is so marked, shall be entered on a list in this act called "the list of votes marked by the presiding officer."

The said declaration, in this act referred to as "the declaration of inability to read," shall be made by the voter at the time of polling, before the presiding officer, who shall attest it in the form hereinafter mentioned, and no fee, stamp, or other payment shall be charged in respect of such declaration, and the said declaration shall be given to the presiding officer at the time of voting.

27. If a person, representing himself to be a particular elector named on the register, applies for a ballot paper after another person has voted as such elector, the applicant shall, upon duly answering the questions and taking the oath permitted by law to be asked of and to be administered to voters at the time of polling, be entitled to mark a ballot paper in the same manner as any other voter, but the ballot paper (in this

act called a tendered ballot paper) shall be of a colour differing from the other ballot papers, and instead of being put into the ballot box, shall be given to the presiding officer, and endorsed by him with the name of the voter and his number in the register of voters, and set aside in a separate packet, and shall not be counted by the returning officer. And the name of the voter and his number on the register shall be entered on a list, in this act called the tendered votes list.

28. A voter who has inadvertently dealt with this ballot paper in such manner that it cannot be conveniently used as a ballot paper, may, on delivering to the presiding officer the ballot paper so inadvertently dealt with, and proving the fact of the inadvertence to the satisfaction of the presiding officer, obtain another ballot paper in the place of the ballot paper so delivered up (in this act called a spoilt ballot paper), and the spoilt ballot paper shall be immediately cancelled.

29. The presiding officer of each station, as soon as practicable after the close of the poll, shall, in the presence of the agents of the candidates, make up into separate packets, sealed with his own seal and the seals of such agents of the candidates as desire to affix their seals,—

(1.) Each ballot box in use at his station, unopened, but with the key attached; and
(2.) The unused and spoilt ballot papers, placed together; and
(3.) The tendered ballot papers; and
(4.) The marked copies of the register of voters, and the counterfoils of the ballot papers; and
(5.) The tendered votes list, and the list of votes marked by the presiding officer, and a statement of the number of the voters whose votes are so marked by the presiding officer under the heads "physical incapacity," "Jews," and "unable to read," and the declarations of inability to read;

and shall deliver such packets to the returning officer.

30. The packets shall be accompanied by a statement made by such presiding officer, showing the number of ballot papers entrusted to him, and accounting for them under the heads of ballot papers in the ballot box, unused, spoilt, and tendered ballot papers, which statement is in this act referred to as the ballot paper account.

Counting Votes.

31. The candidates may respectively appoint agents to attend the counting of the votes.

32. The returning officer shall make arrangements for counting the votes in the presence of the agents of the candidates as soon as practicable after the close of the poll, and shall give to the agents of the candidates appointed to attend at the counting of the votes notice in writing of the time and place at which he will begin to count the same.

33. The returning officer, his assistant and clerks, and the agents of the candidates, and no other person, except with the

sanction of the returning officer, may be present at the counting of the votes.

34. Before the returning officer proceeds to count the votes, he shall, in the presence of the agents of the candidates, open each ballot box, and, taking out the papers therein, shall count and record the number thereof, and then mix together the whole of the ballot papers contained in the ballot boxes. The returning officer, while counting and recording the number of ballot papers and counting the votes, shall keep the ballot papers with their faces upwards, and take all proper precautions for preventing any person from seeing the numbers printed on the backs of such papers.

35. The returning officer shall, so far as practicable, proceed continuously with counting the votes, allowing only time for refreshment, and excluding (except so far as he and the agents otherwise agree) the hours between seven o'clock at night and nine o'clock on the succeeding morning. During the excluded time the returning officer shall place the ballot papers and other documents relating to the election under his own seal and the seals of such of the agents of the candidates as desire to affix their seals, and shall otherwise take proper precautions for the security of such papers and documents.

36. The returning officer shall endorse "rejected" on any ballot paper which he may reject as invalid, and shall add to the endorsement "rejection objected to," if an objection be in fact made by any agent to his decision. The returning officer shall report to the clerk of the crown in chancery the numbers of ballot papers rejected and not counted by him under the several heads of—

1. Want of official mark;
2. Voting for more candidates than entitled to;
3. Writing or mark by which voter could be identified;
4. Unmarked or void for uncertainty;

and shall on request allow any agents of the candidates, before such report is sent, to copy it.

37. Upon the completion of the counting, the returning officer shall seal up in separate packets the counted and rejected ballot papers. He shall not open the sealed packet of tendererd ballot papers or marked copy of the register of voters and counterfoils, but shall proceed, in the presence of the agents of the candidates, to verify the ballot paper account given by each presiding officer by comparing it with the number of ballot papers recorded by him as aforesaid, and the unused and spoilt ballot papers in his possession and the tendered votes list, and shall reseal each sealed packet after examination. The returning officer shall report to the clerk of the crown in chancery the result of such verification, and shall, on request, allow any agents of the candidates, before such report is sent, to copy it.

38. Lastly, the returning officer shall forward to the clerk of the crown in chancery (in manner in which the poll books are by any existing enactment required to be forwarded to such clerk, or as near thereto as circumstances admit) all the packets of ballot papers in his possession, together with the

said reports, the ballot paper accounts, tendered votes lists, lists of votes marked by the presiding officer, statements relating thereto, declarations of inability to read, and packets of counterfoils, and marked copies of registers, sent by each presiding officer, endorsing on each packet a description of its contents and the date of the election to which they relate, and the name of the county or borough for which such election was held; and the term poll book in any such enactment shall be construed to include any document forwarded in pursuance of this rule.

39. The clerk of the crown shall retain for a year all documents relating to an election forwarded to him in pursuance of this act by a returning officer, and then, unless otherwise directed by an order of the House of Commons, or of one of her Majesty's superior courts, shall cause them to be destroyed.

40. No person shall be allowed to inspect any rejected ballot papers in the custody of the clerk of the crown in chancery, except under the order of the House of Commons or under the order of one of her Majesty's superior courts, to be granted by such court on being satisfied by evidence on oath that the inspection or production of such ballot papers is required for the purpose of instituting or maintaining a prosecution for an offence in relation to ballot papers, or for the purpose of a petition questioning an election or return; and any such order for the inspection or production of ballot papers may be made subject to such conditions as to persons, time, place, and mode of inspection or production as the house or court making the same may think expedient, and shall be obeyed by the clerk of the crown in chancery. Any power given to a court by this rule may be exercised by any judge of such court at chambers.

41. No person shall, except by order of the House of Commons or any tribunal having cognizance of petitions complaining of undue returns or undue elections, open the sealed packet of counterfoils after the same has been once sealed up, or be allowed to inspect any counted ballot papers in the custody of the clerk of the crown in chancery; such order may be made subject to such conditions as to persons, time, place, and mode of opening or inspection as the house or tribunal making the order may think expedient; provided that on making and carrying into effect any such order, care shall be taken that the mode in which any particular elector has voted shall not be discovered until he has been proved to have voted, and his vote has been declared by a competent court to be invalid.

42. All documents forwarded by a returning officer in pursuance of this act to the clerk of the crown in chancery, other than ballot papers and counterfoils, shall be open to public inspection at such time and under such regulations as may be prescribed by the clerk of the crown in chancery, with the consent of the Speaker of the House of Commons, and the clerk of the crown shall supply copies of or extracts from the said documents to any person demanding the same, on payment of such fees and subject to such regulations as may be sanctioned by the treasury.

43. Where an order is made for the production by the clerk of the crown in chancery of any document in his possession relating to any specified election, the production by such clerk or his agent of the document ordered, in such manner as may be directed by such order, or by a rule of the court having power to make such order, shall be conclusive evidence that such document relates to the specified election; and any endorsement appearing on any packet of ballot papers produced by such clerk of the crown or his agent shall be evidence of such papers being what they are stated to be by the endorsement. The production from proper custody of a ballot paper purporting to have been used at any election, and of a counterfoil marked with the same printed number and having a number marked thereon in writing, shall be primâ facie evidence that the person who voted by such ballot paper was the person who at the time of such election had affixed to his name in the register of voters at such election the same number as the number written on such counterfoil.

General Provisions.

44. The return of a member or members elected to serve in parliament for any county or borough shall be made by a certificate of the names of such member or members under the hand of the returning officer endorsed on the writ of election for such county or borough, and such certificate shall have effect and be dealt with in like manner as the return under the existing law, and the returning officer may, if he think fit, deliver the writ with such certificate endorsed to the postmaster of the principal post office of the place of election, or his deputy, and in that case he shall take a receipt from the postmaster or his deputy for the same; and such postmaster or his deputy shall then forward the same by the first post, free of charge, under cover, to the clerk of the crown, with the words "Election writ and return" endorsed thereon.

45. The returning officer shall, as soon as possible, give public notice of the names of the candidates elected, and, in the case of a contested election, of the total number of votes given for each candidate, whether elected or not.

46. Where the returning officer is required or authorised by this act to give any public notice, he shall carry such requirement into effect by advertisements, placards, handbills, or such other means as he thinks best calculated to afford information to the electors.

47. The returning officer may, if he think fit, preside at any polling station, and the provisions of this act relating to a presiding officer shall apply to such returning officer with the necessary modifications as to things to be done by the returning officer to the presiding officer, or the presiding officer to the returning officer.

48. In the case of a contested election for any county or borough, the returning officer may, in addition to any clerks, appoint competent persons to assist him in counting the votes.

49. No person shall be appointed by a returning officer for

the purposes of an election who has been employed by any other person in or about the election.

50. The presiding officer may do, by the clerks appointed to assist him, any act which he is required or authorised to do by this act at a polling station except ordering the arrest, exclusion, or ejection from the polling station of any person.

51. A candidate may himself undertake the duties which any agent of his if appointed might have undertaken, or may assist his agent in the performance of such duties, and may be present at any place at which his agent may, in pursuance of this act, attend.

52. The name and address of every agent of a candidate appointed to attend the counting of the votes shall be transmitted to the returning officer one clear day at the least before the opening of the poll; and the returning officer may refuse to admit to the place where the votes are counted any agent whose name and address has not been so transmitted, notwithstanding that his appointment may be otherwise valid, and any notice required to be given to an agent by the returning officer may be delivered at or sent by post to such address.

53. If any person appointed an agent by a candidate for the purposes of attending at the polling station or at the counting of the votes dies, or becomes incapable of acting during the time of the election, the candidate may appoint another agent in his place, and shall forthwith give to the returning officer notice in writing of the name and address of the agent so appointed.

54. Every returning officer, and every officer, clerk, or agent authorised to attend at a polling station, or at the counting of the votes, shall, before the opening of the poll, make a statutory declaration of secrecy, in the presence, if he is the returning officer, of a justice of the peace, and if he is any other officer or an agent, of a justice of the peace or of the returning officer; but no such returning officer, officer, clerk, or agent as aforesaid shall, save as aforesaid, be required, as such, to make any declaration or take any oath on the occasion of any election.

55. Where in this act any expressions are used requiring or authorising or inferring that any act or thing is to be done in the presence of the agents of the candidates, such expressions shall be deemed to refer to the presence of such agents of the candidates as may be authorised to attend, and as have in fact attended, at the time and place where such act or thing is being done, and the non-attendance of any agents or agent at such time and place shall not, if such act or thing be otherwise duly done, in anywise invalidate the act or thing done.

56. In reckoning time for the purposes of this act, Sunday, Christmas Day, Good Friday, and any day set apart for a public fast or public thanksgiving, shall be excluded; and where anything is required by this act to be done on any day which falls on the above-mentioned days such thing may be done on the next day, unless it is one of the days excluded as above mentioned.

57. In this act—

The expression "district borough" means the borough of Monmouth and any of the boroughs specified in Schedule E. to the act of the session of the 2nd and 3rd years of the reign of King William the Fourth, chapter 45, intituled "An Act to amend the Representation of the People in England and Wales;" and

The expression "polling place" means, in the case of a borough, such borough or any part thereof in which a separate booth is required or authorized by law to be provided; and

The expression "agents of the candidates," used in relation to a polling station, means agents appointed in pursuance of sect. 85 of the act of the session of the 6th and 7th years of the reign of her present Majesty, chapter 18.

Modifications in Application of Part I. of Schedule to Scotland.

58. In Scotland, the place of election shall be a convenient room situate in the town in which the writ for the election would, if this act had not passed, have been proclaimed.

59. In Scotland, the candidates may respectively appoint agents to attend at the polling stations. The ballot papers and other documents other than the return required to be sent to and kept by the clerk of the crown in chancery, shall, in Scotland, be kept by the sheriff clerks of the respective counties in which the returns (including those for burghs) are made, and the provisions of this schedule relating thereto shall be construed as if the sheriff clerk were substituted for clerk of the crown in chancery.

60. In Scotland, the term "district borough" shall mean the combined burghs and towns specified in Schedule E. of the act of the session of the 2nd and 3rd years of the reign of King William the Fourth, chapter 65, intituled "An Act to amend the Representation of the People in Scotland;" and in Schedule A. of the Representation of the People (Scotland) Act, 1868. 31 & 32 Vict. c. 48.

61. The provisions of the act of the session of the 2nd and 3rd years of the reign of King William the Fourth, chapter 65, intituled "An Act to amend the Representation of the People in Scotland," in so far as they relate to the fixing and announcement of the day of election, the interval to elapse between the receipt of the writ and the day of election, the period of adjournment for taking the poll in the case of Orkney and Shetland, and of the district of burghs comprising Kirkwall, Wick, Dornoch, Dingwall, Tain, and Cromarty, and to the keeping open of the poll for two consecutive days in the case of Orkney and Shetland, shall remain in full force and effect, anything in this act or any other act of parliament now in force notwithstanding; but nothing herein contained shall be construed to exclude Orkney and Shetland or Orkney or Shetland, or the said district of burghs, or any of the burghs in the said district, from any of the benefits and obligations of the other portions of this act.

Modifications in Application of Part I. of Schedule to Ireland.

62. The expression "clerk of the crown in chancery" in this schedule shall mean, as regards Ireland, "the clerk of the crown and hanaper in Ireland."

63. A presiding officer at a polling station in a county in Ireland need not be a freeholder of the county.

PART II.

RULES FOR MUNICIPAL ELECTIONS.

64. In the application of the provisions of this schedule to municipal elections the following modifications shall be made:—

(a) The expression "register of voters" means the burgess roll of the burgesses of the borough, or, in the case of an election for the ward of a borough, the ward list; and the mayor shall provide true copies of such register for each polling station:

(b) All ballot papers and other documents which, in the case of a parliamentary election, are forwarded to the clerk of the crown in chancery, shall be delivered to the town clerk of the municipal borough in which the election is held, and shall be kept by him among the records of the borough; and the provisions of Part I. of this schedule with respect to the inspection, production, and destruction of such ballot papers and documents, and to the copies of such documents, shall apply respectively to the ballot papers and documents so in the custody of the town clerk, with these modifications; namely,

(*a*.) An order of the county court having jurisdiction in the borough, or any part thereof, or of any tribunal in which a municipal election is questioned, shall be substituted for an order of the House of Commons or of one of her Majesty's superior courts; but an appeal from such county court may be had in like manner as in other cases in such county court:

(*b*.) The regulations for the inspection of documents and the fees for the supply of copies of documents of which copies are directed to be supplied, shall be prescribed by the council of the borough with the consent of one of her Majesty's principal secretaries of state; and, subject as aforesaid, the town clerk, in respect of the custody and destruction of the ballot papers and other documents coming into his possession in pursuance of this act, shall be subject to the directions of the council of the borough:

(*c*.) Nothing in this schedule with respect to the day of the poll shall apply to a municipal election.

Modifications in Application of Part II. of Schedule to Scotland.

65. In part two of this schedule as applying to Scotland—

The expression "register of voters" means the register, list, or roll of persons entitled to vote in a municipal election made up according to the law for the time being in force.

The expression "county court" means the sheriff court.

The expression "town clerk" includes the clerk appointed by the commissioners of police under the act of the session of the 13th and 14th years of the reign of her present Majesty, chapter 33, intituled "An Act to make more effectual provision for regulating the police of towns and populous places in Scotland, and for paving, draining, cleansing, lighting, and improving the same," and of the General Police and Improvement (Scotland) Act, 1862.

Modifications in Application of Part II. of Schedule to Ireland.

66. In part two of this schedule as applying to Ireland—

The expression "register of voters," in addition to the meaning specified in such part, means, in relation to any municipal borough subject to the provisions of a local act requiring an annual revision of the lists of voters at municipal elections, the register of voters made in conformity with the said provisions of such local act, and in relation to municipal boroughs to which Part II. of the Local Government (Ireland) Act, 1871, applies, the list to be made under the provisions of section 27 of the said act, and in relation to other municipal boroughs a list which the town clerk of every municipal borough is hereby authorised and directed to make, in like manner in every respect as if the provisions of the said section were applicable to and in force within such municipal borough.

The expression "county court" means the civil bill court.

The expression "town clerk" includes clerk to the commissioners, municipal commissioners, town commissioners, or township commissioners of any municipal borough, and any person executing the duties of such town clerk.

The expression "council of the borough" includes commissioners, municipal commissioners, and town commissioners of the town, and township commissioners of the township.

The expression "one of her Majesty's principal secretaries of state" means the chief secretary of the lord lieutenant of Ireland.

SECOND SCHEDULE.

NOTE.—The forms contained in this schedule, or forms as nearly resembling the same as circumstances will admit, shall be used in all cases to which they refer and are applicable, and when so used shall be sufficient in law.

Writ for a County or Borough at a Parliamentary Election.

** The name of the Sovereign may be altered when necessary.*

† Insert "sheriff" or other returning officer.

‡ This preamble to be omitted except in case of a general election.

§ Except in a general election, insert here in the place of A. B., deceased, *or otherwise, stating the cause of vacancy.*

* Victoria, by the grace of God, of the United Kingdom of Great Britain and Ireland, Queen, Defender of the Faith, to the † of the county [*or* borough] of , greeting:

‡ Whereas by the advice of our Council we have ordered a parliament to be holden at Westminster on the day of next. We command you that, notice of the time and place of election being first duly given, you do cause election to be made according to law of members [*or* a member] to serve in parliament for the said county [*or* the division of the said county, *or* the borough, *or as the case may be*] of § and that you do cause the names of such members [*or* member] when so elected, whether they [*or* he] be present or absent, to be certified to us, in our chancery, without delay.

Witness ourself at Westminster, the day of in the year of our reign, and in the year of our Lord 18 .

Label or Direction of Writ.

To the † of .

A writ of a new election of members [*or* member] for the said county [*or* division of a county *or* borough, *or as the case may be*].

Endorsement.

Received the within writ on the day of 18 .

(Signed) *A. B.*,

High Sheriff [*or* Sheriff *or* Mayor, *or as the case may be*].

Certificate endorsed on the Writ.

I hereby certify, that the members [*or* member] elected for in pursuance of the within-written writ, are [*or* is] *A. B.* of in the county of and *C. D.* of in the county of .

(Signed) *A. B.*

High Sheriff [*or* Sheriff, *or* Mayor, *or as the case may be*].

Note.—A separate writ will be issued for each county as defined for the purposes of a parliamentary election.

Form of Notice of Parliamentary Election.

The returning officer of the of will, on the day of now next ensuing, between the hours of and , proceed to the nomination, and, if there is no opposition, to the election, of a member [*or* members] for the said county [*or* division of a county *or* borough] at the*

** Note.* Insert description of place and room.

Forms of nomination paper may be obtained at *, between the hours of and on .

Every nomination paper must be signed by two registered electors as proposer and seconder, and by eight other registered electors as assenting to the nomination.

Every nomination paper must be delivered to the returning officer by the candidate proposed, or by his proposer and seconder, between the said hours of and on the said day of at the said *.

Each candidate nominated, and his proposer and seconder, and one other person selected by the candidate, and no other persons, are entitled to be admitted to the room.

In the event of the election being contested, the poll will take place on the day of .

(Signed) *A. B.*
Sheriff [*or* Mayor, *or as the case may be*].
day of 18 .

Take notice, that all persons who are guilty of bribery, treating, undue influence, personation, or other corrupt practices at the said election will, on conviction of such offence, be liable to the penalties mentioned in that behalf in "The Corrupt Practices Prevention Act, 1854," and the Ballot Act, 1872, and the acts amending the said acts.

* *Note.*—Insert description of place and room.

Form of Nomination Paper in Parliamentary Election.

We, the undersigned A. B. of in the of and C. D. of in the of , being electors for the of , do hereby nominate the following person as a proper person to serve as member for the said in parliament:

Surname.	Other Names.	Abode.	Rank, Profession, or Occupation.
BROWN ..	JOHN	52, George St., Bristol.	Merchant.
JONES ..	*or* WILLIAM DAVID ..	High Elms, Wilts.	Esquire.
MERTON ..	*or* Hon. GEORGE TRAVIS, commonly called Viscount.	Swanworth, Berks.	Viscount.
SMITH ..	*or* HENRY SYDNEY ..	72, High St., Bath	Attorney.

(Signed) A. B.
C. D.

We, the undersigned, being registered electors of the do hereby assent to the nomination of the above-mentioned John Brown as a proper person to serve as member for the said in parliament.

(Signed) E. F. of
G. H. of
I. J. of
K. L. of
M. N. of
O. P. of
Q. R. of
S. T. of

NOTE.—Where a candidate is an Irish peer, or is commonly known by some title, he may be described by his title as if it were his surname.

Form of Nomination Paper in Municipal Election.

NOTE.—The form of nomination paper in a municipal election shall as nearly as circumstances admit be the same as in the case of a parliamentary election.

Form of Ballot Paper.

Form of Front of Ballot Paper.

Counterfoil No.			
	1	BROWN (John Brown, of 52, George St., Bristol, merchant.)	
NOTE: *The counterfoil is to have a number to correspond with that on the back of the Ballot Paper.*	2	JONES (William David Jones, of High Elms, Wilts, Esq.)	
	3	MERTON (Hon. George Travis, commonly called Viscount Merton, of Swanworth, Berks.)	
	4	SMITH (Henry Sydney Smith, of 72, High St., Bath, attorney.)	

Form of Back of Ballot Paper.

No. .
Election for county [*or* borough, *or* ward].
18 .

NOTE.—The number on the ballot paper is to correspond with that in the counterfoil.

Directions as to printing Ballot Paper.

Nothing is to be printed on the ballot paper except in accordance with this schedule.

The surname of each candidate, and if there are two or more candidates of the same surname, also the other names of such candidates, shall be printed in large characters, as shown in the form, and the names, addresses, and descriptions, and the number on the back of the paper, shall be printed in small characters.

Form of Directions for the Guidance of the Voter in voting, which shall be printed in conspicuous Characters, and placarded outside every Polling Station and in every Compartment of every Polling Station.

The voter may vote for candidate.

The voter will go into one of the compartments, and, with the pencil provided in the compartment, place a cross on the right hand side, opposite the name of each candidate for whom he votes, thus X

The voter will then fold up the ballot paper so as to show the official mark on the back, and leaving the compartment will, without showing the front of the paper to any person, show the official mark on the back to the presiding officer, and then, in the presence of the presiding officer, put the paper into the ballot box, and forthwith quit the polling station.

If the voter inadvertently spoils a ballot paper, he can return it to the officer, who will, if satisfied of such inadvertence, give him another paper.

If the voter votes for more than candidate , or places any mark on the paper by which he may be afterwards identified, his ballot paper will be void, and will not be counted.

If the voter takes a ballot paper out of the polling station, or deposits in the ballot box any other paper than the one given him by the officer, he will be guilty of a misdemeanor, and be subject to imprisonment for any term not exceeding six months, with or without hard labour.

Note.—These directions shall be illustrated by examples of the ballot paper.

Form of Statutory Declaration of Secrecy.

I solemnly promise and declare, That I will not at this election for do anything forbidden by sect. 4 of the Ballot Act, 1872, which has been read to me.

Note.—The section must be read to the declarant by the person taking the declaration.

Form of Declaration of inability to read.

I, A. B., of , being numbered on the register of voters for the county [*or* borough] of, do hereby declare that I am unable to read.

A. B. his mark.

day of .

I, the undersigned, being the presiding officer for the polling station for the county [*or* borough] of , do hereby certify, that the above declaration, having been first read to the above-named A. B., was signed by him in my presence with his mark.

(Signed) C. D.,
Presiding officer for polling station for the county [*or* borough] of .
day of .

THIRD SCHEDULE.

Provisions of Registration Acts referred to in Part III. of the foregoing Act.

Session and Chapter.	Title.	Part applied.
	As to England.	
6 & 7 Vict. c. 18 ..	An Act to amend the law for the registration of persons entitled to vote, and to define certain rights of voting, and to regulate certain proceedings in the elections of members to serve in parliament for England and Wales.	Sections 85 to 89, both inclusive.
	As to Ireland.	
13 & 14 Vict. c. 69	An Act to amend the laws which regulate the qualification and registration of parliamentary voters in Ireland, and to alter the law for rating immediate lessors of premises to the poor rate in certain boroughs.	Sections 92 to 96, both inclusive.

FOURTH SCHEDULE.

Acts relating to England.

NOTE.—This schedule, so far as respects acts prior to the 10th year of the reign of George the Third, refers to the edition prepared under the direction of the lord chancellor, intituled "The Statutes, Revised Edition."

A description or citation of a portion of an act is inclusive of the words, section, or other part first or last mentioned, or otherwise referred to as forming the beginning or as forming the end of the portion comprised in the description or citation.

Portions of acts which have already been specifically repealed, are in some instances included in the repeal in this schedule, in order to preclude henceforth the necessity of looking back to previous acts.

Extent of Repeal.

7 Hen. 4 (statute of the seventh year)—chapter 15.

8 Hen. 6 (statutes of the eighth year of King Henry VI.)—chapter 7, from "and such as have the greatest number" to "shall lose their wages" and from "and that in every writ that shall hereafter go forth" to the end of the chapter.

23 Hen. 6 (here begin the statutes made at Westminster in the twenty-third year)—chapter 14.

7 & 8 Will. 3, c. 25 (An Act for the further regulating elections of members to serve in parliament, and for the preventing irregular proceedings of sheriffs and other officers in the electing and returning such members)—sects. 3 and 4, and sect. 5 down to "writing the same."

* 10 Will. 3, c. 7 (An Act for preventing irregular proceedings of sheriffs and other officers in making the returns of members chosen to serve in parliament)—so much as is unrepealed.

2 Geo. 2, c. 24 (An Act for the more effectual preventing bribery and corruption in the elections of members to serve in parliament)—sects. 3 and 9.

18 Geo. 2, c. 18 (An Act to explain and amend the laws touching the elections of knights of the shire to serve in parliament for that part of Great Britain called England)—sect. 5 from "or shall vote more than once," to the end of that section, and sects. 9 to 16.

19 Geo. 2, c. 28 (An Act for the better regulating of elections of members to serve in parliament for such cities and towns in that part of Great Britain called England as are counties of themselves)—sect. 4, from "or shall vote more than once," to end of that section, and sects. 6 to 12.

3 Geo. 3, c. 15 (An Act to prevent occasional freemen from voting at elections of members to serve in parliament for cities and boroughs)—sect. 7.

11 Geo. 3, c. 55 (*An Act the title of which begins with the words* "An Act to incapacitate," *and ends with the words* "New Shoreham, in the county of Sussex")—the whole act.

---

* 10 & 11 W. 3, in running headings in ordinary editions.

21 Geo. 3, c. 54 (An Act for the better regulating elections of citizens to serve in parliament for the city of Coventry)—sects. 7 to 9 and 14.

22 Geo. 3, c. 31 (An Act for the preventing of bribery and corruption in the election of members to serve in parliament for the borough of Cricklade in the county of Wilts)—the whole act.

25 Geo. 3, c. 84 (*An Act the title of which begins with the words* "An Act to limit the duration," *and ends with the words* "to serve in parliament")—the whole act, except sect. 1 down to "make a return of such person or persons," and sect. 3 in so far as that part of a section and section relate to the universities.

33 Geo. 3, c. 64 (*An Act the title of which begins with the words* "An Act to explain and amend an act," *and ends with the words* "time and place of election")—the whole act, except so far as it relates to the universities.

34 Geo. 3, c. 73 (An Act for directing the appointment of commissioners to administer certain oaths and declarations required by law to be taken and made by persons offering to vote at the election of members to serve in parliament)—the whole act.

42 Geo. 3, c. 62 (An Act for extending the provisions of an act made in the 34th year of the reign of his present Majesty, intituled "An Act for directing the appointment of commissioners to administer certain oaths and declarations required by law to be taken and made by persons offering to vote at the election of members to serve in parliament," to all oaths now required by law to be taken by voters at elections for members to serve in parliament)—the whole act.

43 Geo. 3, c. 74 (An Act for further regulating the administration of the oath or affirmation required to be taken by electors of members to serve in parliament, by an act passed in the 2nd year of King George the Second, intituled "An Act for the more effectual preventing bribery and corruption in the election of members to serve in parliament)—the whole act.

44 Geo. 3, c. 60 (An Act for the preventing of bribery and corruption in the election of members to serve in parliament for the borough of Aylesbury in the county of Buckingham)—the whole act.

11 Geo. 4 & 1 Will. 4, c. 74 (An Act to prevent bribery and corruption in the election of burgesses to serve in parliament for the borough of East Retford)—the whole act.

2 & 3 Will. 4, c. 45 (An Act to amend the representation of the people in England and Wales)—sects. 58 to 60; sects. 62, 63, 65, 67; part of sect. 68, namely, from "shall if required thereby" down to "poll at each compartment, and," and from "and in case the booths shall be situated in different places" to "lawfully closed;" and sect. 69; and sect. 71 from "and that all deputies" to "candidates at such election," and from "provided also, that the sheriff" to the end of the section; and sects. 72, 73 and 74.

2 & 3 Will. 4, c. 64 (An Act to settle and describe the divisions of counties and the limits of cities and boroughs in England and Wales, in so far as respects the election of members to serve in parliament)—sects. 29 to 33, and so much of sect. 34 as relates to taking the poll.

5 & 6 Will. 4, c. 36 (An Act to limit the time of taking the poll in boroughs at contested elections of members to serve in parliament to one day)—the whole act, except sect. 2, down to "in the forenoon," and from "and the polling" to "in the afternoon;" and sects. 7 to 9.

5 & 6 Will. 4, c. 76 (An Act to provide for the regulation of municipal corporations in England and Wales)—the words "openly assemble and" in sect. 30; sect. 32 from "by delivering to the mayor and assessors" to the end of that section, and so much of the rest of that section as relates to assessors; sect. 33 from "and shall be so divided" to "poll at each compartment, and," and from "and in case the booths" to "at each place;" the words "Are you the person whose name is signed as A. B. to the voting paper now delivered in by you" in sect. 34, and sect. 35 from "and the mayor shall cause the voting papers" to end of that section, and so much of the rest of that section as relates to assessors; and so much of sects. 43, 44, and 46 as relates to assessors.

6 & 7 Will. 4, c. 102 (An Act for rendering more easy the taking the poll at county elections)—the whole act.

6 & 7 Vict. c. 18 (An Act to amend the law for the registration of persons entitled to vote and to define certain rights of voting, and to regulate certain proceedings in the election of members to serve in parliament for England and Wales)—sect. 79 from "Provided always, that it shall not be lawful" to end of that section; sect. 80; so much of sect. 81 as relates to a commissioner or commissioners; sects. 83, 84, and 91, sects. 94 to 96, and sects. 98 and 99.

16 & 17 Vict. c. 15 (An Act to limit the time of taking the poll in counties at contested elections for knights of the shire to serve in parliament in England and Wales to one day)—the whole act, except sect. 2, down to "in the afternoon of such day," and sect. 3.

16 & 17 Vict. c. 68 (An Act to limit the time for proceeding to election in counties and boroughs in England and Wales, and for polling at elections for the universities of Oxford and Cambridge, and for other purposes)—sects. 2, 3, 7, and 8.

17 & 18 Vict. c. 102 ("The Corrupt Practices Prevention Act, 1854")—sect. 11 and Schedule B.

22 Vict. c. 35 ("The Municipal Corporation Act, 1859")—so much of sect. 7 as relates to the form of nomination paper and so much of sect. 8 as relates to assessors.

25 & 26 Vict. c. 95 (An Act to amend the law relating to polling places in the boroughs of New Shoreham, Cricklade, Aylesbury, and East Retford)—the whole act.

30 & 31 Vict. c. 102 ("The Representation of the People Act, 1867")—sect. 35; sect. 37 from "where in any place" to end of that section; sect. 39.

31 & 32 Vict. c. 58 ("The Parliamentary Electors Registration Act, 1868")—sects. 4 to 16, 24, 26, 34, and 36.

31 & 32 Vict. c. 125 ("The Parliamentary Elections Act, 1868")—sect. 40, from "provided always" to the end of that section.

FIFTH SCHEDULE.

Acts relating to Scotland.

A description or citation of a portion of an act is inclusive of the words, section or other part first or last mentioned, or otherwise referred to as forming the beginning or as forming the end of the portion comprised in the description or citation.

Extent of Repeal.

2 & 3 Will. 4, c. 65 (An Act to amend the representation of the people in Scotland) — sects. 24 and 25; sect. 26; sect. 27 from the words "and each substitute so superintending" to the end of that section; sect. 28 from the words "and shall within three days" to the end of that section; sect. 29 the words "the market cross or some other convenient and open place in or immediately adjoining," and from the words "and if no more than one candidate" to the end of that section; sect. 30 the words "the market cross or some other convenient and open place in or immediately adjoining," and from the words "and if no more candidates" down to the words "Saturdays and Sundays," and from the words "and the sheriff who proclaimed the writ" to the end of that section; sects. 32, 33, and 39; sects. 43, 47, and 48.

3 & 4 Will. 4, c. 76 (An Act to alter and amend the laws for the election of the magistrates and councils of the royal burghs in Scotland)—sect. 8, so far as it provides that the election shall be by "open" poll, and from the words "and each poll clerk shall enter" to the end of that section; sect. 10, so far as it relates to poll-books; sect. 11, so far as it relates to voting by lists; and the words "assemble in the town hall or other public room of such burgh and," and from the words "and the provost" to the end of that section; section 15, so far as inconsistent with this act; sect. 18; sect. 36, from the commencement to "provided always, that;" and sect. 38.

3 & 4 Will. 4, c. 77 (An Act to provide for the appointment and election of magistrates and councillors for the several burghs and towns of Scotland which now return or contribute to return members to parliament and are not royal burghs)—sect. 4, so far as it provides that the election shall be by open poll; and from the words "and each poll clerk shall enter" to the end of that section; sect. 8, and sect. 9 from the words "assemble in the town hall" to the words "in each such burgh or town;" so much of the section as relates to voting by lists, and from the words "and such town clerk" to the end of that section; sect. 11, so far as inconsistent with this act; and sects. 18 and 34.

4 & 5 Will. 4, c. 86 (*An Act the title of which begins with the words* "An Act to explain certain provisions," *and ends with the words* "to return members to parliament, and are not royal burghs")—the whole act.

4 & 5 Will. 4, c. 87 (*An Act the title of which begins with the words* "An Act to explain certain provisions," *and ends with the words* "of the royal burghs of Scotland")—the whole act.

4 & 5 Will. 4, c. 88 (An Act for the more effectual registration of persons entitled to vote in the election of members to serve in parliament)—the whole act.

5 & 6 Will. 4, c. 78 (*An Act the title of which begins with the words* "An Act to explain and amend an Act," *and ends with the words* "and to diminish the expenses thereof")—sects. 1 and 2; sect. 5 from "and after the poll" to "the declaration"; sects. 6, 7, 8, 12, 13 and 15.

13 & 14 Vict. c. 33 (An Act to make more effectual provision for regulating the police of towns and populous places in Scotland, and for paving, draining, cleansing, lighting, and improving the same)—sects. 7 to 11 and 13 to 26, sects. 29 and 30, so far as their provisions are inconsistent with the provisions of this act, and Schedules (A.), (B.), and (C.).

16 & 17 Vict. c. 28 (An Act to amend the law as to taking the poll at elections of members to serve in Parliament for Scotland)—sects. 1 and 10.

18 & 19 Vict. c. 24 (*An Act the title of which begins with the words* "An Act to amend an Act," *and ends with the words* "in county elections in that country")—the whole act.

24 & 25 Vict. c. 83 (An Act to amend the law regarding the registration of county voters in Scotland)—Schedule (D.) annexed to the act from the words "and that I am possessed" to the end of the said schedule.

25 & 26 Vict. c. 101 (*An Act the title of which begins with the words* "An Act to make more effectual provision for regulating the police," *and ends with the words* "and also for promoting the public health thereof")—sects. 46, 47 and 50, so far as their provisions are inconsistent with the provisions of this act.

28 & 29 Vict. c. 92 (An Act to shorten the time for the election of members for the Ayr district of burghs)—the whole act.

31 & 32 Vict. c. 48 (An Act for the amendment of the representation of the people in Scotland)—sect. 24 from the words "and in the case of a poll being demanded" to the words "the said sheriff of the county of Peebles;" and sects. 44 and 54; and sect. 59 from the words "oath of possession" to the end of that section.

31 & 32 Vict. c. 58 (*An Act the title of which begins with the words* "An Act to amend the law of registration," *and ends with the words* "other purposes relating thereto")—sect. 13.

SIXTH SCHEDULE.

Acts relating to Ireland.

A description or citation of a portion of an act is inclusive of the words, section, or other part first or last mentioned, or otherwise referred to as forming the beginning or as forming the end of the portion comprised in the description or citation.

Acts of the Parliament of Ireland.

Extent of Repeal.

10 Hen. 7, c. 22 (An Act confirming all the statutes made in England)—so much of the same as extends to Ireland the provisions of the acts

of the parliament of England following; namely,—7 Hen. 4, c. 15, 8 Hen. 6, c. 7, from "and such as have the greatest number" to "shall lose their wages," and from "and that in every writ that shall hereafter go forth" to the end of the chapter, 23 Hen. 6, c. 14.

35 Geo. 3, c. 29 (An Act for regulating the election of members to serve in parliament, and for repealing the several acts therein mentioned)—sect. 3, sects. 5 to 13, sects. 15 to 18, sect. 20.

Acts of the Parliament of the United Kingdom.

Extent of Repeal.

1 Geo. 4, c. 11 (An Act for the better regulation of polls, and for making further provision touching the election of members to serve in parliament for Ireland)—sects. 2, 3, sect. 5, from the words "and that such sheriff" to the end of that section, sects. 6 to 21, sect. 23, sects. 41, 42.

9 Geo. 4, c. 82 (An Act to make provision for the lighting, cleansing and watching of cities, towns, corporations and market towns in Ireland in certain cases)—so much of sects. 12 and 16 as prescribes the mode of election of commissioners.

4 Geo. 4, c. 55 (An Act to consolidate and amend the several acts now in force, so far as the same relate to the election and return of members to serve in parliament for counties of cities and counties of towns in Ireland)—sect. 33 from the words "and that such sheriffs" to the end of that section, sects. 34 to 47, sects. 49 to 59, sects. 60 to 62, sects. 64, 65, sects. 68 to 70, 72, 76, 77.

2 & 3 Will. 4, c. 88 (An Act to amend the representation of the people of Ireland)—sect. 30, sect. 48, and sects. 49 to 54.

3 & 4 Vict. c. 108 (An Act for the regulation of municipal corporations in Ireland)—sect. 64 from the words "by delivering to the mayor or barrister" to the end of that section, and so much of that section as relates to assessors; sect. 65 from "and shall be so divided" to "poll at each compartment," and from "in case the booths" to "at each place;" the words "are you the person whose name is signed as A. B. to the voting paper now delivered in by you," in sect. 66; sect. 68 from "and the mayor shall cause the voting papers" to the end of that section, and so much of the rest of that section as relates to assessors; and so much of sect. 70 as relates to ward assessors.

6 & 7 Vict. c. 93 (An Act to amend an act of the 3rd and 4th years of her present Majesty for the regulation of municipal corporations in Ireland)—sect. 23.

9 & 10 Vict. c. 19 (An Act to amend an act of the 2nd and 3rd years of his late Majesty, by providing additional booths or polling places at elections in Ireland where the number of electors whose names shall begin with the same letter of the alphabet shall exceed a certain number)—the whole act.

13 & 14 Vict. c. 68 (An Act to shorten the duration of elections in Ireland, and for establishing additional places for taking the poll thereat)—sect. 1, sect. 3, sect. 4, sects. 10 to 14, so much of sect. 15 as prescribes the interval between the election and the polling, sect. 16, sect. 19 from "and that all the deputies" to "at the expense of the candidates," sect. 20, sect. 22.

13 & 14 Vict. c. 69 (An Act to amend the laws which regulate the qualification and registration of parliamentary voters in Ireland, and to alter the law for rating immediate lessors of premises to the poor rate in certain boroughs)—sects. 86, 98, 99; sect. 100, sects. 101, 102, sects. 104, 105.

17 & 18 Vict. c. 102 (The Corrupt Practices Prevention Act, 1854)—sect. 11, and Schedule B.

17 & 18 Vict. c. 103 (The Towns Improvement (Ireland) Act, 1854)—so much of sect. 24 as incorporates the sections of 10 & 11 Vict. c. 16, following; that is to say, sects. 23, 26, 27; sect. 28 from the words "and shall be conducted in manner following" to "carefully preserved by the presiding officer, and," and the question numbered I., sect. 30 from "the returning officer" to "each person and," and sect. 31, and so much of any act as incorporates the part of the said sect. 24 hereby repealed.

25 & 26 Vict. c. 62 (An Act to amend the law relating to the duration of contested elections for counties in Ireland, and for establishing additional places for taking the poll thereat)—part of sect. 4, namely, so much as prescribes the interval between the day fixed for the election and the polling; sect. 5, sects. 8 to 10.

25 & 26 Vict. c. 92 (An Act to limit the time for proceeding to elections in counties and boroughs in Ireland)—sect. 1, and sect. 2 from the words "and in every city or town" to the end of that section.

31 & 32 Vict. c. 49 (An Act to amend the representation of the people in Ireland)—sect. 12 from the words "several boroughs" to the word "Cork," and the words "and county of the city of Limerick."

31 & 32 Vict. c. 112 (An Act to amend the law of registration in Ireland)—sects. 4 to 30; sect. 38.

PARLIAMENTARY ELECTIONS (RETURNING OFFICERS) ACT, 1875.

38 & 39 Vict. c. 84.

An Act to regulate the Expenses and to control the Charges of Returning Officers at Parliamentary Elections. [13th August, 1875.]

Whereas it is expedient to amend the law relating to the expenses and charges of returning officers at parliamentary elections:

Be it enacted by the Queen's most excellent Majesty, by and with the advice and consent of the lords spiritual and temporal, and commons, in this present parliament assembled, and by the authority of the same, as follows:

1. The Ballot Act, 1872, as modified by this act, and this act shall be construed as one act. *Construction of act.*

This act shall apply only to parliamentary elections.

Payments to returning officers.

2. The returning officer at an election shall be entitled to his reasonable charges, not exceeding the sums mentioned in the first schedule to this act, in respect of services and expenses of the several kinds mentioned in the said schedule, which have been properly rendered or incurred by him for the purposes of the election.

The amount of such charges shall be paid by the candidates at the election in equal several shares, or where there is only one candidate, by such candidate. If a candidate is nominated without his consent, the persons by whom his nomination is subscribed shall be jointly and severally liable for the share of the charges for which he would be liable if he were nominated with his consent.

A returning officer shall not be entitled to payment for any other services or expenses, or at any greater rates than as in the said schedule mentioned, any law or usage to the contrary notwithstanding.

Returning officer may require deposit or security.

3. The returning officer, if he think fit, may, as hereinafter provided, require security to be given for the charges which may become payable under the provisions of this act in respect of any election.

The total amount of the security which may be required in respect of all the candidates at an election shall not in any case exceed the sums prescribed in the third schedule to this act.

Where security is required by the returning officer it shall be apportioned and given as follows; viz.,

(1.) At the end of the two hours appointed for the election the returning officer shall forthwith declare the number of the candidates who then stand nominated, and shall, if there be more candidates nominated than there are vacancies to be filled up, apportion equally among them the total amount of the required security:

(2.) Within one hour after the end of the two hours aforesaid, security shall be given, by or in respect of each candidate then standing nominated, for the amount so apportioned to him:

(3.) If in the case of any candidate security is not given or tendered as herein mentioned, he shall be deemed to be withdrawn within the provisions of the Ballot Act, 1872:

(4.) A tender of security in respect of a candidate may be made by any person:

(5.) Security may be given by deposit of any legal tender or of notes of any bank being commonly current in the county or borough for which the election is held, or with the consent of the returning officer, in any other manner:

(6.) The balance (if any) of a deposit beyond the amount to which the returning officer is entitled in respect of any candidate shall be repaid to the person or persons by whom the deposit was made.

4. Within 21 days after the day on which the return is made of the persons elected at the election, the returning officer shall transmit to every candidate or other person from whom he claims payment either out of any deposit or otherwise of any charges in respect of the election, or to the agent for election expenses of any such candidate, a detailed account showing the amounts of all the charges claimed by the returning officer in respect of the election, and the share thereof which he claims from the person to whom the account is transmitted. He shall annex to the account a notice of the place where the vouchers relating to the account may be seen, and he shall at all reasonable times and without charge allow the person from whom payment is claimed, or any agent of such person, to inspect and take copies of the vouchers.

The accounts of a returning officer may be taxed.

The returning officer shall not be entitled to any charges which are not duly included in his account.

If the person from whom payment is claimed objects to any part of the claim, he may, at any time within 14 days from the time when the account is transmitted to him, apply to the court as defined in this section for a taxation of the account, and the court shall have jurisdiction to tax the account in such manner and at such time and place as the court thinks fit, and finally to determine the amount payable to the returning officer and to give and enforce judgment for the same as if such judgment were a judgment in an action in such court, and with or without costs at the discretion of the court.

The court for the purposes of this act shall be in the city of London the Lord Mayor's Court, and elsewhere in England the County Court, and in Ireland the Civil Bill Court, having jurisdiction at the place of nomination for the election to which the proceedings relate.

The court may depute any of its powers or duties under this act to the registrar or other principal officer of the court.

Nothing in this section shall apply to the charge of the returning officer for publication of accounts of election expenses.

5. Every person having any claim against a returning officer for work, labour, materials, services, or expenses in respect of any contract made with him by or on behalf of the returning officer for the purposes of an election, except for publication of accounts of election expenses,

Claims against a returning officer.

shall, within 14 days after the day on which the return is made of the person or persons elected at the election, transmit to the returning officer the detailed particulars of such claim in writing, and the returning officer shall not be liable in respect of anything which is not duly stated in such particulars.

Where application is made for taxation of the accounts of a returning officer, he may apply to the court as defined in this act to examine any claim transmitted to him by any person in pursuance of this section, and the court after notice given to such person, and after hearing him, and any evidence tendered by him, may allow or disallow, or reduce the claim objected to, with or without costs, and the determination of the court shall be final for all purposes, and as against all persons.

Use of ballot boxes, &c. provided for municipal elections.

6. In any case to which the 14th section of the Ballot Act, 1872, is applicable, it shall be the duty of the returning officer, so far as is practicable, to make use of ballot boxes, fittings, and compartments provided for municipal or school board elections, and the court, upon taxation of his accounts, shall have regard to the provisions of this section.

Notices to be given by returning officers.

7. There shall be added to every notice of election to be published under the provisions of the Ballot Act, 1872, the notification contained in the 2nd schedule to this Act with respect to claims against returning officers.

Saving of the universities.

8. Nothing in this act shall apply to an election for any university or combination of universities.

Commencement and duration of act.

9. This act shall come into operation on the 1st day of October, 1875, and continue in force until the 31st day of December, 1880, and no longer, unless parliament shall otherwise determine.

Short title.

10. This act may be cited for all purposes as the "Parliamentary Elections (Returning Officers) Act, 1875.

Not to apply to Scotland.

11. This act shall not apply to Scotland.

SCHEDULES.

FIRST SCHEDULE.

Charges of Returning Officers.

The following are the maximum charges to be made by the returning officer, but the charges are in no case to exceed the sums actually and necessarily paid or payable.

Part I.—Counties and District or Contributory Boroughs.

This Part of this Schedule applies to an election for a county or for either of the boroughs of Aylesbury, Cricklade, Monmouth, East Retford, Stroud, and New Shoreham, or for any borough or burgh consisting of a combination of separate boroughs, burghs, or towns.

	£ s. d.
For preparing and publishing the notice of election	2 2 0
For preparing and supplying the nomination papers	1 1 0
For travelling to and from the place of nomination, or of declaring the poll at a contested election, per mile.	0 1 0
For hire or necessary fitting up of rooms or buildings for polling, or damage or expenses by or for use of such rooms or buildings.	The necessary expenses, not exceeding at any one polling station the charge for constructing and fitting a polling station.
For constructing a polling station, with its fittings and compartments, in England.	7 7 0
And in Ireland the sum or sums payable under the provisions of the 13th and 14th Victoria, chap. 68, and 35th and 36th Victoria, chap. 33.	
In Ireland the returning officer shall use a court house where one is available as a polling station, and his maximum charge for using and fitting the same shall in no case exceed 3*l.* 3*s.*	
For each ballot box required to be purchased	1 1 0
For the use of each ballot box, when hired	0 5 0
For stationery at each polling station	0 10 0
For printing and providing ballot papers, per thousand	1 10 0
For each stamping instrument	0 10 0
For copies of the register........................	The sums payable by statute for the necessary copies.
For each presiding officer........................	3 3 0
For one clerk at each polling station where not more than 500 voters are assigned to such station.	1 1 0

	£ s. d.
For an additional clerk at a polling station for every number of 500 voters, or fraction thereof beyond the first 500 assigned to such polling station.	1 1 0
For every person employed in counting votes, not exceeding six such persons where the number of registered electors does not exceed 3,000, and one for every additional 2,000 electors.	1 1 0
For making the return to the clerk of the Crown ..	1 1 0
For the preparation and publication of notices (other than the notice of election).	Not exceeding for the whole of such notices 20*l.*, and 1*l.* for every addition 1,000 electors above 3,000.
For conveyance of ballot boxes from the polling stations to the place where the ballot papers are to be counted, per mile.	0 1 0
For professional and other assistance in and about the conduct of the election.	In a contested election not exceeding 25*l.*, and an additional 3*l.* for every 1,000 registered electors or fraction thereof above 3,000 and up to 10,000, and 2*l.* for every 1,000 or fraction thereof above 10,000. In an uncontested election, one-fifth of the above sums.
For travelling expenses of presiding officers and clerks, per mile.	0 1 0
For services and expenses in relation to receiving and publishing accounts of election expenses, in respect of each candidate.	2 2 0
For all other expenses	In a contested election, not exceeding 10*l.*, and an additional 1*l.* for every 1,000 electors or fraction thereof above 1,000. In an uncontested election, nil.

NOTE.—*Travelling expenses are not to be allowed in the case of any person unless for distances exceeding two miles from the place at which he resides.*

PART II.—BOROUGHS.

This Part of the Schedule applies to all boroughs not included in Part I. of this Schedule.

	£ s. d.
For preparing and publishing the notice of election	2 2 0
For preparing and supplying the nomination papers	1 1 0
For hire or necessary fitting up of rooms or buildings for polling, or damage or expenses by or for use of such rooms or buildings.	The necessary expenses not exceeding at any one polling station the charge for constructing and fitting a polling station.
In England, for constructing a polling station, with its fittings and compartments, not exceeding two in number.	7 7 0
For each compartment required to be constructed, when more than two be used.	1 1 0
For the use of each compartment hired, when more than two are used.	0 5 0
And in Ireland, in lieu of the charges payable in respect of the foregoing last three services, the sum or sums payable under the provisions of 13th and 14th Victoria, chap. 68, and 35th and 36th Victoria, chap. 33.	
For each ballot box required to be purchased	1 1 0
For the use of each ballot box, when hired	0 5 0
For stationery at each polling station	0 10 0
For printing and providing ballot papers, per 1,000.	1 10 0
For each stamping instrument	0 10 0
For copies of the register........................	The sums payable by statute for the necessary copies.
For each presiding officer........................	3 3 0
For one clerk at each polling station where not more than 500 voters are assigned to such station.	1 1 0
For an additional clerk at a polling station for every number of 500 voters, or fraction thereof beyond the first 500 assigned to such station.	1 1 0
For every person employed in counting votes, not exceeding six such persons where the number of registered electors does not exceed 3,000, and one for every additional 2,000 electors.	1 1 0
For making the return to the clerk of the Crown ..	1 1 0
For the preparation and publication of notices (other than the notice of election).	Not exceeding for the whole of such notices 10*l*., and 1*l*. for every additional 1,000 electors above 1,000.

	£ s. d.
For professional and other assistance in and about the conduct of the election.	In a contested election, not exceeding 20*l.*, an additional 2*l.* for every 1,000 registered electors or fraction thereof above 1,000 and up to 10,000, and 1*l.* additional for every 1,000 or fraction thereof above 10,000. In an uncontested election one-fifth of the above sum.
For services and expenses in relation to receiving and publishing accounts of election expenses, in respect of each candidate	1 1 0
For all other expenses	Not exceeding 10*l.*, and an additional 1*l.* for every 1,000 electors above the first 1,000.

NOTE to PARTS I. and II. of SCHEDULE I.

The above sums are the aggregate charges, the amount of which is to be apportioned among the several candidates or other persons liable for the same.

SECOND SCHEDULE.

1. NOTIFICATION to be added to the NOTICE of ELECTION.

Take notice, that by the Parliamentary Elections (Returning Officers) Act, 1875, it is provided that every person having any claim against a returning officer for work, labour, materials, services, or expenses in respect of any contract made with him by or on behalf of the returning officer, for the purposes of an election (except for publications of account of election expenses), shall, within fourteen days after the day on which the return is made of the person or persons elected at the election, transmit to the returning officer the detailed particulars of such claim in writing, and the returning officer shall not be liable in respect of anything which is not duly stated in such particulars.

THIRD SCHEDULE.

MAXIMUM Amount of SECURITY which may be required by a RETURNING OFFICER.

——	County or District of Contributory Borough.	Borough.
	£	£
Where the registered electors do not exceed 1,000	150	100
Where the registered electors exceed 1,000 but do not exceed 2,000	200	150
Where the registered electors exceed 2,000 but do not exceed 4,000	275	200
Where the registered electors exceed 4,000 but do not exceed 7,000	400	250
Where the registered electors exceed 7,000 but do not exceed 10,000	550	300
Where the registered electors exceed 10,000 but do not exceed 15,000	700	450
Where the registered electors exceed 15,000 but do not exceed 20,000	800	500
Where the registered electors exceed 20,000 but do not exceed 30,000	900	600
Where the registered electors exceed 30,000	1,000	700

If at the end of the two hours appointed for the election, not more candidates stand nominated than there are vacancies to be filled up, the maximum amount which may be required is one-fifth of the maximum according to the above scale.

RULES.

MICHAELMAS TERM, 1868.

GENERAL RULES *made by Sir Samuel Martin, Knight, one of the Barons of the Exchequer; Sir James Shaw Willes, Knight, one of the Justices of the Common Pleas; and Sir Colin Blackburn, Knight, one of the Justices of the Queen's Bench; the Judges for the time being for the trial of Election Petitions in England, pursuant to the Parliamentary Elections Act*, 1868.

I. The presentation of an election petition shall be made by leaving it at the office of the master nominated by the Chief Justice of the Common Pleas, and such master or his clerk shall (if required) give a receipt which may be in the following form:—

Received on the day of , at the master's office, a petition touching the election of A. B., a member for , purporting to be signed by (*insert the names of petitioners*). C. D., *Master's Clerk.*

With the petition shall also be left a copy thereof for the master to send to the returning officer, pursuant to sect. 7 of the act.

II. An election petition shall contain the following statements:—

1. It shall state the right of the petitioner to petition within sect. 5 of the act.

2. It shall state the holding and result of the election, and shall briefly state the facts and grounds relied on to sustain the prayer.

III. The petition shall be divided into paragraphs, each of which, as nearly as may be, shall be confined to a distinct portion of the subject, and every paragraph shall be numbered consecutively, and no costs shall be allowed of drawing or copying any petition not substantially in compliance with this rule, unless otherwise ordered by the court or a judge.

IV. The petition shall conclude with a prayer, as, for instance, that some specified person should be declared duly returned or elected, or that the election should be declared void, or that a return may be enforced (as the case may be), and shall be signed by all the petitioners.

V. The following form, or one to the like effect, shall be sufficient:—

In the Common Pleas.

"The Parliamentary Elections Act, 1868."

Election for [*state the place*] holden on the day of , A.D.

The petition of A., of [*or* of A., of , and B., of , *as the case may be*] whose names are subscribed.

1. Your petitioner A. is a person who voted [*or* had a right to vote, *as the case may be*] at the above election [*or* claims to have had a right to be returned at the above election, *or* was a candidate at the above election]; and your petitioner B. [*here state in like manner the right of each petitioner*].

2. And your petitioners state that the election was holden on the day of A.D. when A. B., C. D., and E. F. were candidates, and the returning officer has returned A. B. and C. D. as being duly elected.

3. And your petitioners say that [*here state the facts and grounds on which the petitioners rely*].

Wherefore your petitioners pray that it may be determined that the said A. B. was not duly elected or returned, and that the election was void [*or* that the said E. F. was duly elected and ought to have been returned, *or as the case may be*]. (Signed) A.
B.

VI. Evidence need not be stated in the petition, but the court or a judge may order such particulars as may be necessary to prevent surprise and unnecessary expense, and to insure a fair and effectual trial in the same way as in ordinary proceedings in the Court of Common Pleas, and upon such terms as to costs and otherwise as may be ordered.

VII. When a petitioner claims the seat for an unsuccessful candidate, alleging that he had a majority of lawful votes, the party complaining of or defending the election or return shall, six days before the day appointed for trial, deliver to the master, and also at the address, if any, given by the petitioners and respondent, as the case may be, a list of the votes intended to be objected to, and of the heads of objection to each such vote, and the master shall allow inspection and office copies of such lists to all parties concerned; and no evidence shall be given against the validity of any vote, nor upon any head of objection not specified in the list, except by leave of the court or judge, upon such terms as to amendment of the list, postponement of the inquiry, and payment of costs, as may be ordered.

VIII. When the respondent in a petition under the act, complaining of an undue return and claiming the seat for some person, intends to give evidence to prove that the election of such person was undue, pursuant to the 53rd section of the act, such respondent shall, six days before the day appointed for trial, deliver to the master, and also at the address, if any, given by the petitioner, a list of the objections to the election upon which he intends to rely, and the master shall allow inspection and office copies of such lists to all parties concerned; and no evidence shall be given by a respondent of any objection to the election not specified in the list, except by leave of the court or judge, upon such terms as to amendments of the list, postponement of the inquiry, and payment of costs, as may be ordered.

IX. With the petition petitioners shall leave at the office of the master a writing, signed by them or on their behalf, giving the name of some person entitled to practise as an attorney or agent in cases of election petitions whom they authorize to act as their agent, or stating that they act for themselves, as the case may be, and in either case giving an address, within three miles from the General Post Office, at which notices addressed to them may be left; and if no such writing be left or address given, then notice of objection to the recognizances, and all other notices and proceedings may be given by sticking up the same at the master's office.

X. Any person returned as a member may at any time after he is returned send or leave at the office of the master a writing, signed by him or on his behalf, appointing a person entitled to practise as an attorney or agent in cases of election petitions to act as his agent in case there should be a petition against him, or stating that he intends to act for himself, and in either case giving an address, within three miles from the General Post Office, at which notices may be left, and in default of such writing being left in a week after service of the petition, notices and proceedings may be given and served respectively by sticking up the same at the master's office.

XI. The master shall keep a book or books at his office in which he shall enter all addresses and the names of agents given under either of the preceding rules, which book shall be open to inspection by any person during office hours.

XII. The master shall upon the presentation of the petition forthwith send a copy of the petition to the returning officer, pursuant to sect. 7 of the act, and shall therewith send the name of the petitioners' agent, if any, and of the address, if any, given as prescribed, and also of the name of the respondent's agent, and the address, if any, given as prescribed, and the returning officer shall forthwith publish those particulars along with the petition.

The cost of publication of this and any other matter required to be published by the returning officer shall be paid by the petitioner or person moving in the matter, and shall form part of the general costs of the petition.

XIII. The time for giving notice of the presentation of a petition and of the nature of the proposed security shall be five days, exclusive of the day of presentation.

XIV. Where the respondent has named an agent or given an address, the service of an election petition may be by delivery of it to the agent, or by posting it in a registered letter to the address given at such time that, in the ordinary course of post, it would be delivered within the prescribed time.

In other cases the service must be personal on the respondent, unless a judge, on an application made to him not later than five days after the petition is presented on affidavit showing what has been done, shall be satisfied that all reasonable effort has been made to effect personal service and cause the matter to come to the knowledge of the respondent, including, when practicable, service upon an agent for election expenses, in which case the judge may order that what has been done shall be considered sufficient service, subject to such conditions as he may think reasonable.

XV. In case of evasion of service the sticking-up a notice in the office of the master of the petition having been presented, stating the petitioner, the prayer, and the nature of the proposed security, shall be deemed equivalent to personal service if so ordered by a judge.

XVI. The deposit of money by way of security for payment of costs, charges and expenses payable by the petitioner shall be made by payment into the Bank of England to an account to be opened there by the description of "The Parliamentary Elections Act, 1868, Security Fund," which shall be vested in and drawn upon from time to time by the Chief Justice of the Common Pleas for the time being, for the purposes for which security is required by the said Act, and a bank receipt or certificate for the same shall be forthwith left at the master's office.

XVII. The master shall file such receipt or certificate, and keep a book open to inspection of all parties concerned, in which shall be entered from time to time the amount and the petition to which it is applicable.

XVIII. The recognizance as security for costs may be acknowledged before a judge at chambers or the master in town, or a justice of the peace in the country.

There may be one recognizance acknowledged by all the sureties, or separate recognizances by one or more, as may be convenient.

XIX. The recognizance shall contain the name and usual place of abode of each surety, with such sufficient description as shall enable him to be found or ascertained, and may be as follows:—

Be it remembered that on the day of , in the year of our Lord 18 , before me [*name and description*], came A. B. of [*name and description as above prescribed*], and acknowledged himself [*or severally acknowledged themselves*] to owe to our sovereign lady the Queen the sum of one thousand pounds [*or the following sums*] (that is to say) the said C. D. the sum of £ , the said E. F. the sum of £ , the said G. H. the sum of £ , and the said J. K. the sum of £ , to be levied on his [*or* their respective] goods and chattels, land and tenements, to the use of our said sovereign lady the Queen, her heirs and successors.

The condition of this recognizance is that if [*here insert the names of all the petitioners, and if more than one, add* or any of them] shall well and truly pay all costs, charges and expenses in respect of the election petition signed by him [*or* them], relating to the [*here insert the name of the borough or county*] which shall become payable by the said petitioner [*or* petitioners, or any of them] under the Parliamentary Elections Act, 1868, to any person or persons, then this recognizance to be void, otherwise to stand in full force. (Signed) [*Signatures of sureties.*]

Taken and acknowledged by the above-named [*names of sureties*] on the day of , at , before me,

C. D., a justice of the peace [*or as the case may be*].

XX. The recognizance or recognizances shall be left at the master's office by or on behalf of the petitioner in like manner as before prescribed for the leaving of a petition forthwith after being acknowledged.

XXI. The time for giving notice of any objection to a recognizance under the 8th section of the act shall be within five days from the date of service of the notice of the petition and of the nature of the security, exclusive of the day of service.

XXII. An objection to the recognizance must state the ground or grounds thereof, as that the sureties, or any and which of them, are insufficient, or that a surety is dead, or that he cannot be found, or that a person named in the recognizance has not duly acknowledged the same.

XXIII. Any objection made to the security shall be heard and decided by the master, subject to appeal within five days to a judge, upon summons taken out by either party to declare the security sufficient or insufficient.

XXIV. Such hearing and decision may be either upon affidavit or personal examination of witnesses or both, as the master or judge may think fit.

XXV. If by order made upon such summons the security be declared sufficient, its sufficiency shall be deemed to be established within the meaning of the 9th section of the said act, and the petition shall be at issue.

XXVI. If by order made upon such summons an objection be allowed and the security be declared insufficient, the master or judge shall in such order state what amount he deems requisite to make the security sufficient, and the further prescribed time to remove the objection by deposit shall be within five days from the date of the order, not including the day of the date, and such deposit shall be made in the manner already prescribed.

XXVII. The costs of hearing and deciding the objections made to the security given shall be paid as ordered by the master or judge, and in default of such order shall form part of the general costs of the petition.

XXVIII. The cost of hearing and deciding an objection upon the ground of insufficiency of a surety or sureties shall be paid by the petitioner, and a clause to that effect shall be inserted in the order declaring its sufficiency or insufficiency unless at the time of leaving the recognizance with the master there be also left with the master an affidavit of the sufficiency of the surety or sureties sworn by each surety before a justice of the peace, which affidavit any justice of the peace is hereby authorized to take, or before some person authorized to take affidavits in the Court of Common Pleas, that he is seised or possessed of real or personal estate, or both, above what will satisfy his debts of the clear value of the sum for which he is bound by his recognizance, which affidavit may be as follows:—

In the Common Pleas.

"Parliamentary Elections Act, 1868."

I, A. B., of [*as in recognizance*] make oath and say that I am seised or possessed of real [*or* personal] estate above what will satisfy my debts of the clear value of £ .

Sworn, &c.

XXIX. The order of the master for payment of costs shall have the same force as an order made by a judge, and may be made a rule of the Court of Common Pleas, and enforced in like manner as a judge's order.

XXX. The master shall make out the election list. In it he shall insert the name of the agents of the petitioners and respondent, and the addresses to which notices may be sent, if any. The list may be inspected at the master's office at any time during office hours, and shall be put up for that purpose upon a notice board appropriated to proceedings under the said act, and headed "Parliamentary Elections Act, 1868."

XXXI. The time and place of the trial of each election petition shall be fixed by the judges on the rota, and notice thereof shall be given in writing by the master by sticking notice up in his office, sending one copy by the post to the address given by the petitioner, another to the address given by the respondent, if any, and a copy by the post to the sheriff, or in case of a borough having a mayor, to the mayor of that borough, fifteen days before the day appointed for the trial.

The sheriff or mayor, as the case may be, shall forthwith publish the same in the county or borough.

XXXII. The sticking up of the notice of trial at the office of the master shall be deemed and taken to be notice in the prescribed manner within the meaning of the act, and such notice shall not be vitiated by any miscarriage of, or relating to, the copy or copies thereof to be sent as already directed.

XXXIII. The notice of trial may be in the following form:—

"Parliamentary Elections Act, 1868."

Election petition of . County [*or* borough] of .

Take notice that the above petition [*or* petitions] will be tried at on the day of and on such other subsequent days as may be needful.

Dated the day of .

Signed, by order, A. B.
The master appointed under the above act.

XXXIV. A judge may from time to time, by order made upon the application of a party to the petition, or by notice in such form as the judge may direct to be sent to the sheriff or mayor, as the case may be, postpone the beginning of the trial to such day as he may name, and such notice when received shall be forthwith made public by the sheriff or mayor.

XXXV. In the event of the judge not having arrived at the time appointed for the trial, or to which the trial is postponed, the commencement of the trial shall *ipso facto* stand adjourned to the ensuing day, and so from day to day.

XXXVI. No formal adjournment of the court for the trial of an election petition shall be necessary, but the trial is to be deemed adjourned, and may be continued from day to day until the inquiry is concluded; and in the event of the judge who begins the trial being disabled by illness or otherwise, it may be recommenced and concluded by another judge.

XXXVII. The application to state a special case may be made by rule in the Court of Common Pleas when sitting, or by a summons before a judge at chambers, upon hearing the parties.

XXXVIII. The title of the court of record held for the trial of an election petition may be as follows:—

"Court for the trial of an election petition for the [county of *or* borough of *as may be*] between petitioner, and respondent." And it shall be sufficient so to entitle all proceedings in that court.

XXXIX. An officer shall be appointed for each court for the trial of an election petition, who shall attend at the trial in like manner as the clerks of assize and of arraigns attend at the assizes.

Such officer may be called the registrar of that court. He by himself, or in case of need, his sufficient deputy, shall perform all the functions incident to the officer of a court of record, and also such duties as may be prescribed to him.

XL. *The reasonable costs of any witness shall be ascertained by the registrar of the court, and the certificate allowing them shall be under his hand.*—Repealed.

XLI. The order of a judge to compel the attendance of a person as a witness may be in the following form:—

Court for the trial of an election petition for [*complete the title of the court*], the day of . To A. B. [*describe the person*]. You are hereby required to attend before the above court at [*place*] on the day of , at the hour of [*or* forthwith, *as the case may be*], to be examined as a witness in the matter of the said petition, and to attend the said court until your examination shall have been completed.

As witness my hand. A. B., judge of the said court.

XLII. In the event of its being necessary to commit any person for contempt, the warrant may be as follows:—

At a court holden on , at , for the trial of an election petition for the county [*or* borough] of , before Sir Samuel Martin, Knight, one of the barons of her Majesty's Court of Exchequer, and one of the judges for the time being for the trial of election petitions in England, pursuant to the Parliamentary Elections Act, 1868.

Whereas A. B. has this day been guilty, and is by the said court adjudged to be guilty, of a contempt thereof. The said court does therefore sentence the said A. B. for his said contempt to be imprisoned in the gaol for calendar months, and to pay to our Lady the Queen a fine of £ , and to be further imprisoned in the said gaol until the said fine be paid; and the court further orders that the sheriff of the said county [*or as the case may be*] and all constables and officers of the peace of any county or place where the said A. B. may be found, shall take the said A. B. into custody and convey him to the said gaol, and there deliver him into the custody of the gaoler thereof, to undergo his said sentence; and the court further orders the said gaoler to receive the said A. B. into his custody, and that he shall be detained in the said gaol in pursuance of the said sentence. A. D.

Signed the day of .

S. M.

XLIII. Such warrant may be made out and directed to the sheriff or other person having the execution of process of the superior courts, as the case may be, and to all constables and officers of the peace of the county or place where the person adjudged guilty of contempt may be found, and such warrant shall be sufficient without further particularity, and shall and may be executed by the persons to whom it is directed or any or either of them.

XLIV. All interlocutory questions and matters, except as to the sufficiency of the security, shall be heard and disposed of before a judge, who shall have the same control over the proceedings under the Parliamentary Elections Act, 1868, as a judge at chambers in the ordinary proceedings of the superior courts, and such questions and matters shall be heard and disposed of by one of the judges upon the rota, if practicable, and if not, then by any judge at chambers.

XLV. Notice of an application for leave to withdraw a petition shall be in writing, and signed by the petitioners or their agent.

It shall state the ground on which the application is intended to be supported.

The following form shall be sufficient:—

Parliamentary Elections Act, 1868.

County [*or* borough] of petition of [*state petitioners*] presented day of .

The petitioner proposes to apply to withdraw his petition upon the following ground [*here state the ground*], and prays that a day may be appointed for hearing his application.

Dated this day of . (Signed)

XLVI. The notice of application for leave to withdraw shall be left at the master's office.

XLVII. A copy of such notice of the intention of the petitioner to apply for leave to withdraw his petition shall be given by the petitioner to the respondent, and to the returning officer, who shall make it public in the county or borough to which it relates, and shall be forthwith published by the petitioner in at least one newspaper circulating in the place.

The following may be the form of such notice:—

Parliamentary Elections Act, 1868.

In the election petition for in which is petitioner and respondent.

Notice is hereby given, that the above petitioner has on the day of lodged at the master's office notice of an application to withdraw the petition, of which notice the following is a copy—[*set it out*].

And take notice that by the rule made by the judges any person who might have been a petitioner in respect of the said election, may within five days after publication by the returning officer of this notice, give notice in writing of his intention on the hearing to apply for leave to be substituted as a petitioner. (Signed)

XLVIII. Any person who might have been a petitioner in respect of the election to which the petition relates, may within five days after such notice is published by the returning officer, give notice in writing, signed by him or on his behalf, to the master of his intention to apply at the hearing to be substituted for the petitioner, but the want of such notice shall not defeat such application, if in fact made at the hearing.

XLIX. The time and place for hearing the application shall be fixed by a judge, and whether before the Court of Common Pleas or before a judge, as he may deem advisable, but shall not be less than a week after the notice of the intention to apply has been given to the master as hereinbefore provided, and notice of the time and place appointed for the hearing shall be given to such person or persons, if any, as shall have given notice to the master of an intention to apply to be substituted as petitioners, and otherwise in such manner and at such time as the judge directs.

L. Notice of abatement of a petition, by death of the petitioner or surviving petitioner, under section 37 of the said act, shall be given by the party or person interested, in the same manner as notice of an application to withdraw a petition, and the time within which application may be made to the court or a judge, by motion or summons at chambers, to be substituted as a petitioner, shall be one calendar month, or such further time as upon consideration of any special circumstances the court or a judge may allow.

LI. If the respondent dies or is summoned to parliament as a peer of Great Britain by a writ issued under the great seal of Great Britain, or if the House of Commons have resolved that his seat is vacant, any person entitled to be a petitioner under the act in respect of the election to which the petition relates, may give notice of the fact in the county or borough by causing such notice to be published in at least one newspaper circulating therein, if any, and by leaving a copy of such notice signed by him or on his behalf with the returning officer, and a like copy with the master.

LII. The manner and time of the respondent's giving notice to the court that he does not intend to oppose the petition, shall be by leaving notice thereof in writing at the office of the master, signed by the respondents six days before the day appointed for trial, exclusive of the day of leaving such notice.

LIII. Upon such notice being left at the master's office, the master shall forthwith send a copy thereof by the post to the petitioner or his agent, and to the sheriff or mayor, as the case may be, who shall cause the same to be published in the county or borough.

LIV. The time for applying to be admitted as a respondent in either of the events mentioned in the 38th section of the act shall be within ten days after such notice is given as hereinbefore directed, or such further time as the court or a judge may allow.

LV. Costs shall be taxed by the master, or at his request by any master of a superior court, upon the rule of court or judge's order by which the costs are payable, and costs when taxed may be recovered by execution issued upon the rule of court ordering them to be paid; or, if payable by the order of a judge, then by making such order a rule of court in the ordinary way and issuing execution upon such rule against the person by whom the costs are ordered to be paid, or in case there be money in the bank available for the purpose, then to the extent of such money by order of the Chief Justice of the Common Pleas for the time being, upon a duplicate of the rule of court.

The office fees payable for inspection, office copies, enrolment, and other proceedings under the act, and these rules, shall be the same as those payable, if any, for like proceedings according to the present practice of the Court of Common Pleas.

LVI. The master shall prepare and keep a roll properly headed for entering the names of all persons entitled to practise as attorney or agent in cases of election petitions, and all matters relating to elections before the court and judges, pursuant to the 57th section of the said act, which roll shall be kept and dealt with in all respects as the roll of attorneys of the Court of Common Pleas, and shall be under the control of that court, as to striking off the roll and otherwise.

LVII. The entry upon the roll shall be written and subscribed by the attorney or agent, or some attorney authorized by him in writing to sign on his behalf, who shall therein set forth the name, description, and address in full.

LVIII. The master may allow any person upon the roll of attorneys for the time being, and during the present year any person whose name or the name of whose firm is in the law list of the present year as a parliamentary agent, to subscribe the roll, and permission to subscribe the roll may be granted to any other person by the court or a judge upon affidavit, showing the facts which entitle the applicant to practise as agent according to the principles, practice, and rules of the House of Commons in cases of election petitions.

LIX. An agent employed for the petitioner or respondent shall forthwith leave written notice at the office of the master, of his appointment to act as such agent, and service of notices and proceedings upon such agent shall be sufficient for all purposes.

LX. No proceeding under the Parliamentary Elections Act, 1868, shall be defeated by any formal objection.

LXI. Any rule made or to be made in pursuance of the act, if made in term time shall be published by being read by the master in the Court of Common Pleas, and if made out of term by a copy thereof being put up at the master's office.

Dated the 21st day of November, 1868.

Samuel Martin.
J. S. Willes.
Colin Blackburn.
The judges for the trial of election petitions in England.

Additional General Rule

Made by Sir Samuel Martin, Knight, one of the Barons of the Exchequer; Sir James Shaw Willes, Knight, one of the Justices of the Common Pleas; and Sir Colin Blackburn, Knight, one of the Justices of the Queen's Bench; the Judges for the time being for the trial of Election Petitions in England, pursuant to the Parliamentary Elections Act, 1868.

That notice of the time and place of the trial of each election petition shall be transmitted by the master to the Treasury, and to the Clerk of the Crown in Chancery; and that the Clerk of the Crown in Chancery shall, on or before the day fixed for the trial, deliver, or cause to be delivered, to the registrar of the judge who is to try the petition, or his deputy, the poll books, for which the registrar or his deputy shall give, if required, a receipt: And that the registrar shall keep in safe custody the said poll books until the trial is over, and then return the same to the Crown Office.

Dated the 19th day of December, 1868.

SAMUEL MARTIN.
J. S. WILLES.
COLIN BLACKBURN.
The judges for the trial of election petitions in England.

ADDITIONAL GENERAL RULES

Made by the Judges for the time being for the trial of election petitions in England, pursuant to the Parliamentary Elections Act, 1868.

I. All claims at law or in equity to money deposited or to be deposited in the Bank of England for payment of costs, charges, and expenses payable by the petitioners pursuant to the 16th General Rule, made the 21st of November, 1868, by the judges for the trial of election petitions in England, shall be disposed of by the Court of Common Pleas or a judge.

II. Money so deposited shall, if and when the same is no longer needed for securing payment of such costs, charges, and expenses, be returned or otherwise disposed of as justice may require, by rule of the Court of Common Pleas or order of a judge.

III. Such rule or order may be made after such notice of intention to apply, and proof that all just claims have been satisfied or otherwise sufficiently provided for as the court or judge may require.

IV. The rule or order may direct payment either to the party in whose name the same is deposited, or to any person entitled to receive the same.

V. Upon such rule or order being made, the amount may be drawn for by the Chief Justice of the Common Pleas for the time being.

VI. The draft of the Chief Justice of the Common Pleas for the time being shall, in all cases, be a sufficient warrant to the Bank of England for all payments made thereunder.

Dated the 25th day of March, 1869.

SAMUEL MARTIN.
J. S. WILLES.
COLIN BLACKBURN.
The judges for the trial of election petitions in England.

Additional General Rules

Made by the Judges for the time being for the trial of election petitions in England, pursuant to the Parliamentary Elections Act, 1868, for the more effectual execution of the said Act.

1. A copy of every order (other than an order giving further time for delivering particulars, or for costs only), or, if the master shall so direct, the order itself, or a duplicate thereof, also a copy of every particular delivered, shall be forthwith filed with the master, and the same shall be produced at the trial by the registrar, stamped with the official seal. Such order and particular respectively shall be filed by the party obtaining the same.

The petitioner or his agent shall, immediately after notice of the presentation of a petition and of the nature of the proposed security shall have been served, file with the master an affidavit of the time and manner of service thereof.

3. The days mentioned in rules 7 and 8, and in any rule of court or judge's order, whereby particulars are ordered to be delivered, or any act is directed to be done so many days before the day appointed for trial, shall be reckoned exclusively of the day of delivery, or of doing the act ordered and the day appointed for trial, and exclusively also of Sunday, Christmas Day, Good Friday, and any day set apart for a public fast or public thanksgiving.

4. When the last day for presenting petitions, or filing lists of votes or objections, under rules 7 and 8, or recognizances, or any other matter required to be filed within a given time, shall happen to fall on a holiday, the petition or other matter shall be deemed duly filed if put into the letter box at the master's office at any time during such day; but an affidavit, stating with reasonable precision the time when such delivery was made, shall be filed on the first day after the expiration of the holidays.

5. Rule 10 is hereby revoked, and in lieu thereof it is ordered that the amount to be paid to any witness whose expenses shall be allowed by the judge, shall be ascertained and certified by the registrar; or in the event of his becoming incapacitated from giving such certificate, by the judge.

6. After receiving notice of the petitioner's intention to apply for leave to withdraw, or of the respondent's intention not to oppose, or of the abatement of the petition by death, or of the happening of any of the events mentioned in the 38th section of the act, if such notice be received after notice of trial shall have been given, and before the trial has commenced, the master shall forthwith countermand the notice of trial. The countermand shall be given in the same manner, as near as may be, as the notice of trial.

Dated the 27th day of January, 1875.

G. Pigott.
Robt. Lush.
George E. Honyman.
Judges for the time being on the rota for the trial of election petitions in England.

INDEX.

*** *The figures in parentheses apply to the number of the Section of the Act.*

THE END.

www.ingramcontent.com/pod-product-compliance
Lightning Source LLC
Chambersburg PA
CBHW031404270326
41929CB00010BA/1318

* 9 7 8 3 3 3 7 1 5 9 9 5 5 *